MANY WORLDS:
A RUSSIAN LIFE

Many Worlds:
A Russian Life

Sophie Koulomzin

ST. VLADIMIR'S SEMINARY PRESS
CRESTWOOD, NY 10707
1980

Library of Congress Cataloging in Publication Data

Koulomzin, Sophie.
  Many Worlds.

     1. Koulomzin, Sophie.   2.   Orthodox Eastern
Church, Russian—Biography.   I.   Title.
BX597.K64A35   281.9'3   [B]   80-19332
  ISBN 0-913836-72-9

PRINTED IN THE UNITED STATES OF AMERICA
BY
ATHENS PRINTING COMPANY
461 Eighth Avenue
New York, NY 10001

CONTENTS

"Is it really the end of all this? Will it just disappear —
not be there any more? All this . . ." A shiver ran down my
back.

I was thirteen years old, and it was a summer evening in
1917 at Voltchy, our country place. I was running barefoot
down the big grassy slope leading from our house to the
kitchen garden, when I sud-
denly stopped. The sun was
setting. Clumps of trees pressing on all sides threw long
shadows. The heat of the day
was over, and my toes felt the
dew on the grass. A faint
fragrance from the many rose
beds filled the air. I believe I can pinpoint to this one moment
my first realization that the entire way of life I knew was
coming to an end. But it was so frightening to face the completely unknown and unimaginable future that I shrugged off
my fear and ran on to tell my mother that supper was ready.

The Happy Kingdom

Voltchy, the golden dream of our childhood, our country
home where we stayed every year from June to October, was
located, roughly speaking, in the middle of a triangle formed
by the cities of Kursk, Voronezh, and Kharkov. It is not a very
picturesque part of Russia. There are no mountains, no woods,
no lakes there. Vast undulating plains, "steppes," stretch out
in all directions. This is the wheat belt, the most fertile part
of European Russia, with a top layer of rich black soil several
feet thick. We grew up with a sense of vastness all around
us, an endless open horizon on all sides, the green and golden

waves of the wheat fields rippling in the wind like a sea. Winters were cold and snow-bound, summers clear and hot, with enough rain for good crops.

Our home was not an old family estate. My father was the second son in his family. By the time he was twenty-two years old, he had completed his education, had gone through the three months of compulsory military service for college graduates, and had made the traditional "grand tour" around the world. A piece of land some ten thousand acres large was situated too far from the old estate to be farmed economically. For years it had been rented out, but now the leaseholder lost interest, and my grandfather assigned to his second and unmarried son the job of building up an estate of his own.

On a fine May day in 1880 my father rode the twenty miles separating the new land from his old home. He found a few fields waiting to be prepared for sowing in the fall and a thatched hut with an earthen floor. On the first market day in a nearby large village, he bought a horse, a cart, some equipment and food supplies, hired a married couple for the farm and housework, and began his lifework.

By the time I remember Voltchy, about thirty years later, it was a fairly large and self-sufficient estate with some sixty buildings scattered over the hillside: kitchen, dairy, stables for riding horses, stables for workhorses, cattle sheds, carpenter's shop, smithy, steam flour-mill, pigsties, poultry yards, cottages for employees with small gardens, dormitories for seasonal workers, school building, barns, granaries, etc. At the bottom of the hill rose the tall "cranes" of the draw-wells that provided all the water needed on the estate.

Our own whitewashed brick house stood on the top of a gentle slope. It was a one-story building on one side and had two floors on the other, with several porches and balconies. The flower garden, park, orchard and vegetable garden stretched for some thirty acres all around. The trees seemed old and shady to me, and the whole place stood there as if it had existed for ages.

Compared to the old country homes of Western Europe, Voltchy was unpretentious and not very beautiful — as a matter of fact rather raw. No architect had a hand in designing the main house. My father planned it and a local contractor built it. As the family grew it was enlarged. At the time I remember it, there were twelve large rooms on the main floor and a few smaller ones in the basement. The wooden floors were either painted or waxed, the inner walls white-washed. Almost all the furniture was home-made of bird's-eye birch by our carpenter and upholstered in bright chintzes or linens embroidered by the girls of the estate. My mother did much of the designing and decorating herself, inspired by the many Russian and foreign art magazines she received. I remember the telephone being installed, a party line, so that all the neighbors were hooked on the same line and could listen and join in the conversation. We had no electricity yet in the country and used kerosene lamps. The kerosene lamps were not turned off when we left the room, and the whole house stood brightly illuminated in the evenings. Water was supplied from deep wells bored at the foot of the hillside and it was a man's full-time job to drive a team of oxen hitched to a wooden barrel on wheels. The barrel was filled by means of well sweeps, then slowly driven up to the house, piped into a reservoir in the basement and then pumped by hand into the two bathrooms on the main floor.

My mother's absorbing interest was the garden, especially the rose garden. A trained gardener with numerous assistants spent all their time on it, but gathering the roses and arranging the flowers was my mother's own job, into which she drew all her willing and unwilling children and most of the tutors and governesses, who were generally much more willing, since they were city bred and handling flowers was still a pleasure. Our record, as I remember, was one thousand roses, cut and arranged in vases in one day. For me, throughout my childhood, the park provided all the fascination of imaginary play: climbing trees, making tree houses, treasure caves, and forts, and even having trees for playmates.

For all the members of our family, my parents, my three older brothers, my sister and me, Voltchy was the core of our life, the object of our greatest loyalty and love, a love quite difficult to explain reasonably. In the memoirs he wrote after the Revolution, my father said that by 1907 it had become quite clear to him that large landownership in Russia was doomed and that the national economy based on it was heading toward a catastrophe. It became obviously impractical to invest money and work in the estate, and the reasonable solution would be to sell Voltchy, especially since prices for land were high and the sale would bring us a real fortune. My father was certainly not a sentimental man, yet he felt a deep distaste at the thought of selling the estate. He realized that for him land was not a marketable commodity; it represented a value that he could not measure in terms of profit. Feeling that this should not be his personal decision, he held a family conference with us all. The mere suggestion of the sale of Voltchy was so unanimously and violently rejected that my father gave up any thought of doing it. In his memoirs he wrote: "My ancestors owned this land by right and I decided that if I have to lose it, I want to be deprived of it by law, not sell my own home for profit. Now, fifteen years later, living in exile and poverty, having lost everything, I do not regret my decision."

We came to Voltchy every year in May, and it was a two-and-a-half day journey by train from St. Petersburg to the station closest to Voltchy. From there we drove fifteen miles in a large coach drawn by four horses hitched abreast in the usual Russian style. The train arrived late in the evening, and after the excitement of meeting the coachman, the horses, the coach, there came a monotonous two-hour drive through the night with nothing to see except the flicker of the oil lanterns. We dozed, woke up, dozed again, slid into each other's laps. The old coach was stuffy and smelly. Then suddenly, after a seeming eternity, the horses' hoofs thudded over the little wooden bridge of the driveway. Even now, after sixty-five years, I can hear the sound. We are home, the house is lit up like a Christmas tree. Old Alexei picks me up, half asleep as I am, and carries me through the dark hall into the dining room. On the dining table the brightly polished red-copper samovar purrs away. A supper of cold chicken, bread and butter and honey and all kinds of country goodies waits for us. The windows are wide open and the fragrance of lilac in bloom pours in. And the nightingales!

A deafening symphony of nightingales fills the air, for our Kursk nightingales are famous in all Russia. We are home, we are home! The happiness of that moment seems to give us a foretaste of what heaven must be like.

If the material furnishings in Voltchy were far more modest than those of any well-equipped country home today, the same cannot be said of the people who made up our household, nor of their cultural interests, which made us part of the intellectual life of a far larger world. Hundreds of books in many languages and for all age levels lined the walls of the hall and the dining room. English, French and German magazines were regularly received. Friends and visitors from all parts of the world came occasionally, and I do not remember a time when several foreign languages were not spoken at mealtimes. Trips abroad, including the quite young children and some of the domestic staff, were frequent, but whether we were in Rome or in beautiful Schwarzwald or anywhere else, we always waited eagerly for our return to Voltchy.

During the last years before World War I, our family in Voltchy consisted of my parents and their five children. Andrei, my eldest brother, eleven years older than myself, was a student at the Imperial Alexander Lyceum, from which my father and both my grandparents had also graduated. Alexander, four years younger, was in the older grades of "Reformierte Schule", a well-known private German day-school in St. Petersburg. My sister Mania, in her mid-teens, my brother Iuri and I were taught at home. Iuri was two years older than I.

I have to digress here to tell more about Iuri and our rather special friendship. In 1909 our family made one of its trips abroad, the purpose of which, I believe, was to enable my mother to avoid the harsh Petersburg winter. My father felt that she worried too much if she did not have the children with her, so that Mania, Iuri and I, accompanied by Gania, our nurse, went to Rome with her. Though I was only six years old, I still remember some impressions of Rome, the Piazza d'Espagna, the Colosseum, the catacombs. The day before our departure for Russia, at a farewell luncheon given

us at the home of my mother's friends, eight-year old Iuri
complained of a bad headache. It grew worse rapidly. He had
to be taken home and when the doctor came he diagnosed
meningitis. For days it was uncertain whether Iuri would live.
He screamed with pain or was unconscious most of the time.
I do not know what arrangements were made, but we stayed
in the hotel suite we had. Mother, Gania and a trained nurse
took care of Iuri; several doctors came daily. My sister and I
were taken into a friend's house. My father came from Russia.

Very gradually Iuri began to get better, but he could not
move. At last I was allowed to come and see him. He lay flat
in the big bed, the room darkened by shutters. He looked very
small, very white. I had been told beforehand not to sit on
his bed nor jiggle it, for every movement hurt him badly. So
I stood by his bed and looked at him. Iuri looked pleased and
smiled. "I'll show you a trick," he whispered. I watched, but
nothing happened. "Isn't it good?" he asked. "Oh fine, Iuri!
How did you do it? It's really good," was my wily and tactful
feminine response. Only when Gania took me out, did I learn
from her that for the first time since he was ill Iuri was able
to move his head very slightly.

Time went on, school was out and my older brothers and
their tutor joined us in Rome. Iuri improved enough to sit
in an armchair and we moved from the hotel to the home of
friends who had already left for the summer. The Roman heat
was oppressive and it was decided we would all go for the
summer to a water resort in Germany, where Iuri could undergo therapy in the famous swimming pools. We children
were all disappointed in not going back to Voltchy for the
summer and one day, egged on by my twelve-year old sister
Mania, Iuri attempted to get up from his armchair and crashed
to the floor, scaring us terribly, for the doctor had said any
shock or blow on the head could cause a relapse.

Badenweiler was a charming resort in the hills of Schwarzwald and for some reason very popular among Russians. We
found many friends there and had a very good time. Iuri was
brought to Badenweiler on a stretcher, but rapidly progressed
to a stroller, so that he could join us on our hikes. One of
the main attractions was a rocky mountain slope where one

could find amethysts, beautiful semiprecious crystals, from light lavendar to deep violet in color. Local jewelry shops specialized in setting them. My older brothers climbed up to the steeper, more inaccessible places and found some really fine stones. Iuri would be taken out of his stroller and settled in the sand at the foot of the slope where it was practically impossible to find an amethyst. I remember being so worried by this that I carried out quite a complicated strategy: I found a nice crystal, hid it in the palm of my hand, came back to Iuri, pretended to look for stones near him, unobtrusively dropped mine, and slowly moved away again. When I heard his joyful shout, I was as pleased as he was and never told him what I had done.

Iuri recovered completely, but his illness left its traces. Physically he remained somewhat clumsy and not very well coordinated in his movements, so that he never took part in any sports. He was very bright intellectually, but remained nervous and high-strung, easily upset emotionally. I think all this influenced our friendship very deeply; it became rather exclusive, like that of twins. We lived, played, studied, and worked together, with no other friends. I developed a somewhat maternal attitude to Iuri and felt that I had to protect him.

In Voltchy at meal times some twelve or fourteen people met at the table. Besides the immediate family there was our elderly French governess, Mademoiselle Benzenger, whose special responsibility was Mania, but who gradually took over Iuri and me. Mademoiselle Benzenger's grandfather was an officer in Napoleon's army who was lost in the Russian campaign. His wife, bringing her baby son with her, came to Russia to look for him. All her efforts failed and she stayed in Russia and married a Russian landowner. Her French son went back to France to finish his medical education, but then returned to Russia, became a Russian citizen, joined the Orthodox Church, and served as a medical officer in the Russian army. All his children maintained their bi-national status. For our Mademoiselle Benzenger, also called Marianna Vasilievna, Russian and French were equally familiar. She also spoke faultless English, German and Italian and had lived for long periods abroad. She had no degrees, but was one of the most cultured and well-read women I ever knew.

Every summer we were joined by Dorothy Gibson, a charming girl in her late teens from one of the professional English families who formed the foreign community in Petersburg. She was our companion and playmate whose only duty was to speak and read English with us. Almost every summer there also was a German tutor for my brothers and some special teacher coaching us in subjects in which we had not done too well in the winter. In addition there was usually a kind of "combination medical person," who worked as a physical therapist with Iuri, as a "masseuse" for my mother, and as a medical assistant in the small infirmary that served the needs of the neighborhood.

We aways tend to idealize our childhood, to see it as a kind of Golden Age. In my memory the little world of Voltchy, only a few years before the explosion of the Revolution in 1917, which brought with it the complete upheaval and breakdown of Russian society, was a happy kingdom which gave little sign of the tensions and problems boiling under its peaceful surface. It was certainly not classless, for in its community, circles were moving within circles. Each category of people fullfilled quite different functions and had its own style of life, but throughout my childhood I felt a comfortable relationship of mutual affection and mutual responsibility.

Around the circle of our family moved the circle of all the people who served us, "servants" as they were called then. It was a structured world too, with its own "upper class" — our nurse Gania, my mother's personal maid Luisa, the butler Peter, the dressmaker who joined our household for the summer. They had their meals separately from the others and were more intimate with us. The larger group had its own dining room in a separate building near the kitchen, where the cook and the woman in charge of the laundry were the ruling authorities.

I think I was closer to this world of our servants than any of my brothers or sister because of my nurse Gania. In my parents' eyes Gania also belonged to the servants' group, even though personally appreciated and respected, but for me she meant almost as much as my mother or Iuri, certainly much more than any of the teachers and governesses.

Gania came to us two years before I was born. She was fifteen years old, had just graduated from an orphanage school and was engaged as a nursery maid to help our old nanny. By the time I remember her she was our only nurse and ruled the nursery with supreme authority. Later I learned that when I was five years old, she had become secretly engaged to our butler Peter. She told him that she would not marry him until she had finished bringing me up. Then came World War I and Peter was drafted into the army. He came back to us after the Revolution in 1917, and we celebrated their wedding soon after the Communists came to power. Together we went through the hard times of famine and terror, and Peter and Gania saw my mother and me off when we escaped from Russia. We left them; they never left us.

In my early childhood Gania was a stern but just ruler of the nursery. It must have been hard for my mother to avoid being jealous sometimes, for however much we loved her, she still belonged to a different world than we. She would leave the world of the adults when she came to see us in the evening, to hear us say our prayers, when she took us on some special outing, or even when she played games with us. But Gania was part of our own world; she was with us always, all day long, and slept in our nursery. Every evening, after our mother had left, we waited for Gania to come and tuck us in. With the rather typical child's sense of privacy of feelings, we never said anything if my mother tucked us in, but as soon as her footsteps died away we called for Gania and let her do it all over again in her own way.

Since we did not attend school and had few friends our own age, Iuri and I created a rich world of fantasy, and our imaginary games lasted for weeks and months. We had an imaginary land of our own, an imaginary society in which each one of us impersonated different persons, even an imaginary religion with its priestly rites. Curiously Gania's presence never disturbed us; she was so much part of our life that we could play as if she were not there. Years later I asked her if she remembered our games. "I don't know," she said. "You were always talking away about some silly things . . ." She was just not interested and perhaps because of this we felt completely unselfconscious with her.

Yet I was very conscious of her love and understanding. An Easter Sunday stands out in my memory. Traditionally the whole family clan, grandparents, uncles, aunts, and cousins, gathered at our home for the midday meal on Easter Sunday. I was eagerly looking forward to it; perhaps it was the first time that I was allowed to join the grownups. Impatiently I peeked into the big dining room to look for my place. Horror! Tragedy! No places were set for Iuri and me, for I always recognized our places because of our special oilcloth placemats, and there were none! The whole surface of the table was one big expanse of an immaculate white tablecloth. It was a moment of utter despair and grief. I ran away as fast as I could, hid myself in my father's empty study, deep in the well under his big writing desk, behind the wastepaper basket, and cried my heart out. Gania found me there, led by some sixth sense. I could only sob brokenly and say, "They don't want us at the table!" She went to ask Peter, understood what had happened ("I thought they would not want their placemats on such a special occasion!" was his embarrassed explanation at her assault), and in a few minutes everything was made all right. My face washed, and in a clean frock, I was again re-established in a safe and happy world.

As years went on and lessons, teachers, and tutors became more important in our life, my relationships with Gania changed too. She had a kind of wistful sympathy for me when I had to work hard on my lessons and there was nothing she could do to help me. I felt that I had to comfort her and make her feel that everything was all right, that I was not really tired. Gradually we became friends on an equal footing and discussed many things: social conditions, religion, life. Gania was a sincere, believing Christian but she had a lively intelligence and she asked questions.

Because of Gania I became conscious in a childish way of class and social distinctions and the injustices involved in them. Why were the meals of the servants different from ours? Why was Gania's salary so small? Why did she have so few days off? Why could my mother scold her and even shout at her? Why didn't Peter, Luisa, and others have rooms of their own, but only screened off corners in a passage or the pantry?

Another man on our household staff in Voltchy represented a completely different generation and a different type of person. The first thatched hut with the earthen floor that had been my father's home when he started work in Voltchy was now inhabited by Alexei, his wife and their numerous children. Alexei was the first member of the Voltchy household staff. By the time my father had settled to live full time in Voltchy, he felt the need of some kind of houseman, someone to clean his rooms, polish his boots, take care of the house. He saw a good-natured looking young fellow oiling the threshing machine and decided this was sufficient training for the kind of houseman he needed. Alexei stayed with us for over thirty years until Voltchy ceased to exist. He was eight years old when serfdom was abolished in Russia; he was illiterate and all of us five children had tried unsuccessfully to teach him to read and write. He had been a soldier under the famous General Skobeleff in the Turkish war of the 1870's. At the time I remember him Alexei was close to seventy years old. His job was to trim all the lamps in the house, ring the bell for meals and bring the dishes in from the kitchen building. I remember well the sunny yard, the red-brick kitchen and old Alexei in his white apron, a covered dish in each hand, trotting along with knees slightly bent and all the dogs jumping around him in the everlasting hope that some day he would let a dish fall and their patience would be rewarded. Alexei had a short yellow-white beard, rounded shoulders and small, twinkling blue eyes.

In my childish arrogance I thought I'd teach Alexei some science. "What do you think causes lightning, Alexei?" I asked rather smugly. "Well," he said, "I guess it's clouds knocking against each other." Suddenly I felt that my textbook definitions of "positive and negative charges" was neither more clear nor more convincing. I still remember the confused embarrassment I felt at the moment.

A still wider circle of relationships around us was that of the country community as a whole.

Voltchy was a new estate. There was no village around it, no tradition of interdependence left over from the days of serfdom. The "estate" included many employees and their families who lived in small private houses built for them and most of whom remained there for many years. My father had built a small school with a full-time teacher during the winter months. My mother spent considerable time and effort on medical work. A doctor came approximately once a month or in case of emergency, but every day my mother had to see several patients at her little pharmacy. Some of the sick came from quite a distance; some were cases where she applied treatments prescribed by the doctor, whereas others had had minor accidents that needed first aid. My older sister was supposed to conduct a handicraft class with older girls and teach them embroidery, but I believe this project never developed successfully. My own project was the children's lending library. I began by lending my own books, but the response was so good and I got so interested in the work that I asked my mother to give me as my namesday present a boxful of new children's paperback books. The library was a great success. Some twelve or fifteen children came every day to exchange books and I had lots of fun playing librarian. I always enjoyed my contacts with the village children, probably because I never attended school and missed contact with children my own age.

The red-letter day of the summer for me was September 17, my namesday. I always felt that my very best presents were given to me on that day, some of them made by our carpenter Igor and others store-bought ones that my mother brought back from St. Petersburg after seeing off my brothers to their schools. All the presents would be laid out on a small table in the dining room, decorated with a large wreath of oak leaves. A big cake, the "krendel," was always the centerpiece, and around it were laid out all the presents given me by all the members of the family. Of course, I was not allowed to go into the dining room until the entire family gathered there, and as I pranced at the closed door in my fresh, crisp white frock, my excitement reached an almost painful level.

In the afternoon a big party was held for all the estate children, usually some fifty or sixty of them. This involved preliminary shopping at Perkhunov's, the general store at the big village where we attended church on Sundays. It was the only shop in the village and it sold everything — tools, harness, candy, kerosene, drygoods, stationery, even perfume. The store was cool and dark, with its own penetrating aroma which I've never encountered since, and what wouldn't I give to smell it again! We bought pounds and pounds of candy, hair-ribbons for girls, whistles and tops for boys, big loaves of a special kind of white bread, large tins of jam, mints and ginger cookies.

The tea party started at four o'clock, but some children had been hanging around since morning. Tea was served on long trestle tables in the yard, and after tea we had games, the part I liked best. Ours was certainly not a democratic society, but looking back at it now I believe that there was considerable sensitivity and mutual respect. A small incident stands out vividly in my memory. We were playing tag, and two boys a little older than I were running with me, holding my hands and helping me run faster and faster. "We are carrying you, aren't we, Sonichka?" one of them yelled and at that moment he released my hand and blew his nose in the ageless regular peasant manner without the use of handkerchief. I remember my instant hesitation, as he grasped my hand again, and my immediate inner reaction: "I must not show in any way that I mind holding his hand; I might hurt his feelings just as we are having such a good time together."

Usually village children were not allowed in our yard or garden, but there was one other occasion for companionship that I enjoyed very much. My mother, my older brothers and our many guests played tennis quite a lot, and village children were hired to pick up the balls. I was allowed to join them and was paid at the same rate — three kopeks a set, as I still remember. Though my being with them meant that one child less was hired, the other children seemed to like this arrangement because when the grownups had finished playing, we stayed on and had a good time at the swings.

A still wider circle was formed by our relationships with the neighboring villages. Almost every day a few peasants came to see my father. It might be to discuss conditions of renting land or a loan to be made or a payment deferred, or to ask for advice on some legal matter. They would talk about methods of farming or fire insurance (a new practice at this time) or about some building project. My father was a fervent partisan of the agricultural reform introduced by Stolypin in the 1900's, which allowed peasants to break away from the traditional village community and purchase or rent a separate lot of land that they would then farm individually. It is among those individual farmers that my father witnessed a remarkable improvement in methods of farming, in the use of better implements, in productivity and wealth, while "community farming" remained crippled by the nearsighted, ignorant and conservative decisions of the village assembly. I understand that my father was a well-respected landowner, not sentimental, yet fair and sober in his judgment. Of course, vestiges of old customs persisted. Sometimes my father would thoroughly lose his temper when a visitor started off his business by kneeling and bowing down to the earth in the traditional Russian obeisance, but the image I remember best is of my father and a peasant sitting together on the steps of the shady porch, absorbed in a conversation that interested both of them.

Other visitors came to see my mother. I have already mentioned the small dispensary where she worked several hours daily. At other times people came to ask for material help. Some were what one might call "professional beggars" who for some special reason of health, or old age, or death in the family were unable to provide for themselves. These were given clothes, made by a sewing group that worked in winter, a little money and a note to the estate manager for food supplies. A very different type of people were "the burnt-out ones" — victims of a fire. In those pre-insurance days, whenever a peasant household was destroyed by fire, the family, borrowing if necessary a horse and cart, made the rounds of a wide neighborhood, collecting help. They came in dignity, expecting to be assisted, and were received with sympathy. In their case the note to the estate manager would include building materials, seed, and other things necessary to reestablish the victim of the disaster. Accidents connected with work were also dealt with in this patriarchal way. I remember the case of a young girl who tried to jump over the opening at the top of the threshing machine into which sheaves of wheat are thrown. She slipped and fell. The man working at the place pulled her out but she lost her foot. I remember her coming into our yard a few months later, on crutches, asking my parents' help to be outfitted with an artificial limb. She came as a petitioner, asking my parents to help her out of charity.

The pattern of community relationship in Voltchy was different from that of landowners whose old country places were part of "their" village, a village of their former serfs. In my uncle's country place, in 1910, fifty years after the abolition of serfdom, engaged couples still kept up the custom of asking my grandmother for permission to get married. The point of the custom, of course, was that she was bound by the same tradition to give the young people a present, a kind of dowry. Smilingly my grandmother wondered what would happen if she refused to give her permission. She never had the courage to try it.

Alexandrovka, the country home of my maternal grandparents Sabouroff in central Russia, was also of the patriarchal, traditional type. The old frame house was surrounded by some sixty acres of wooded grounds. Its most striking feature was the long wide avenues, carefully sanded, edged by huge old birch trees, maples and oaks. High, high up the branches intertwined and formed arches like those of a Gothic cathedral. A white church stood nearby, and around it, in the shade of trees, stood the white marble crosses of the family cemetery. Alexandrovka was adored by the whole Sabouroff family: my great-grandmother, whose marble bust with the inscription "Genius Loci" stood in the park; my grandfather Andrei Sabouroff, an active statesman of the "Emancipation era" of the 1860's who became Minister of Education in the reign of Alexander II; my charming grandmother, a very popular and cosmopolitan hostess of St. Petersburg society; and their three daughters. The eldest daughter, a beautiful and gifted girl, died at the age of sixteen. My mother was the youngest and married my father when she was eighteen. The middle one, my Aunt Mary, died in the United States at the age of 93. For all of them Alexandrovka was the joy and the hub of their life. My mother and my aunt, aged fourteen and sixteen, started the village school and taught there until my mother's marriage. Later on my aunt created a home industry for the village women: Russian artisan embroidery that sold very well abroad. The women's good earnings actually changed their position within the home, the husbands willingly helping with the home chores to give wives more time for paid work. While Voltchy always produced a good income, the farming in Alexandrovka was always in the red, and the charming country home was maintained at the price of gradually selling parts of the land.

At the time of the Revolution of 1917, violence and hatred exploded in Alexandrovka, unparalleled by anything that took place in Voltchy. The Alexandrovka house was burned down and pillaged by the villagers. The library books were torn page by page and scattered in the wind. The portrait of the child who died was pulled down and her eyes poked through; the old trees were all cut down. At a meeting of the villagers a man shouted at my aunt: "We've had enough of your sucking our blood!" "Stephan, when did I suck your blood?" she answered mildly. "If I had not taught you to read and write, you'd still be illiterate today!" There was a ripple of laughter in the crowd at this exchange, but the bitter resentment was still there.

The changeover at Voltchy, on the other hand, was quiet and gradual. After the Communists came to power the estate was nationalized and dismantled. A Soviet Committee came and took away all the contents of the main house. Old Alexei, when requested to turn over the keys, kept one back. For days after this, he would penetrate into the house at night and withdraw those things he thought we would care most about: letters, photographs, etc. He then hid everything in a hole he made in the earthen floor of his cottage and later tried to send the things to us. Nothing reached us, of course, except a rumor that poor old Alexei was shot, accused of trying to hide my older brothers.

I often wondered at the contrast. Was my father's businesslike, fair efficiency better understood or better respected than the somewhat sentimental and unrealistic idealism practised in Alexandrovka? Or was it the heritage of serfdom, the feeling of the villagers that this particular property belonged to them by right? It is always wrong to generalize, but I often wondered about this when I witnessed the enmity shown by underprivileged nations to Americans who had given much material help. Perhaps "philanthropy" is always resented?

In July 1914 my parents went abroad to spend a month or two in Badenweiler in Germany for a treatment my mother had to undergo. My brother Iuri and I were sent with Mademoiselle Benzenger to Pokrovskoye, the old Shidlovsky estate, to stay with our Uncle Kolia and Aunt Katia Shidlovsky. Pokrovskoye was always a second home to us.

"Is it really going to be war? I mean, a real war, just like in a book?" I was rather confused. Grown-ups were speaking of ultimatums, mobilizations and other things I did not understand very well. But war? To me, a child of the 1900's, war meant something big and heroic, that made you feel hot all over. War was glory, self-sacrifice and death; it made you want to die, to die for Russia. I was walking with Aunt Katia up the road leading to the church. She was worried and somehow I felt war did not mean to her what I always thought it to be. "Is it really war," I pressed on, "like the Japanese one?"

"A mighty more serious one, I am afraid," she answered. "More like the one of 1812." The sun was setting and all the western side of the sky was a dull red and looked like a huge fire somewhere far away. One by one the stars came up in the sky. The air was growing cool and damp. My aunt tried to explain the situation to me: Serbia, Austria, Germany, France, England, Belgium, Russia. She tried to explain what war meant and told me that I ought not to wish for it. But deep down in my heart I still felt excited. War, Russia — what great words! Our brothers, our cousins, would be heroes; they would go and fight for Russia.

Next morning I had a chance to come closer to what real war was like, the real war "just like in a book." Mobilization was declared and the rented part of the orchard was crowded with recruits and their families buying apples on their way to the railway station. I will never forget some of the faces I saw there.

An old peasant woman, some sixty years old, came with her son, a handsome boy in his early twenties. She clung to him, sobbing, and would not let him go. Self-consciously and shyly he tried to soothe her and his face had a tender and pitying expression. Suddenly a song burst forth not far away, the song which recruits always sing on their last day home. The recruits were leaving. With an effort the boy tore himself away and ran to join the others. The woman remained.

A little further on a whole family was waiting for somebody to join them before following the recruits to the station. A young boy and a still smaller baby girl were sitting on the cart. They looked frightened and bewildered by the unusual scene and watched with open mouths and half-dried tears. An older girl of about fourteen sat next to them. She had also cried and her pale little face was swollen and tear-stained. An old woman was wailing, "keening" in the traditional Russian way. A young woman stood silently, leaning on the cart. She did not cry and her eyes looked dull and dry. Her face was still and stony with such a blank expression of hopelessness that it made me feel cold. Was this day the first crack in the happy world of my childhood?

For several days there was no news from my parents. Uncle Kolia, an excitable and high-strung but kindly gentleman, was in his element. "Of course they'll get stranded in Germany. They will be treated as civilian prisoners of war, for the duration! Who knows when we will see them again? Agitatedly he paced our schoolroom, where Mademoiselle Benzenger, serene and calm, presided over our lessons. He struck a dramatic attitude: "Ne craignez rien, Mademoiselle! Les enfants de mon frère sont mes enfants!"

My parents did go through rather anxious days. My mother had just undergone an operation. As the international situation became more and more threatening, my father asked the doctor whether she could stand the journey to Russia. The doctor answered that she should stay in bed for at least another week. When my father said that they could not wait, the doctor gave him a few ampules of morphine and showed how to inject them. "If anything goes wrong, she'll be better off completely unconscious," he said.

My parents had a hectic trip with several train changes through war-ready Germany, with crowds demonstrating and booing foreigners. In Berlin, abandoning all their heavy luggage, they managed to get on a train which proved to be the very last one to leave Germany for Russia. Years later, during the times of hunger and cold after the Revolution, these mysterious trunks left somewhere in Berlin became a family myth. We loved listing all the things these trunks might contain and imagining that some day we would get them.

Father and Mother finally made it to St. Petersburg on the very day when my eldest brother Andrei left for the front line. He had graduated from the Imperial Alexander Lyceum in the spring and was doing his military service when war was declared. His regiment was among the first to leave to take part in the advance into East Prussia that ended in the disastrous encirclement and defeat of the Russian army. In the middle of the night my parents watched as my brother's regiment marched, with its band in front, to the Warsaw station. Men and horses were loaded on a freight train with their supply of hay. The whistle blew at seven A.M. My father saw some of the railway guards make the sign of the cross, blessing the train with all these young men leaving for war. There were tears in many eyes.

Iuri and I were having our French lesson with Mademoiselle on the sunny veranda. It was one of those beautiful lazy mornings when the last thing one would want to do is to study French grammar. The only sound to be heard was the humming of bees and the clicking of Mademoiselle's knitting needles. Suddenly I heard footsteps and one of my cousins came in. She gave us an envelope addressed in Mother's hand. The French lesson, the heat, Mademoiselle — all was forgotten. We knew already that my parents had arrived safely in St. Petersburg, but we had had no letters from them yet.

"My darling little girl, here we are safe and sound..." Suddenly I saw at the bottom of the page, a few words hastily scrawled in pencil, in a different handwriting: "Dear Iuri and Sonia, we are leaving this night for the front. Don't be afraid. And if I don't see you again, remember,— it is for Russia. Pray for me. God bless you. Love, Andrei." Iuri was reading over my shoulder and suddenly he left the room. I followed and found him on his bed, his face buried in the pillow. There we lay, side by side, for a long time and I thought again and again: Andrei, Russia.

A week later my parents returned, my mother looking frail, and we settled down to spend the fall in Voltchy. The optimism and enthusiasm of the first days of war were dimmed. News from the front was confusing and disturbing. Obviously something had gone wrong. After the first two postcards there had been no news from Andrei. My father received no answer to his official inquiries. My mother went back to Petersburg.

October evenings are long in the country. We had supper, my father read aloud to us and then it was time for bed. Suddenly at about eleven P.M. the telephone bell rang. Fifteen-year-old Mania was the first to reach the big wall instrument. It was a telegram transmitted by the friendly old postmaster in Volokonovka — the large village where the railway station and the post office were located.

After the endless slow dictation of the date, the number, the sender's official address, my father's name and address, came the text: "Your son Andrei safe, lightly wounded, commended for bravery in action, decorated Cross of St. George." As the dictation ended the old postmaster's trembling voice added: "Permit me to add my congratulations to your joy..." Mania's joyful screams brought everyone running, half-undressed, whether in nightgown, pajamas or robe. Mademoiselle always insisted that she did *not* kiss my father. "We embraced, yes, but we did not kiss!"

Much later we learned the details of the feat that earned my brother his St. George Cross. In action he was sent as an orderly with some message. After delivering it, on his way back, because of changes in the positions of the troops, he found himself at night in enemy territory. Riding along, rifle in hand, trying to find his way, he approached a house. He dismounted, entered, and found some thirty or forty German soldiers, many of them wounded, and a German doctor. Aiming his rifle at them he announced that the area was in the hands of the Cossacks and that he was making the Germans his prisoners of war. The doctor answered that some of the men were heavily wounded and could not be moved. Andrei chose eighteen men who were not wounded, or only very lightly, and ordered them to march in front of him. He followed on horseback and kept up an uninterrupted flow of artistic German swear words, which he had acquired to perfection during his years in the German high school in Petersburg. He sincerely believed that it was the language he used that brought him safely through German-occupied territory, back to the Russian positions where he turned over his prisoners to the appropriate authorities and then tried to make himself scarce because he thought he would be in trouble for being late. A few days later my brother's commandant received an official paper announcing that my brother was awarded the Cross of St. George for his outstanding action.

In the fall of 1914 we returned to Petersburg, and the usual routine was resumed for us children.

Our family lived in our own house in a small side-street at the end of the Kameno-Ostrovsky Prospect. We occupied the whole middle floor, actually two apartments joined into one. One end of the apartment was our children's world: a large nursery where Gania and I slept, a small adjoining room for Iuri, a classroom, the children's bathroom, a large room for Mademoiselle Benzenger and a room for my sister, all of them opening onto a small hall. The central part of the apartment, with windows facing the street, consisted of my father's large study, a ballroom, my mother's drawing room, and my parents' bedroom. Across the corridor, with windows facing the yard, were my older brothers' rooms and the dining room. Several small rooms beyond my parents' bedroom, my mother's dressing room, bathroom, sewing room, and pantry, joined the front rooms to the wing containing the servants' quarters, the kitchen and the laundry. Though cars were beginning to be used more and more in cities, we still held on to our horse-drawn carriages, to our stables and our coachman Vasily. He wore the traditional heavily padded Russian coachman's garb. It made him look so fat that I was greatly surprised when I first saw him out of uniform, and discovered he was a slight and skinny fellow.

Of all that I have received in my childhood, I am most grateful for the excellent and systematic education which was given us. The credit for it goes fully to my mother and to the painstaking and sustained attention she gave to our lessons. She did not have a high opinion of the school education of the time and merely resigned herself to it in the case of my older brothers, as a formal education was needed for any career or profession. Because of Iuri's physical handicaps, resulting from meningitis, the doctor supported her in postponing his school attendance. Thus, a kind of home-school was set up for us, with teachers carefully selected by my mother, and the curriculum determined by the examinations we had to pass at the end of each year at the public school, called "gymnasia" in Russia.

Our lessons began each morning, with teachers arriving at nine and ten A.M. German, Latin, science, and French were the morning subjects, each one two or three times a week. At 11 A.M. we took a "French walk" with Mademoiselle. Lunch was at 12:30. From 1 to 3 P.M. we took a long walk — rain, shine or snow — three times a week with a young English girl, and three times a week with a young German teacher. These last were finally dropped during the war, because Iuri and I rebelled at talking German in the streets and having people give us dirty looks. From 3 to 4 P.M. we did homework. At 4 P.M. we had a break for afternoon tea, then two more lessons with tutors: mathematics, Russian, history, or geography. One more hour of homework before family dinner at 7:30, half an hour's recreation after dinner, and then bedtime, when my mother came to spend some time with us. Evening prayers, Bible reading, and catechism with her replaced formal lessons in religious instruction. Once a week the routine was interrupted by a dancing class held in the ballroom, with some twenty children attending — little girls in white dresses, long black stockings and slippers, and boys in sailor suits. Another group met once a week for an art class.

Our homework was carefully supervised. If we had not finished our assignments by dinner time, Mademoiselle investigated: either we had been lazy and were reprimanded, or a tutor had given us too much to do, and she tactfully notified him or her to decrease the workload.

This routine lasted six days a week, all winter long, with very few interruptions. Somehow in the midst of it all, my mother found time to read aloud to us or to take us on trips to museums and places of interest like the Mint, or the State Paper Works. Birthdays and namesdays were celebrated by parties and we were invited to parties in our friends' houses. We attended church on Sunday mornings and were free to play all Sunday afternoon.

There seemed to be no major problems of discipline in this carefully planned routine. The only punishment I remember is being "forbidden to read" for a day, or a few days, or a week, which, I suppose, was equivalent to "No TV" today. I never misbehaved sufficiently to call upon myself the capital punishment of "being sent to Father," but Iuri did several times. He said to me after one such expedition that the corridor leading from the nursery to the study was a very convenient one because there were so many corners and so many pieces of furniture at which you could grab and hold on. "But what did Papa *do* to you?" I asked awe-struck. "Well, nothing much, really. He looked at me kind of severely and told me to sit down and think. And then he came up and said 'Now, I don't want this to happen again, you hear.' Then he put me out and gave me a little kick with his knee in my behind."

We loved our father, but he was a figure of awe to us. His study was carefully soundproofed, with a cork floor and a rug in the corridor in front of it, a padded door and heavy curtains on both sides of it. The study itself was somewhat dark, with old Dutch and Flemish pictures in heavy frames covering all the walls. He was an ardent collector. I must have been nine or ten years old when, quite consciously, I undertook a campaign to make friends with father. He allowed me to stay quietly in his study and read there, nestling in the corner of the rug-covered sofa. I started asking him questions about some of the pictures he had bought recently and he asked me which one I liked best. I still remember the mental effort I made trying to guess which picture *he* would like me to like best!

Iuri and I missed the companionship of real school life, and the examinations coming at the end of the year caused great excitement. Quite accidentally these examinations were my first contact with the problem of feminism. Yearly examinations taken at a public boys' school were necessary for Iuri so that he would not be handicapped by the time he attended the senior grades. My parents asked the principal of the school whether I could take these examinations too, since we were studying together. The answer was that they would have to submit a special application for imperial approval. And, added the principal, he would be grateful to my parents if they would go through with this formality, for it would open the doors to many young women eager to study at the University. To be accepted there they had to have a diploma of studies completed at a classical public school. This they could obtain by passing examinations at a boys' public school as "externs." My parents applied for the necessary permission for me, and we were greatly impressed to see our names and the mention of the authorization granted in very small print in the newspaper. Thus I became the first girl admitted at the age of ten as an "extern" to the examinations at the Sixth Classical Male Gymnasium of St. Petersburg.

Wide stone steps, dividing as they swept majestically upwards, a uniformed "Swiss" doorman at the entrance, uniformed teachers, the important-looking corpulent principal with gold-rimmed glasses, also uniformed, who received my mother and me in his austere study . . . As ill luck would have it, Iuri got sick the day we had to go for the first time, and I had to face the ordeal by myself. Whenever I went down the corridors or entered a classroom, I heard all the crew-cut, uniformed youngsters whisper excitedly, "The girl, the girl!" Though I looked young for my ten years, even the teachers seemed to recognize in my person a sign of the times. When, during an oral examination, in geography, I failed to remember the name of some volcano on Indonesian islands, the teacher murmured in a loud aside, "Thank God, women have not outdistanced men in everything..." And the nice math teacher who, when I finished the written part of the exam, gallantly accompanied me back to my mother, upon his return to the classroom, looked reproachfully at the boys and said: "So many of you, and one girl was the quickest of you all."

Probably because Iuri and I were somewhat isolated in our companionship and were well endowed with imagination, we gradually created a whole world of our own. It was a world of play and we never confused it with reality, but as years went by the play became so absorbing, so diversified and all-embracing, that it acquired a reality of its own.

We lived in an imaginary land. My part of it was the mountains; Iuri's the plains. I was a mountaineer and to climb my mountains I used my hoop (the plain wooden hoop which my imagination supplied with sharp steel teeth, or cogs). The same hoop could be used in fighting enemies and making prisoners. From our ancient Greek history textbook we took the name Zevgitia for the mountains and Polymarchia for the plains. We had our own cities, of which I remember the names Pelkil and Pak. Our father's involvement in political and government work influenced our play too. Iuri, bearing the name of Prince Gromoff, was president. I held the modest title of "archivarius" — keeper of archives — with the rather strange name of Count Pochka. We both published weekly newspapers, written in pencil in huge block characters. We had meetings of the state council at which we decided vital matters concerning our lands. We had elaborate banquets with dishes made from the stuff Gania procured for us from the kitchen, with long speeches, toasts, and dances to the music of the wonderful old music box, with its cogged cylinder and steel disks peppered with little holes that set the cylinder in motion. We gave and received decorations. We had a scale of ranks, or grades, and had to pass examinations for our advancement.

Somehow wedged into this imaginary world was the family of our dolls and teddy-bears. They were an imaginary "Imperial Family." The uniformed monkey Petka was respectfully called the "czar." We loved Petka more than any other of our stuffed animals and he seemed to us a natural leader. Each one of them had a personality of his own that we accepted as such and would not think of changing.

We even had a religion of our own, with one of the plaster masks in the classroom (used as a model during art classes) as our god. The real fun was the elaborate ceremonies and rituals, with Iuri as high priest, draped in a nightgown and my sashes, chanting hymns, and I as everything else. Bits of Gania's celluloid hairpins, tied to a string, flared and smoked terrifically, as we swung them like incense burners.

The only person who occasionally joined us in our games was my brother Alexander or Sandik, almost 6 years older than Iuri. On marvelous Sunday afternoons he would help us build fantastic flying boats, submarines, etc., on which we went on journeys of discovery out of chairs, tables, blackboards, and stepladders. To have to tidy up without his help was a small price to pay for the fun. He helped us carve a state seal for our state papers and made up a secret code for us to use. One winter he taught us French wrestling, with two of us wrestling against him. Quite often this ended with my two much heavier brothers sitting on top of me, the lightweight, and pounding each other. That same winter our family doctor found, whether correctly or no, I don't know, that I had a "displaced kidney," and parental investigation condemned our wrestling bouts as the cause of the trouble, and forbade them. The word "Pochka" means "kidney" in Russian, and in our games with Iuri I acquired the honorary title of "Count Pochka."

I suppose all children's games are equally fantastic and equally fascinating for the children who play them. What I think was somewhat unusual about ours was that they lasted for years, and that our imaginary play penetrated all of our life.

Iuri and I were undivided in all our attempts to face problems and to understand things. My mother was a very sensitive and emotionally intense person in her spiritual and religious life. Her thinking was shaped both by our own background and the whole way of life of the Russian Orthodox Church as well as by Protestant piety of the Anglican type. The writings of Vladimir Soloviev and Henry Drummond were her favorites. Throughout our childhood our reading included many English children's books that she had loved herself: Charlotte M. Younge's *Daisy Chain* and *The Heir of Radcliffe, Tom Brown's Schooldays, Eric* or *Little by Little, Ada and Girty, The Wide, Wide World.* Some of them were too old-fashioned for us and at the fifth or sixth pious death-scene we hooted derisively, but the books did influence us and ingrained a sense that there is "goodness" and "badness" in life, and that we wanted to be on the side of "good" and had to work for it.

I remember that once, at the beginning of Great Lent, Iuri and I decided that each morning we would read the New Testament and choose a verse that we would try to carry out all day long. Our first attempt was unsuccessful because by the end of the day neither of us could remember the verse we had chosen. What could we do to remember it? I suggested that each day we change around some piece of furniture in our room, so that whenever we enter it, something would look unfamiliar and remind us of our resolve. Turning this over in his mind, Iuri must have felt that he would be expected to do most of the moving and vetoed the suggestion. We finally agreed to write out the verse and pin the slips of paper to our handkerchiefs. Of course, our plan was to be kept completely secret, for it would lose all value if we showed off. Our handwritings were large at the time, the nursery safety pins were large too, and we soon discovered that if we had to blow our nose in public, it was difficult to keep our secret. We became frustrated and the plan quickly petered out.

Every year the last week before Easter stood out as a very special time: long church services, no lessons, no secular reading for pleasure, no guests, special food. On Holy Wednesday afternoon we made a long trip in our carriage to a factory suburb, to go to confession to a priest at the church there. My mother had known him for years when he had a parish nearby, and she did not want to go to a different confessor. It was a once-a-year event and we took it very seriously. One year my mother consigned all five of us to my father's study. "Collect your thoughts," she said. "Think and prepare yourself for confession." She left the room and we began to argue about the best way to "collect our thoughts." At first the older ones announced that I was disqualified: I was not yet seven years old and would not be going to confession. "But I'll receive Communion tomorrow!" I argued spiritedly. "I can think about that." They were doubtful but finally let me stay. Then we decided that we were getting in each other's way and that we needed privacy to collect our thoughts. So each one of us made himself a little house under a separate table where each one could meditate in peace. Upon her return my mother scolded us for playing silly games instead of taking our repentance seriously, but I do remember that, sitting under my table, I *was* thinking very seriously and sincerely about my sinfulness and unworthiness to receive Jesus Christ.

Until we were twelve Iuri and I were not allowed to attend the Easter night service, so we worked out a ritual of our own to celebrate the great feast. Gania procured for us some of the Easter food — a small "kulich" and "pascha" and some sliced meat. We kept back a few of the eggs that we helped dye on Thursday afternoon, and with all of this we set our own little "Easter table" in the nursery. We went to bed at the usual time, but secretly set our alarm clock for ten minutes to midnight. I suppose all the adults went to church, for we were never interrupted or supervised during our celebration. As soon as we woke up we put on our warm dressing gowns and opened the small hinged windowpane that was left for ventilation in the winter double windows. Holding our breath we listened. On the stroke of midnight all the church bells in town began to ring. The deep silvery tones floated into the room. Christ is risen! Christ is risen! Iuri and I stood before the icon in the corner of the nursery, with its small red vigil light burning brightly. We sang the Easter hymn "Hristos

Voskrese" and solemnly exchanged the threefold Easter kiss.
We gave each other our presents and then settled down to
our feast. One year my father, who had a heart condition,
was too unwell to attend church on Easter night. He joined
us in the ceremony and I heard him say later that it was the
best Easter celebration he had ever taken part in.

World War I brought a few changes into our way of life
and, as far as I was concerned, widened my experience of
life. My mother conscientiously reduced her social life. No
more balls were given or attended. Because of this, the only
ball I remember was the one given in the last winter before
the war for my oldest brother's twenty-first birthday. I enjoyed it tremendously, although I was only ten years old
and my mother allowed me to stay up only until 10 P.M.
But my brother's friends and classmates were my staunch
friends too, and after curfew time they would hide me in a
corner and stand in front of it every time my mother passed
by. Then my cousin, a guards' officer who was the "director"
of the ball, invited me to dance with him, and in an intricate
form of the quadrille that he directed, set me up on his
shoulders to avoid the crush. For a ten-year-old it was surely
the ultimate excitement.

With the beginning of the war many luxurious private
homes were converted into hospitals for the wounded. We
were most closely connected with the one organized in the
palace of the Princess Helen of Altenburg, a close friend of
my mother's. At first my mother tried to make herself useful
as a nurse's aid, but she soon realized that, untrained and
physically unsuited to the work as she was, she was not much
help. She then turned her attention to the convalescent soldiers and organized classes for them. She proved to be an excellent teacher and the classes became very popular. She
discovered that some of the soldiers were illiterate and she
drew Iuri and me in to become her assistants in teaching them
to read and write. This hospital work became part of our
weekly routine and we both made good friends among the
wounded.

Gradually my mother became involved in assisting those
who had been blinded, a special branch of work among the

wounded. Their situation did not become less tragic when, medically speaking, their wounds were healed. They had to be taught to adapt to their new condition, to learn to live, to move about, to take care of themselves as blind men. They had to be taught some skill or profession, they had to learn to read and write in Braille. My mother started a small private Training Home for some twenty to thirty blinded soldiers and gave all her time to it. Especially tragic was the situation of those soldiers who had lost their sight not because of a wound, but as a result of drinking denaturated alcohol, to which they turned as the sale of liquor had been forbidden since the beginning of war. These men had no right to a pension of any kind and faced a life of destitution.

Iuri and I often came to visit the Training Home. I remember particularly one soldier who was fond of dancing: with his cane he would "feel out" a wide circle to make sure there was nothing in his way and then, to the music of an accordion played by another blind soldier, he would throw himself into the spirited whirl of the Russian folk dance, stamping, kicking, bending his knees in the traditional *prisiadka*, the tempo getting faster and faster.

In 1916, after a short-term course at the Military School (Imperial Corps of Pages), my second brother, Sandik, enlisted in the same regiment where my eldest brother Andrei was by then an officer.

The first year of the war remains in my mind as a time of patriotic enthusiasm, untroubled by any doubts, even though the losses were heavy and many young men we knew were killed. Yet there was no disillusionment or hesitation in our minds: the deaths were heroic, the war was a "holy war," a war "for Russia." Only very gradually did we begin to experience a sense of frustration, of doubt, a feeling that things were somehow going wrong. It was rather like a fog coming up in which you are uncertain of finding the right way.

This general mood coincided rather strangely with the first fissure I recognized in the structure of our family life, the solidity and happiness of which seemed to me so absolute until then. In 1916 my eldest brother Andrei married. I remember my mother speaking to me of the girl even before

Andrei became engaged: she was a fairy princess, with deep blue eyes; she was beautiful and wonderful, an angel entering Andrei's life. The night Andrei came home to tell us that his proposal had been accepted, my mother brought him to the nursery and woke me up to give me the great news. I accepted everything like a fairy story with a happy ending. Unfortunately the young couple's happiness did not last. Whatever the reasons, my sister-in-law became dissatisfied. Andrei was back at the front lines. The life of a beautiful, attractive young woman, temporarily husbandless, surrounded by young officers on leave and looking for excitement, is not easy, and less than a year after their wedding their marriage collapsed. My sister-in-law had several charming and good-looking younger sisters and brothers. Their rather rigidly pious and moralistic widowed mother brought them up quite strictly and my mother felt they would set us a good example. As a matter of fact the teen-age sisters were completely intoxicated by the unexpected freedom of wartime. Nursing opened to them a whole new world of intimacy and fun with young men of varied social background. My seventeen-year-old sister Mania was drawn into this set, the precursor of the "roaring twenties." Smoking, drinking and breaking many rigid rules of pre-war society seemed fascinating. At thirteen, I was puzzled by their behavior and their unfamiliar new standards. I remember being especially confused by a kind of trade the girls established with my brother Iuri: they would teach him words of the "dirty" songs they knew in exchange for smutty words he would teach them from his vocabulary. This did not fit in with my previous experience of family friendship.

My parents' silver anniversary, which was celebrated on January 10, 1917, stands out for me as a landmark. I thought it would be such a happy occasion, a time of happiness and celebration, and yet as the day went on I felt that something was wrong. There was just no taste of happiness to the day. I later learned that at that very time my brother's wife had definitely left him and asked him for a divorce. A few weeks later the February Revolution of 1917 took place.

CHAPTER TWO

At the time of the Revolution in February 1917, I was thirteen years old, old enough to sense the atmosphere of "malaise" and frustration that was prevalent all around, yet child enough to feel secure and comfortable in the daily routine of our life. Rumors of the first disturbances and conflicts in the streets of Petersburg did not concern us too much.

The Break 1917-1920

On February 27th, however, my father, who was unwell, received an urgent phone call from his colleagues at the State Duma and left our home to join them. He did not return for ten days and during this time the radical break in the history of Russia took place. Father phoned several times to give news. My eldest brother and some of his officer friends called my father trying to discover what was happening and what they, as guard-regiment officers, should do. There was a feeling of uncertainty, of confusion, of lack of confidence in any kind of leadership. The Czar abdicated. Would his brother, Grand Duke Michael, become czar? No. Who, then, rules the country? No one seemed to know. Whom should we obey? asked the officers, and there seemed to be no answer. It seemed that the Duma was the only body that had any reality to it, and yet all the news our father gave us indicated their own confusion and helplessness. The Duma set up a Provisional Committee (of which my father was a member) which tried to create a Provisional Government. But revolutionary crowds broke into the building occupied by the Duma and a Soviet of Workers' Deputies was created then and there.

39

Until that day the word "Soviet" meant to us simply "council," but from then on it became a symbol of a new regime which was falling more and more under Communist leadership. The liberals created a Provisional Government with Kerensky as its most outstanding member. My father did not take part in it and it did not seem to inspire much confidence in anyone. Right from the beginning the Soviet was in opposition to the Provisional Government and its plans to call a Constitutional Assembly.

The only form of violence I saw at that time was a crowd mobbing the police station across the street from our house. Next morning we saw footprints in the deep snow that covered the roof of the building. They led to an attic of the house next door and I fervently hoped that whoever had escaped would reach safety.

That year we stayed in town longer than usual. The weather was hot and my most vivid memory of the time is dust, crowds and sunflower seeds. Sunflower seeds have always been a popular treat and spitting out the seeds had a certain proletarian elegance. Now all the public buildings, all places of gathering, all movie houses and theatres seemed to be covered with a layer of sunflower seed husks. And so many places one had known, of cold dignity and grandeur, typical of classical Petersburg, were now crowded and dirty. The crowds looked different from any people I had seen before: soldiers did not look like soldiers, working men seemed to be on an unending holiday. Meetings and rallies took place, speakers jumped up and harangued the crowds. I guess it was a sign of my sister's and my adaptability and liveliness that we rather enjoyed getting involved in these street meetings, argued and merrily heckled the speakers. What I really enjoyed most that spring was the branches of lilac blossoms sold on street corners. Usually we left the city before lilacs were in bloom and their sweet freshness, the sheer quantity of the blossoms, seemed a promise of better things.

Our summer in Voltchy was undisturbed, although we realized it would be our last one there. We read in the newspapers the fiery speeches made by Kerensky. On our party line that served as a kind of broadcasting system, we caught the news of General Kornilov's attempt to gain control of the government and of its failure. My mother directed all her energy into putting up preserves for the coming winter, when food shortages were expected. She was pretty naive and inexperienced in planning the food supplies. She mobilized all the household to shell peas, cut beans and dry vegetables. How bitterly we regretted in the days to come that her stocks did not include flour, cereals, bacon, ham, lard, preserved meats, and other basics of which we remained deprived for years, but she never thought that such food supplies would not be sent us from the country as usual. Fortunately she did stock up on jam, syrups, jellies and sugared fruit which in time provided a lot of calories.

In the fall we did not return to Petersburg. The Russian army was in collapse, the Germans were advancing and my father thought Petersburg would soon be taken. My mother felt that there was more chance of my father being arrested in Petersburg, where he was well known and where many of his colleagues were already imprisoned. She found a very pleasant furnished apartment in Moscow which belonged to the manager of the largest department store in the city. He was an Englishman, and was going back to England. There were five or six large rooms, attractively furnished, and our considerably reduced household moved into it. Gania, Vasilissa (a daughter of old Alexei) and Maria the laundress were our staff. My parents, Mania, Iuri and I made up the family.

In October 1917 my father was still in Petersburg where he took part in a Pre-Parliamentary Committee that was to prepare the work of the Constitutional Assembly. On October 25th a crowd of soldiers invaded the meeting room and chased out all the delegates, using rifle butts to encourage their exit. A cruiser stationed on the river Neva took a few shots at the Winter Palace, Kerensky's residence, defended by the Women's Battalion and students of a Military School. Kerensky fled and the whole regime of the Provisional Government disintegrated. The Communist, or Bolshevik, Party and its organ, the Soviet of Workers' and Peasants' Deputies, became the ruling government of Russia.

All did not go as smoothly in Moscow. We arrived there in mid-October and did not settle down immediately because first my mother and then Iuri got a light form of diphtheria. Mania and I roamed in our still unfamiliar new home. On a dark October evening, we could see from the windows the angry glow of a house on fire. A sudden crash of heavy guns made us start. It was answered by the measured tac-tac-tac of machine guns. We could not make out from which side the sounds came.

"Mania, Mania, is it the end? Can't we help in some way?"

Flushed and angry my sister walked up and down the room. "Shut up, won't you? Don't you think it is bad enough as it is? Help them? I'd do anything to help!"

We knew that for days fighting had been going on between large groups of soldiers and much smaller ones made up mostly of high school boys and cadets. And again no leadership, no support. We sat alone in that little apartment high above the unfamiliar, unknown city, without really knowing what was going on.

Only once did I actually see any fighting in our street. I tried to look out of the window, but the street was too narrow, and from our sixth-floor apartment I could only get a glimpse of the opposite pavement. I saw a woman caught between the two parties. She flattened herself against the wall, trying to hide from the bullets, crawling slowly on until she disappeared into a yard.

We did not know then how the fighting was going, or how it ended. But one day the shooting stopped and there was silence. We listened to it with sinking hearts.

That first winter of 1917/18 in Moscow was difficult in many ways, but life still remained measurable according to normal standards. It was frightening to see lists of executed people posted in the streets, some of whom were familiar. Our style of life was drastically reduced. Vasilissa went back to the country and Maria had to be dismissed. My mother and I attempted to do the family laundry ourselves, and I must admit that the results of our enthusiastic efforts were rather discouraging. Gania, of course, stayed with us and Peter returned from the army. We celebrated their wedding as best we could, my parents giving them the traditional blessing and my father acting as best man. There was a wedding dinner after church and Vasilissa giggled all the time at having to "sit next to the master." Gania and Peter settled down in the small room behind the kitchen — not as our paid servants any more, but all members of one family. Peter found work in a factory and learned how to mend shoes, which brought him quite a good additional income. Gania cooked for all of us. My parents could still draw on small monthly amounts from their bank account. Food stuffs were still sent from Voltchy, or brought to Moscow by our faithful old Alexei. Iuri and I continued to take lessons and in the spring of 1918 passed our exams at a private school.

We did not feel isolated from the outside world, for there was quite a large group of foreigners in Moscow, most of them American YMCA secretaries who were trying to continue their work for German prisoners of war and to organize "Y" clubs in the Russian army. They were all frequent visitors at our English-speaking home. My special friend was Chapin W. Huntington, an attaché at the American Embassy, who used his subscription at the Embassy library to provide me with juvenile books such as Charlotte M. Younge's *Daisy Chain*. The librarian must have been really puzzled by his strange tastes. The interests of all the young men were divided: for hours they would discuss with my father politics, the past and future of Russia, and world prospects, and respectfully listen. Deprived of the tribune he was used to, he enjoyed having them as an audience. Then, with equal enthusiasm they joined the company of English-speaking Russian girls of my sister's age, obviously a rather new type of femininity for them. And for these girls, going out with their new friends, attending theatres, having good times according to unfamiliar American patterns, was something new and exciting too. Their parents accepted such unchaperoned "dating" in a bewildered way. It all would have been unheard of in pre-revolutionary days, but how could one refuse to let one's daughters have a good time in these days of gathering darkness?

Mania got a secretarial job in the office of the American

YMCA and worked there until September 1918, when Paul B. Anderson, the last YMCA secretary to remain in Moscow, was arrested. The local staff, including my sister, was arrested too, but their imprisonment lasted only a few days. The American Embassy left and this put an end to my supply of reading matter, but fortunately I found a well-filled bookshelf in our apartment and read in that one winter practically all of Charles Dickens' novels. Soon after the Embassy's departure Peter, grinning happily, presented us with a huge parcel left by Huntington which contained chocolate, condensed milk, sugar, and canned food, as well as some articles of clothing. It was pleasant to get all these things and yet how funny it seemed to be given, for the first time in our life, used clothing. It made us appreciate all the more Huntington's tact in handling the matter.

As time went on, life became more difficult. Our Voltchy estate was nationalized and "expropriated" and no more food could be sent from there. Private funds in banks and the contents of deposit boxes were nationalized. There was not a chance of my father finding a job and he was lucky to be forgotten. As a matter of fact when he made an attempt to register for a job at the City Employment Agency, the girl at the desk stared at him: "Why — are you still alive? Didn't they execute you?" My father gave up the idea of looking for a job and settled down to write his memoirs. Our last source of income was to sell our things and we were somewhat handicapped by our move to Moscow, which meant that we did not have the resource of old trunks and attics crammed with discarded things.

My father took part in one more public assembly, that of the All-Russian Church Sobor (Council) that was called in August 1917 to solve the many problems of church life and administration that arose after the Revolution. Since Peter the Great, at the start of the eighteenth century, the church had been practically subjected to the state, with all the undesirable consequences of such a condition. Now this period came to an end and a new structure had to be set up. The antagonism of the Sovie government to all forms of religion could be foreseen, although no one could guess how intense the persecution would be and how long it would last. The "Sobor" reestablished the post of the Patriarch as head of the church and elected Patriarch Tikhon. It also reorganized the structure of parish administration, creating parish councils with elected lay members and giving these councils a considerable degree of self-government. This allowed the church to exist during long decades of persecution when the central church administration was completely crippled.

From the very beginning the lovable, humble and radiant personality of Patriarch Tikhon attracted the loyalty and affection of church people. In all the divisions and splits of the Russian Orthodox Church in Russia and abroad during the fifty years that followed his death, his image remained unblemished. This is why I cherish the memory of the day when our father took Iuri and me to some function of the "Sobor" and introduced us to the Patriarch, who gave us his blessing.

A ceremony in which I took part impressed me deeply. It must have been soon after the first anniversary of the October Revolution. Since some of the gates leading into the Kremlin were damaged during the fighting, they were draped for the occasion with red cloth. Above the Nikolsky Gate opening into the Red Square, there was an ancient ikon of St. Nicholas set into the stone wall of the tower. Naturally it was hidden by the red draperies, but for some reason after a few days, the cloth became shredded at that place and through the big hole the icon became clearly apparent. At the order of Patriarch Tikhon it was announced in all churches that a service of prayer would be held in front of the icon of St. Nicholas at the Nikolsky Gate. On the appointed day and hour processions started from all the parish churches of Moscow, with priests walking in full vestments, with banners and icons carried by the people and choirs singing as the crowds marched. Never in my life, before or after, have I seen such a crowd. The entire Red Square was crammed as well as all the streets leading into it. The crowd seemed to feel completely in possession of the situation. I noticed that the crowd shouted at a mounted militia man who had neglected to take off his

cap, and he hurriedly removed it. Our father took us to the
elevated round stone platform near the cathedral of St. Basil,
which is at the opposite end of the Red Square from the Nikolsky Gate. We saw from there how the huge ancient banners of the Kremlin cathedrals moved slowly and majestically
through the gates to meet the flood of the smaller banners of
the parish processions. The Patriarch began the service and
the famous choir of the Uspensky Cathedral sang the responses. Of course, we could not hear the Patriarch and even
the singing of the choir barely reached us, but when the
Patriarch's deacon raised his voice to chant the petitions, we
could hear every word. Everything went peacefully and there
were no conflicts. Yet the tension must have been great, for
our parish priest invited us all to make a general confession
and partake of Holy Communion before we set off, "for,"
he said, "who knows what will happen."

The winter of 1918/19 set in. Somehow we managed to
smuggle Iuri, whose health had greatly deteriorated on our
insufficient diet, to join our relatives in the south of Russia.
I missed him badly, for we had been inseparable all our lives,
but I inherited from him a partitioned-off part of the pantry,
with a chair and a desk, which became "my place." This was
the beginning of the endless diaries, stories and reminiscences
I wrote, and in a sense it was the beginning of my own inner
independent life and thought. Curiously I felt somehow separated from the rest of the family and experienced a tremendous compassion for them: for my parents because everything
they believed in and had worked for all their life had broken
down, and for the older young people because I felt that the
change was harder on them than on me, just because they
were older.

There was no question of resuming lessons. The great
problem was to find food and ways of earning money. During
the summer and fall we took long trips into the Moscow
suburbs and came back laden with heavy sacks of squash,
turnips, cabbages or cucumbers. Potatoes were almost impossible to find, but occasionally, if lucky, we brought back
tins of cottage cheese made of skimmed milk. Eggs, milk,
butter, fats, meat, cereals, and fish disappeared from our diet.

The private companies that supplied power, gas and telephone were nationalized and became disorganized. Transport failed and no coal or wood could be delivered. Buildings like ours remained unheated, water pipes burst, elevators did not work, electric lights went off.

My mother tried desperately to learn ways of earning money and I tried to help her. Our attempts were awkward and painful. We tried to make little embroidered handbags. The designs were pretty, the colors well-matched, but we did not have the skill to make them well and neatly. We tried to offer them for sale in different stores, and after just two days of it we became so discouraged that we never entered a store together. I burned with humiliation and shame and hated the condescending smiles of the shopkeepers. Our worst experience, however, was with an agency of school supplies from which we received an order for a Montessori kit of little wooden panels to be painted in different shades of colors. My mother was quite a good amateur painter and thought this would be a job for her. We received from the agency the wooden panels, a few tubes of paint, not quite the right shades, but worst of all they gave us no brushes. And paint brushes were unobtainable in Moscow in 1919. We tried harder than ever and the mess was even worse. At last I wrapped up the package, like an illegitimate baby, took it early in the morning to the door of the agency, left it there and ran away.

Gradually we improved, although our earnings were nothing to boast of. My mother found translation work. Why, of all books, did a Soviet government publishing firm decide to translate the novels of George Eliot in 1919? I cannot imagine, but we plodded conscientiously through *The Mill on the Floss* and *Silas Marner*, and I learned to type to help my mother. I also knitted baby booties from remnants of wool we had, or from yarn obtained by unwinding old sweaters, and sold them in a neighboring park to women with babies. I still hated approaching people to sell something; it felt almost like begging, but the booties sold well and soon I had no more wool left. I was even more self-conscious than before because of my clothes. For two years no one had had any new clothes, but I grew. All my sleeves ended somewhere between my wrist and elbow; my dress and coat were much too short. And my mother's optimistic attempts to make clothes for me from her old dresses or coats were a dismal failure. But even in those miserable, outgrown clothes I somehow remained earmarked as "not of the people," "former upper class," and this called for jeers and mockery by street boys.

We made better money by going to the famous open-air market "Suharevka," where anything and everything could be bought and sold. Peasants brought food stuffs and exchanged them for shoes, evening dresses, furniture, pictures, jewelry, any kind of clothes. The wares were spread on the pavement, on tables and in small sheds. All around the noise and din were terrific: barrel organs played, children ran around, shrilly offering matches, or homemade candy, or cigarettes for sale. Groups of men played cards and gambled. Women sold hot buns at astronomic prices and suspicious-looking sausages. Occasionally the whole market would be surrounded by soldiers, everyone caught was arrested and the goods confiscated, but next day old Suharevka would be as alive as ever.

We went several times to Suharevka taking my mother's old evening gowns, shoes, underwear, sheets. Sometimes the trade was dull, but if we managed to get the attention of a few people and a group formed around us, the sales would improve. Then we would hunt for food stuffs to buy: bread, potatoes, sometimes milk. One day before leaving for Suharevka, my mother remarked pointedly that it was my father's turn to give some of his things to sell. Rather unwillingly he gave his silver cigarette case and a pair of shoes. That would fetch a good price, we felt. We went to our usual place and again there was a lull at first and no one approached us. We cheered up when a few people came closer and began examining our wares. Suddenly a woman cried out: "Watch out! The cigarette case is gone!" We both turned our heads and saw the cigarette case disappear quickly, passed from one person to another in the crowd. We turned around; the shoes were gone too!

What were a pair of old shoes and a cigarette case in

comparison to all my parents had lost! Yet for the first time in my life I saw my mother break down. She began to sob, she trembled, she clutched her throat, she almost fell. I did not know what to do, how to protect her from the gaping crowd. Tears rolled down my face too as I gathered all our scattered things, crammed them into bags and, hitching them on my back, tried to lead my mother away.

Towards the end of the winter my sister Mania left us to join our uncle's family in Petersburg. They had made up their minds to try and escape from Russia and she wanted to go with them. She tried to persuade my parents to do the same, but they were still undecided. Iuri returned from Kiev and found a job in the archives of a museum.

As the winter of 1919/20 set in, the building we lived in grew bitterly cold. It had been a modern building and proved to be the worst kind to live in when practically all facilities were nonexistent. Without gas, without electricity, with no water supply, unheated, with no elevator or telephone, at a time when one could not buy any wood, coal, oil, or candles, it was harder to exist there than in some old-fashioned little cabin of a house.

For a long time we did not touch the furniture, but at last one day when we were miserable with cold, we broke up a kitchen chair to heat the small handmade sheet-iron stove we installed in one of the rooms. Soon after this went a second chair and that started the fun. One after another we broke all the kitchen and bedroom chairs, then all the shelves, the wooden ornaments of the cupboards. Best of all was the wooden partition that divided one of the rooms into three cubicles. By the end of the winter not a cupboard remained with a shelf and we still hunted through our things hoping to find something to burn. We left all the rooms unheated except two. My mother and I slept in the former dining room, my father and Iuri next door, in the former pantry. In our room stood the little stove (called "burzhuika," from the word "bourgeois," used in those days as an abusive word for the former privileged classes) that could be heated with small pieces of wood, paper and all sorts of rubbish. The pipes were led through the pantry and the kitchen and were supposed to heat them too. Peter and Gania slept in their cubicle behind the kitchen. In the daytime the temperature was only a few degrees above freezing point, but in the evening when we heated the little stove it rose to some 40 or 50 degrees (Fahrenheit). We wore heavy coats, caps, shawls, felt boots and woolen gloves all the time.

When we were lucky enough to be able to buy some wood, every log had to be brought up the six flights of stairs. Every pail of water had to be carried upstairs too, and with all the water that was spilled, the stairs were very slippery. Iuri and Gania's husband Peter were out all day; Gania was expecting her first child; my father had a heart condition, and carrying wood and water was my chore. Undernourished as we all were, we found it no easy job and I remember trying to make a mistake as I counted the floors, so that I would have a pleasant surprise when I reached our door.

A spirit of community developed among the families whose back doors opened on the same stairs, bound as we were in our common needs. Occasionally a tenant would appear in our kitchen and whisper to Gania that a "meshechnik" was in the house selling bread. The word means literally the "bag-man" and was applied to peasants who brought bread or flour or potatoes to sell or exchange in the city. This was quite illegal and although the trade was a profitable one it was dangerous too. There was a general rush if on some of the lower floors water could be had, and everybody ran down with jugs and pails. Another topic of general interest was whether bread would be distributed this week. When there was bread, a bell was rung and people ran downstairs to line up and exchange their coupons for the bread ration. If I remember correctly it was four ounces a day, but was distributed very irregularly. This was my favorite chore. The heavy and sticky bread was cut up and weighed into individual rations. My profit for carrying the pile of cut-up pieces upstairs was the crumbs, quite a few of them, and, I am afraid, I occasionally pinched off little pieces of crust.

By that time my mother had found an office job as a typist. She worked until 4 P.M. and then remained an additional two hours for extra pay. She came home about seven bringing with her soup from a Soviet kitchen — an ill-smelling, thin mess which we warmed up and had for supper. After supper she settled down to her translation work and worked late into the night. For me this was the best time of the day. The wood crackled and burnt gaily, the air grew warmer and warmer, the little homemade oil lamp or candle made our poor dismantled room look less forlorn. I would stand on my knees in front of the stove and make potato-peel cakes, quite a feature of our life in those days. You cooked potato peels, put them through a meat-grinder, added a *little* flour and salt, made flat round cakes and toasted them on the iron stove. Sometimes the warmth of the stove and the fatigue got the better of my mother, the papers would slip down to the floor and she went to sleep in her armchair. It always made me happier to see her get a little rest.

But the stove burned well only if the wind blew in a certain direction. If it came from the opposite one, it was better not to heat it. The fire started quite well, but as I looked hopefully on, smoke burst out through the opening, filled the room and the fire went out. The more I tried, the worse it grew. I'd stand for an hour on my knees, blowing and wheezing, smoke drawing tears from my eyes. The thought that my mother would come home, tired and cold, probably with a headache, to an unheated apartment made me miserable. Almost as bad as the smoke was the black, nasty-smelling liquid that oozed and dripped from the pipejoints. I hung little jars to catch the drip, but they quickly overflowed and the inky stuff poured on my head, or some new joint would begin to leak.

I know that both then and now there are many places in the world where people suffer far more from hunger than we did in Moscow in 1920. We were always hungry, we were undernourished, but we still had something to eat every day. That hungry winter became such a time of horror in my mind because the experience we went through really destroyed our family relationships, our family life. At some time we must have decided that we would divide the little food we had into individual rations, each one of us taking care of his own. I think now it was a mistake. We hid our rations from each other and became suspicious. Iuri ate nothing all day long, roamed the streets after work, and on coming home at night gulped down all his food for the day, while I watched him hungrily. Sometimes my father would beg my mother for a little more food and, furiously, I would give him part of my ration so that he would not take my mother's food. I think the men of the family felt that the severe rationing was somehow my mother's fault and resented it. My helplessness, my love and pity for her, were almost more painful than the physical hardships. I tried to think of ways to make her life a little easier. I remember one time when my effort was crowned with success. Somehow, someone brought a few pounds of white flour to my grandmother, who also lived in Moscow. She shared it with us and Gania made the pleasure last by baking each one of us a small roll once a week, if Iuri managed to get yeast. (For some unknown reason yeast was occasionally distributed at his place of work.) At that time my mother had asked me to keep her small daily ration of black bread for her. Secretly I went to the "Suharevka," sold my white roll and for the money bought a much larger piece of black bread. For many days I was able to add a good slice to my mother's ration, so that she even asked me why there seemed to be more bread than usual. I said there had been an additional allocation.

Some time during that winter we reached the decision to try to escape. Mania was already in Petersburg with my uncle's family. They all escaped successfully, in small groups of two or three persons, walking over the ice of the Finnish Bay. My father and Iuri left for Petersburg too, and finally succeeded in crossing the frontier to Estonia, smuggled in a fisherman's boat. Thus they all disappeared from our life. We did not hear from them, and they did not hear from us. We did not know whether or not their attempt to escape succeeded or whether they were alive or not. My mother and I were making plans to escape across the Polish frontier.

The breakup of our family did not cause me any grief. Life had become too horrible. In a diary that I kept during that winter, I wrote on January 13, 1920: "The battle of this winter has cost a lot: my friendship with Iuri is destroyed, nothing remains of my love and respect for Father, home life has become a thing of horror that I almost hate. And my faith in God, what has remained of it? I suppose God exists somewhere and perhaps even watches us with pity, but I can't look at Him to find courage . . . If only there was someone strong enough to help me . . ." One tends to dramatize things at sixteen, but I think the feelings were real.

Towards the end of winter I fell ill. The kindly old doctor shook his head compassionately and said it was "exhaustion and undernourishment." With his prescription mother was able to get a little milk and cereal which she cooked for me on our "burzhuika." Turning over in bed I accidentally upset the saucepan and my mother broke down and cried . . . Early in spring Gania had her baby, but it was stillborn. I was alone with her when her birth pains began and we stayed together waiting for Peter to return from his work and take her to the hospital. I tried to comfort her and help her as best I could, but I do not think the baby could have been saved. The doctor at the hospital said the baby had been dead for a few days. I still have Gania's pencil-scribbled, tear-stained, almost illegible little notes. She wrote me:

> Dear Sonichka, I am sorry I have not written you before. Thank you for the book and for visiting me; too bad they don't let people come in. The babies are kept in a separate room and are brought in for the mothers to nurse them. Then I cannot help feeling sad and I look at them and I think of my lost little girl and I can't stop crying. But at other times I am all right. Don't tell Peter about what I write — it will make him sad, too. I am writing you and tears are dropping on the paper and smearing it. How is Peter? How is he taking it?

But even in that dark winter there were happy and good moments. Such was my friendship with Igor Alexeev, only son of Konstantin Stanislavsky of the Moscow Art Theatre. Somebody recommended my mother as a teacher of English to Igor and he began coming to us for his lessons. He was

twenty-one at the time, very tall, thin, and shy, and because
of his father's position much more comfortably off than we
were. Our friendship started in a rather funny way. During
a lesson my mother called out to me asking me to bring her
fur tippet, of blue velvet with an ermine collar and lined in
soft squirrel fur. I was absorbed in a book and tore myself
away from it to do my mother's bidding. Absentmindedly I
brought the tippet and placed it on his shoulders instead of
my mother's. Standing up he unfolded, tall and gangling,
smiling with embarrassment, the tippet elegantly hanging
down like a theatrical cape. "Th . . . thank you . . ." he stammered, holding on to his good manners, and then all three of
us collapsed with laughter. Quite often after that, he brought
me tickets for plays at the Moscow Art Theatre and these
outings were red-letter days for me.

In the summer of 1920 my mother and I decided to take
a vacation and Igor suggested a place not far from Moscow —
"Pokrovskoye-Streshnevo," the site of a former beautiful
estate. His parents would be spending their vacation there too.
The place was very picturesque, one could get milk from
farmers, and we were able to rent a small attic for two weeks
where my mother could work in peace on her current translation. We met Igor's mother first, Madame Lilina, one of the
leading actresses of the Moscow Art Theatre. She called on
us because she found a pocket handkerchief my mother had
dropped on one of the lanes, and she was sure it must be ours,
because it had embroidered initials and the small crown.
Then she came again with her husband, and since our attic
was too small to receive them, we stayed in the garden chatting
for some time. Stanislavsky made a very strong impression
on me: we exchanged just a few words, but I had the feeling
that during these short minutes he directed a concentrated
beam of attention at me. Of what interest could I be to him,
a teen-age youngster he scarcely knew? But I felt as if he
were actually studying me attentively, and I was extremely
conscious of his amazing personal charm.

During that same vacation I felt for the first time in my
life the stirrings of a romantic feeling, not for Igor, with
whom we remained the best of friends all our life, but for

a friend he brought one evening. I can only remember his
first name, Iuri. The three of us roamed along the beautiful,
tree-lined lanes of the ancient estate. Everything looked like
a setting for the opera *Eugene Onegin*. During the conversation it emerged that Iuri would be leaving for Moscow next
morning, with the 8 A.M. train. I returned late to our attic
that night. For a long time I could not sleep and my pillow
caught quite a few of my tears. Next morning, rather unexpectedly for my mother, I announced that it was indispensable to get some more milk and that I had to do it earlier than
usual. Of course quite accidentally this errand brought me to
the railroad station a short time before the Moscow-bound
train was to stop there. Sure enough, Iuri was waiting for
the train. He saw me, he came to speak to me . . . Then there
was the train. It stopped but Iuri remained talking to me . . .
There was a whistle, the train began to move but Iuri was
still there, talking to me. At last he tore himself away, raced
after the train and leapt up to the steps of the car.

Towards the end of that harsh winter, in a strange way,
things began to improve, or at least I began to feel less desperate. It all started with our parish church and the new
priest that was assigned to it.

I do not know what made his sermons different. Somehow
he managed to make us feel like a community, a fellowship,
almost a family. I remember how he asked us to help clear
away the snow around the church so that we could have our
Easter night procession. Many of us came and he was there
too and worked like any of us. Curiously enough it was my
first experience of working for the church, or being part of
the church, outside of church services. Never until then had
I felt that a parish could be something of which one was
a part. Through old Victorna, the cook in the third floor
apartment and a great authority in church matters, we learned
that Father Vasili lived all alone, his wife had died and he
had no relatives in Moscow. When he came to his room after
serving Divine Liturgy, he had nothing but hot water for
breakfast. Then, on Easter week, soon after I had recovered
from my illness, he called on us and gave me an egg. An egg!
Mother and I said we could not possibly accept it, he should

eat it himself. Father Vasili laughed: "You should see my table," he said, "I have all I could want—eggs, Easter cakes, milk, butter, meat. I am sharing with you of my plenty." Victorna did her job and people had responded generously.

Our plans for escape over the Polish border were taking shape. I could think of nothing else. It seemed to me that my life depended on their success. If we managed to escape a new life would begin. We would live again. I could imagine how we might become a family once more: my father as he used to be, Iuri getting well again, my mother, yes, she'd be working, but not killing herself with work. And I, perhaps . . . perhaps I'd be able to go on with my education. This was my most secret sorrow that I shared with no one; my schooling had stopped when I was fourteen and I felt that I would remain a dunce for life.

Gradually everything was made ready. The smuggler from the village at the Polish border sent us a message that he was willing to help us cross over on a certain date. We agreed on the price to be paid in my mother's jewels. My mother obtained a leave of absence from her office and permission to leave Moscow. We applied for a special pass that had to be presented at the ticket office before buying tickets for towns near the frontier. We had to show up at the village on Tuesday, so we would leave Moscow on Monday. We tried to get our pass on Saturday, but it was too late and they told us to come back on Monday. Our train was leaving at 2 P.M. so we had plenty of time to pick up our pass on Monday morning.

We packed our bags, not more than we could carry ourselves, and Peter took them to the station. He would stand in line at the ticket window until my mother and I turned up, as soon as we had picked up our passes.

The office where the passes were delivered was on Kuznetsky Most, one of the busiest streets in Moscow. My mother went in and I waited outside, walking up and down the street. It seemed an awfully long time. The day was sunny and warm but I felt cold and my mouth was dry. Many people were entering the building, others were leaving it.

Suddenly I saw my mother. She looked upset. Silently we moved out of the crowd.

"You must be brave, Sonia," she said. "Since yesterday no travel passes are given to places close to the Polish frontier. It is a new order. We are trapped."

We were trapped indeed. My older brothers, Mania, father, and Iuri — they were all outside. Somewhere, somehow, they were trying to rebuild their lives. My mother and I alone were trapped. The new life I had dreamed of was not for us.

It was at this very moment, right there on that sunlit street, that something happened to me of which I always think as a kind of miracle. Suddenly I felt very clearly and strangely: "No, no, this is not the end. A new life will begin. It will begin right here and now. A new life . . . it has begun!" My mother's spirit was not broken either. The very same day she began making efforts to find another way of escape.

My new life began for me in very simple ways. The winter cold was over and I lugged pails and pails of water up to our sixth floor and scrubbed our room until it was perfectly clean. That summer of 1920 was a wonderful year for apples — the harvest was quite unusual. At every street corner you could buy large, golden, juicy, sweet apples, and what a difference they made in our diet.

My recent illness worried my mother and she tried to find ways in which my diet could be improved. At a family consultation including darling old grandmother and my mother's sister Aunt Mary, it was decided that I should take a job made available through a friend in a government institution where food rations were part of the salary. It was a very modest little job as filing clerk in an unimportant department of the People's Commissariat of Foreign Trade (Narkomvneshtorg). For my first interview, Granny, Aunt Mary and Mother tried to make me look as grown-up as possible. I am afraid that their ideas of how a grown-up young person should look did not fit in with the way of life in Moscow in 1920 and looking at me in the floor length skirt they lent me, a high-collared shirt-waist and a small hat with a veil covering the upper part of my face, Granny sighed worriedly: "Navrante de distinction!" ("Distressingly distinguished!"). Fortunately I had the sense to discard the costume and went to work in my shabby old grey cotton flannel dress.

The big attraction of the job was that, besides the salary which was quite insignificant, we did get a hot lunch: soup in which you could actually see some cereal grains and a small piece of bread. There were rumors too that occasionally some food supplies like flour or honey or sugar were distributed to employees, but I did not stay long enough at the job for this to happen.

As a matter of routine the questionnaire filled out by a new employee had to be approved by the head of the Commissariat. Quite unexpectedly my application for the position of filing clerk in the Department of Provincial Trading Posts came back with the Commissar's note: "Transfer her to my personal Secretariat." Probably my knowledge of foreign languages — English, French and German — attracted his attention. I was thus catapulted to the very top of the Commissariat and became part of the personal office of the Commissar. To add more glamour to my career, the official translator was sick on the day I started work, the very day when a long message was telegraphed from London reporting on a meeting of the British Parliament where the resumption of trade relations with the USSR was discussed. There was no one else on the staff capable of translating the report into Russian. There was, of course, a special Department of Legal Translations at the Commissariat, but they were always swamped with work and our Commissar Scheinmann wanted to read the report right away. With fear and trembling the senior secretary entrusted the job to me, young-looking for my sixteen years and quite green at the job. Only one of the office girls had a smattering of English and she hovered around me in case I needed help. From my early childhood, English was my second mother tongue and translating a text from English into Russian was as easy as falling off a chair, except when political or professional terms came up that were beyond a young girl's vocabulary. Fortunately the text was simple and in a couple of hours the work was done and taken to Commissar Scheinmann. To my great surprise and,

I must admit, somewhat smug conceit, a few days later a special bonus of two hundred rubles was paid out to me for "outstanding work" by personal order of Commissar Scheinmann.

I worked in this office for about six months. It was a curious environment, quite new to me. Commissar Scheinmann, the prototype of a Communist Commissar, was a fat, greasy, smart, his low forehead slanting back, fond of good food and girls. When he chose an office girl to act as his private secretary she had to come to his home to work at night. It is true that, among other things, it meant enjoying gourmet suppers that he had served to him. He liked using me as interpreter when foreigners came to see him, especially Americans, and with the same oily smile he told them the most blatant lies. Only once did I risk slipping in a sentence in English: "I am translating exactly what I am told to translate," but this did not seem to produce any impression on the interviewers.

The two senior women in the office were very different from each other. Sophia Robertovna Bogomolova, the official chief of staff, was obviously a Socialist Revolutionary of old vintage, severe to herself and to others, devoted to her work. She dressed in the good old bleak style of Russian revolutionaries, her hair severely drawn back, and used no cosmetics. Her manner was dry and impersonal, yet under it I felt personal kindliness, and somehow she seemed to be a person to trust. One day a short notice appeared in the Moscow newspapers about "the well-known member of the State Duma S. Shidlovsky, who had been hiding in Moscow, and now escaped abroad." My mother dropped in at the office looking upset, and told me not to return home that night to avoid a possible arrest. A few days later, Sophia Robertovna, looking very business-like, sent me to fetch some papers from the man in charge of the small department where I had first applied for a job. And this gentleman very kindly spelled out to me the need to be more careful: my mother's visit, her upset manner, could very easily be connected with the notice in the newspapers and this might be dangerous for me. It was not difficult to guess that Sophia Robertovna had asked him to speak to me.

The senior secretary, officially Sophia Robertovna's subordinate, quite often seemed to be the more powerful of the two. She was a young, pretty and friendly Jewish girl, with a head of merrily dancing curls, Rosalie Heifetz by name. She had several brothers and they were all members of the Cheka, as the secret police was called at that time, and therefore possessed arms. She enjoyed telling us how their apartment was searched once and how embarrassed the searching party became when they found the weapons and realized with whom they were dealing. She boasted of the beautiful personal lingerie belonging to the Czar's family which had been distributed to her and to other girls. She also told us the story of her older brother, who played the violin, and, as a little boy, was sent abroad by his parents to join his uncle and aunt living there. He had been mixed up in a political demonstration and a friendly policeman advised the parents to get him safely out of the way. There was some misunderstanding and the relatives were late meeting the train. The boy sat down on his suitcase and began to play his violin and was thus finally found by his uncle. I often wondered in later years whether this could have been Jascha Heifetz, but could never find anything to confirm it.

Another member of the staff was a silent woman who kept to herself. Whenever there was no work for her, she studied a book that she kept in the drawer of her desk and made copious notes. My curiosity pushed me to take a look at her book when she once left it on her desk, and to my amazement discovered that it was a New Testament. I don't remember her name, for in my mind I had dubbed her "The Christian."

There was also a pretty, rather heavy girl, who privately boasted that her Baltic German name had the particle "von" as a sign of nobility. Very willingly she became the private typist of Commissar Scheinmann and entertained us with the description of the good suppers she had at his home.

Somewhat later, another person, Mrs. J., joined the staff, a small elderly lady, rather like a wren, obviously of a good old Moscow family. Instinctively I knew I could trust her. We were birds of a feather and she was the only one who might know my grandmother. One day I told her that if ever anything happened to me and I were suddenly to disappear, would she please not mention that I had any relatives in Moscow. She gave me a quick look and said, without asking any questions, "Yes, yes, of course, I understand."

It was a strange environment and I was in a strange mood. My strongest feeling after the failure of our attempted escape was that I must somehow "educate" myself, that I must develop intellectually. I found an old library with a good collection of books which were freely lent. On my own I worked out a reading program: one day I read the theological works of Vladimir Soloviev, the next one *Das Kapital* by Karl Marx, the third one a manual on higher mathematics. Soloviev I could understand and got carried away by his "Three Conversations" and the wonderful "Story of Antichrist." Karl Marx was tough going and I could never plough through more than a few pages at a time. The book on higher mathematics was a sheer waste of time since I could not understand a word, but I obstinately forced myself to read it. I am naturally an extrovert, spoke freely and the whole staff knew of my reading interests. On the Karl Marx days Rosalie Heifetz beamed at me and showed me her affection. On the Soloviev days, "The Christian" gave me softly encouraging looks.

Our conversations were pretty frank too. One day the question was raised about who would be willing to become a member of the Communist party. One of the office girls said she would not mind becoming a member if it did not involve volunteering for the "subbotniki," volunteer labor on Saturdays, such as unloading trains with medical supplies. I flared up and announced in all my arrogant prudishness that I would never become a party member, but would be quite willing to volunteer for a "subbotnik." Rosalie picked this up immediately and next Saturday, rather self-consciously, I marched to the tune of revolutionary songs to a station where we did some unloading. Even to my inexperienced eyes the work was obviously very inefficiently organized and we mostly just sat around.

On another day our conversation turned to vocations and professions. One of us wanted to be a film star, another to reach a top administrative position. When they asked me what

my ambition was, I tried to answer sincerely and said somewhat shyly that most of all I "wanted to be a mother." At
these words "The Christian" jumped up, crossed the room,
and embraced me.

During my work at the office I witnessed a rather amusing
incident. Some documents had to be taken to the Kremlin,
and I was chosen for the errand. Rosalie was most enthusiastic
over the honor bestowed on me: who knows? Perhaps I would
get a glimpse of Lenin himself! I was simply glad of an ex-
cuse to take a walk. All it amounted to was that I handed
the envelope with the papers to a special agent at one of the
gates leading into the Kremlin. A long line of people were
waiting patiently for their turn to deliver whatever they had
to the guard. The day was cold and drizzly. Suddenly a car
approached, and a tall man stepped out and went straight to
the head of the line. We had no trouble recognizing the well-
known figure of the singer Chaliapin. But the Moscow lines
of those days, called "tails" in Russian, were perhaps the
last outposts of free speech. The line protested violently:
Chaliapin or not, a line is a line and you have to wait for your
turn. At that Chaliapin lost his temper, turned round and
yelled at us, letting us catch the full force of his magnificent
voice. This had its effect. A shabby little old man, with a moth-
eaten beard, stepped out of the line: "Look, comrades," he
said humbly, "There are many of us everywhere, but Chaliapin — there is just *one* Chaliapin in the world. Let him
through!" And the line, recognizing the wisdom of his words,
stepped aside and Chaliapin went in.

Another time the office I worked in provided me with unexpected good news. Scheinman had been replaced by an old
Communist named Lejava, with the title of Deputy, or "Zam-
kom" in the abbreviated Russian used so much then. Lejava
was a revolutionary of the old type, almost ascetic in his way
of life. We heard that it was a matter of principle with him
to keep within his food ration (which, of course, was considerably larger than the one received by ordinary citizens).
There were no more gourmet suppers for night typists. He
shared his room with an old friend, whom we called "Zamzam," equivalent to "Subsub," whose name was Braude.

Braude was a revolutionary who had spent many years in prison under the czarist regime. I don't know why, but it always seemed to me that for both these men the "old days" were a happy memory and that they did not enjoy their new position of power. One day "Zamzam" stopped me in the corridor leading from the typists' room to the Commissar's office. "I have something to show you," he said mysteriously. We stepped into a dark corner, behind one of the big cupboards. "Look!" and he put into my hands an obviously foreign-looking newspaper printed in Russian. Yes, it was a Russian émigré newspaper printed in Reval, and there, right on the front page, was an article by my father! "Oh, thank you, thank you!" I cried. "We didn't know whether he was alive or not. It's just like getting a telegram to say that he is safely abroad and working!" I almost hugged poor old "Zamzam" who shook his head ruefully. "Your father writes in an awfully conservative paper . . ." he sighed.

* * *

We continued to look for a loophole that would enable us to escape. The most promising possibility was connected with the repatriation of German prisoners of war. In addition to the actual war prisoners, there were many civilian prisoners: Germans who had lived in Russia for many years, had been interned during the war, and could now go home. And this was our loophole.

A certain Mr. X was making a lot of money by examining the official lists of Germans to be repatriated. He looked for names of people who were not really going back because they had either left already, or had died, or perhaps did not want to go back. People who wanted to escape from Russia got in touch with Mr. X. He then found among the names officially listed, but actually not there, persons whose age and sex matched those of escapees and inserted their photos and their addresses. It was all very secret and very dangerous. Mr. X. made a lot of money, but he risked his own life and, of course, the people who trusted him risked their lives too.

Mother still had quite a few pieces of jewelry. As a mat-

ter of fact it was more valuable those days than money, and
we had no trouble agreeing on a "price" with Mr. X. He
told us we had to be very careful: there would be no receipts,
no letters; we would not know our new names until the eve
of our flight, nor could he tell us in advance when and how
we would leave. Two or three days ahead of time he would
let us know.

Weeks went by. One day Mr. X. called on us and said:
"The initials of your German names will be H. N. and W. N.
Make sure all your things are marked. You will have to say
that you lived in the town of Simbirsk. Make sure you know
something about it: names of streets, stores, etc. The next
train of prisoners of war leaves in five days. If all goes well,
you will be on it."

We got busy marking our clothes and packing, so that we
could carry everything ourselves. We had to make sure that
none of the things betrayed our identity — no photos, no
books, no souvenirs. The remaining pieces of my mother's
jewelry had to be carefully hidden. Some of them we baked
into a loaf of bread, which we then cut up so that it would
not look suspicious. Peter hollowed out the heels of a pair of
shoes and hid some diamonds inside. We made burnt-sugar
candy and put it into a tin, hiding a little sapphire brooch at
the bottom. We outdid each other in thinking of new hiding
places for these things which would have to see us through
the difficult time of starting a new life abroad.

We went to confession to Father Vasili. I was excited
about the adventure of escaping and yet I was unhappy at the
thought of leaving Russia. Somehow I felt that this was where
I belonged. I sensed that Russia was going through something
terrible and tremendous, riding out a storm, and that God
was leading her through this experience. I wanted to share
her fate; it seemed a betrayal to leave her. During confession
I must have said something about this and about my feeling
of guilt at having to tell so many lies in order to escape. "You
see," said Father Vasili, "this is what's wrong about our life
here today. It is a life of lies. That's why it is right for you
to try to get away."

Next day we went to early Divine Liturgy and received

Communion. Having fasted I was hungry when I came to the office a little earlier than usual. I perched on top of a desk munching a big juicy apple. I felt happy and at peace. Sophia Robertovna went quickly through the office before I had time to get off the desk, but her usually severe face lit up with a smile as she saw my dangling feet. Then Mrs. J. came in. "I'm having my breakfast," I explained apologetically. "I've been to church to receive Communion this morning." Her face changed: "What? Already? The time has come! Well, God bless you and keep you safe!" People knew how to understand each other.

That evening Mr. X. gave us our last instructions. My mother's name would be Helene Neumann; mine would be Wanda Neumann. According to the lists there should have been another daughter, but we were to say that she had died in Simbirsk. We were to present ourselves the following morning at a little building behind the big terminal station from which trains were leaving for the north. A line of people would be waiting there and we should take our place in the line. At 11 A.M. someone would start calling the names on a list. When we heard our names we were to answer "Here!" This was all there was to it. Mr. X. had nothing more to do with us.

Early next morning my mother and I started off on foot. Each one of us carried a bag strapped to her shoulders and a suitcase in each hand. This was the end of our life in Russia; these were all the possessions we had in the world. We were both silent. My mother told me afterwards that she was more frightened, more nervous, than she had ever been in her life. What if something went wrong? What if Mr. X. was a crook? Or had been discovered? Other people we knew who had made such attempts to escape, had been arrested and executed.

We went down the street past our parish church. A small funeral procession was approaching and Father Vasili was standing in the door waiting for it. He saw us and made a sign to my mother to enter. I remained in the street with all our bags and suitcases and my mother went in alone. Father Vasili hurried to an "analoy," took the icon of the Mother of

Our Lord, my mother knelt down and he blessed her with the icon. It was the one called "Odigitria" — Protector of Travelers. As my mother felt the old wooden icon touch her forehead, her panic, her frantic nervousness disappeared. Suddenly she felt at peace.

We reached the big station, went around it as directed and found a shack between two side-tracks. A group of people was lining up and my mother took her place. I remained to the side, guarding our luggage. Now it was my turn to feel scared, probably because I had nothing to do but to wait. I realized that it was not merely a matter of succeeding to escape, but that our life and death were involved, and this was frightening.

Suddenly all was over and my mother was coming back smiling. Our names had been called, no questions asked. Together with some thirty other people we were assigned to a freight car on a train standing by. Our traveling companions — German civilians, men, women, and children — were very efficient and obviously experienced travelers. In a few minutes a "car-warden" was elected and took command. Under his guidance boards were laid across the box car, forming two raised platforms on both sides of the sliding doors, forming a kind of second floor. Women and children were assigned to the upper berths, the men to the lower. We unpacked our bags and used our heavy winter coats to make a bed in the corner assigned to us. It was a cozy little nest. One of the men hung up a small, home-made oil lamp in the middle of the car. The "car-warden" announced that our train would leave some time in the evening after all the lists had been checked again by the Cheka. This left my mother and me with a little gnawing sense of fear.

There were several hours of daylight left, and now came the moment of which I can never think without a stab of grief. Not far from our train, I suddenly saw the trim, neat figure of Gania. She came to tell me "goodbye." I hugged her hard and cried bitterly. Gania clung to me, weeping too. "Gania, Gania, I'll come back, I'll come back! It's not forever. I promise you, I'll come back!" My heart was breaking. I was leaving behind half of myself: Gania, Russia, my childhood. I was separating myself from Russia's fate, from all that was being born in the dark suffering of those days.

I never saw Gania again. She died from tuberculosis in Moscow during World War II. Peter had died earlier. We corresponded until the beginning of the war and she often wrote how much she would have liked to help me bring up my children. She had a son who served in the army, and I was able to get in touch with him after the war. He wrote that by lucky chance he was in Moscow at the time of Gania's death and that she was buried "properly." I think he meant that she had a church funeral.

Emotionally exhausted I went back to our "nest" in the box-car. My mother and I lay down to rest. There was still the check-up to go through. We did not notice how we went to sleep, but when we woke up it was quite dark. The little oil lamp was swinging back and forth under the car roof. Ra-ta-ta, ra-ta-ta, ra-ta-ta clicked the wheels rhythmically. The train was rolling steadily; it must have been moving for quite some time. The Cheka clearance must have been a paper formality. We were off, we were off . . .

Our journey under false names lasted three weeks. For three days we rolled through the birch and pine forests of northwestern Russia. Occasionally the train stopped in the middle of nowhere. People got out, gathered pine cones and lit "samovars" to make tea. Journey-wise mothers hung up diapers they had washed in pans. Suddenly the train would jerk into motion again and everyone scrambled back, gathering wet diapers and smoking samovars, and calling back children, while the car-wardens checked in the passengers of each car.

I had an exciting time in Iamburg, the frontier town, where people and luggage were searched. One of the things we had hidden was a beautiful string of pearls. The string had snapped and I hid the two halves in the pointed toes of my shoes, which were too large for me anyway, since they were my mother's old high-heeled evening slippers. As we were standing in line to be searched, the woman next to me said: "I don't want to interfere, but you know, your shoes do look too big for you, and I heard that this is the first place where they look for things." Obviously this was not a good hiding place, but where else could I hide the pearls at such short notice? I could think of only one place. I bent down as if to adjust my shoes, took out the pearls, and stuffed them into my mouth, one strand in each cheek. I could still speak, and it really did not show too much, especially if I smiled. The woman in the line behind me had a baby in her arms and I could talk and smile to the baby. If only I did not sneeze or cough! The woman who searched looked in my hair, felt all over my clothes. I offered to take off my shoes and she obviously thought this was unnecessary, since I was suggesting it. But she did not, *she did not* say, "open your mouth!"

We were less lucky when two soldiers looked through our luggage. We had been too greedy and had eaten too much of the burnt-sugar candy in the tin! When the soldier opened the tin and looked into it, he saw the sapphire pin!

The soldiers took me away to an office where such things had to be turned in. I was made somewhat anxious by the fact that the office bore the title "Iamburg Agency of *Norkom-vneshtorg* — the institution in which I have been working. What if someone who knew me happened to be there? It was not the pin we cared for but we were afraid of being found out.

The soldiers were good-natured. On the way one of them said: "I'm sorry, miss. Why didn't you give me a wink? I wouldn't have looked then. And just as I found the thing, the officer came in, so I didn't dare put it back."

The other soldier teased him:

"Don't make excuses. Someday you'll go abroad and you will meet this girl and she'll remember the dirty trick you played on her!"

Fortunately the pin was not valuable enough to attract attention and we were lucky enough to leave without further mishap.

Then we crossed the border and our whole "transport" of a thousand prisoners of war and two hundred civilians was unloaded in Narva, Estonia. We arrived in the middle of the night in pouring rain. It took hours for our crowd to be counted, arranged in lines and marched through the town. At last we reached "Ivangorod," an old medieval fortress that was now used as a prisoners' stockade. For another hour we waited in the courtyard and then were assigned to our barracks. All our luggage was still somewhere on trucks. No one knew when it would arrive, so we could not change into dry clothes. All two hundred of us sat on the floor in the huge, dark, empty hall which had just one electric bulb hanging from the ceiling to give us some light. We were hungry, cold, exhausted in our steaming, ill-smelling clothes. Babies yelled and poor old women who could not understand what was happening cried too.

In one corner of the hall a few boards were laid on trestles. My mothers had gone out to try to find out when our luggage would arrive and I was standing alone, leaning on the trestle. Suddenly a door swung open and in the light of a candle, we saw a tall nurse in white and a uniformed American YMCA secretary carrying a huge cauldron of hot cocoa. They set it on the trestles next to me and started serving us. At that moment they came close to my idea of angels.

I knew that as long as we were part of the "transport" I must not let anyone know who we really were, but the temptation to speak to those two people was very strong. I remembered how frequently young YMCA secretaries visited our home in Moscow and what good friends they were. I said something in English and the American stared at me:

"Who are you?" he said.

I was even more troubled than before. When we told so many lies in order to escape, it was a kind of dangerous game, in which all was fair, but here was a friendly person and I did not want to lie. Still I had no right to say who we were. So I said:

"Well, *here* I am called Wanda Neuman," emphasizing the word "here."

"Now, who the devil are you?" said the puzzled young man. But he seemed to understand my difficulty and told me to have my mother come to his office next day. This visit set many wheels in motion and we could continue our journey knowing that in Berlin at the YMCA office, there would be news waiting for us. In years to come the young American,

Sam Keeny, became my very good friend and I will have occasion to speak of him again.

A week later our transport boarded a cargo boat for Stettin. The sea voyage lasted five days, the weather was rough and I was miserably seasick. It was a relief when the journey was over. Slowly and majestically our boat steamed up the river Oder. For everyone, except my mother and me, it was the long-awaited joyous return home. From the windows of the tall apartment buildings along the shores people waved to the returning prisoners of war. We could hear their shouts: "Welcome home! Welcome home!"

The men on the boat were sorting out their personal things — all the things they had carried from POW camp to POW camp, from barrack to barrack, from train to train, during their many-months-long journey from Siberia. Now they were home and these things were useless. Old mattresses, torn blankets, wornout shoes and clothes, broken pots and pans, homemade lamps and chests, rags of all kinds were being thrown overboard. As the boat slowly steamed up the Oder, a trail of floating rubbish was left behind.

For a long time I watched this homecoming. Then silently I went back to my bunk and lay down. My face was wet with tears. This was not homecoming for us. We had lost our homeland, but the memory was alive and would remain so. "Always, always," I thought. "As they sing in church, 'If I forget you, O Jerusalem, let my right hand wither...'"

We spent another six days in a POW campsite in Germany, a kind of quarantine where we were all taken to group hot showers and our clothes were disinfected. Curiously enough, though we managed to remain vermin-free until then, we became lice-infested after the common baths and changing of clothes. Perhaps we were infested already but did not notice it until then.

At last we were all given individual train tickets to whatever place we had indicated in Germany. My mother and I were going to Berlin. It was strange to board an ordinary, clean, well-run train and to mix with the other passengers. On a rainy September morning we walked out of Stettiner Bahnhof in Berlin. We were on our own. We were free.

Leaving our luggage in storage we walked down the busy streets. Everything had a dream-like quality — a "normal looking" city, open well-kept stores, clean well-dressed people, heavy traffic, a foreign yet familiar language. It was rather like being part of a movie.

We went to the office of the American YMCA and found letters from my father and Iuri and Mania waiting for us there. Not all the news was good. My eldest brother Andrei had died in an epidemic during the civil war almost a year before. My father and Iuri had written many times to us in Moscow, but their letters never reached us. It was especially painful that we now learned of Andrei's death through a casual sentence in Iuri's letter: "Of course you already know about Andrei's death..." There was no news of Sandik. Father and Iuri were in Reval, waiting for us. Mania was in Paris and would come to see us in Berlin as soon as she heard from us.

At the office we met three American YMCA secretaries we already knew — Paul B. Anderson, Jim Somerville and Donald Lowrie. They were to remain our friends all our lives, especially Paul. They received us that day with a warmth I will never forget. Dirty and shabby as we were, they took us to one of the best restaurants in town. They reserved a room for us in a hotel. They promised to find us work. They gave us the address of the former Russian Ambassador in Berlin who would help us straighten out our identity. They told us that there were many Russian refugees in Berlin, among them many whom we knew. Life in exile is not easy and we went through many struggles later, but these friends managed to give us an almost dream-like feeling of well-being and friendship during the month we remained in Berlin.

CHAPTER THREE

We spent the month of October 1920 in Berlin. Formal documents had to be obtained to reestablish our identity. Long letters were exchanged between all the members of the family to decide in which country we should settle. Russian friends in Berlin insisted that Estonia would not exist for more than a few months as an independent country. It was madness,

Estonia
1920-1922

they said, to leave Berlin, where both my mother and I were offered work in the American YMCA office. Mania was begging us to come to Paris. She wrote that some kind of funds would be distributed to help Russian émigré families. My father and Iuri wanted us to join them in Estonia. My father had a rather uncertain counselling position with the Estonian government and a steady writing job in the local Russian newspaper. Most of all our decision was influenced by Iuri's state of health. He had suffered from eczema, but after the long years of undernourishment and deprivation his skin condition was so terrible that it could only be compared to a third-degree burn over a large part of his body. A skin specialist, Professor Paldrok, at the university of Dorpat (Tartu) finally diagnosed his condition correctly and prescribed a treatment that was to last three years. Part of the treatment was to take mud-baths in Arensburg, an Estonian island. Iuri had already gone through one year of treatment and there was a marked improvement. My mother did not really care where we settled. After Andrei's death and the uncertainty about Sandik she realized the family would never be reunited in the old way. To be separated from my father and Iuri seemed unthinkable and we decided to go to Estonia.

A day or two after our arrival in Berlin I got sick, with a very high temperature. The German doctor thought it might be typhus, but I improved so quickly at first that he gave up the idea of having me hospitalized in a ward for contagious diseases. Then, suddenly, my temperature rose alarmingly again and he said it might be a typhoid enteric fever. The real reason for the relapse was much simpler: we were still staying in a hotel, my mother did not want to spend money eating in a restaurant and bought herself bread, cheese, sausages, etc. I was supposed to stay on a diet of tea, toast and broth. But after the hungry Moscow years the temptation was too strong and as soon as my mother turned her back I eagerly tasted all the things she had bought. When my relapse caused concern to the doctor I was too embarrassed to admit the truth. Fortunately everything was over in a few days. Another trouble lasted much longer: lice in our hair. We were inexperienced and too embarrassed to deal with the trouble efficiently, and many days went by before my mother gathered enough courage to ask for a remedy at the pharmacy.

That one month in Berlin meant very much for my own growth, both physical and moral. I know now that Berlin in 1920 was a poverty-stricken city, barely beginning to recover from the effects of war, but to me it seemed the epitome of luxury and civilization. I felt as if I were living in one of the foreign novels I read so avidly. New clothes, really new clothes chosen for me... I still remember the pure joy of wearing a raspberry-red knitted jacket which my mother bought for me, overcoming her traditional feeling that one should wear black after a death in the family. My hair began to grow so strongly that it made a natural bang on my forehead. I was very proud of "becoming a woman," as I duly noted in my diary. Our American friends offered me a job at the YMCA office. It seemed almost like a dream come true to enter this world of independence, of being really grown up, of going out to have lunch, or better still, being taken out for lunch by Jim Somerville, who seemed to become something of an admirer of mine. I felt I had to find my way of life in this new world, so very new and exciting. More than ever before and more than in the years to come, I felt on my own, a full-fledged person.

Curiously enough I felt little affinity with the Russian émigrés we met in Berlin. Most of them had not lived the life that we had experienced during the last two or three years in Moscow, the life of "suffering Russia." They simply sorrowed for the "lost paradise," for the "glorious past," while I felt that something new was being born in Russia — not the Communist regime, but a new sense of values, a new kind of relationship between people suffering together.

At the same time I experienced my first contact with the Protestant idealism of American vintage, a much more practical social Christian concept of life and work than the Anglican pietism which I had come to know through my mother. It appealed to my sense of responsibility, a sense of mission in life. I began to set myself goals that I felt I had to achieve. A conversation with Paul Anderson, who became then and remained throughout my life one of my best friends, made a deep impression on me. I realized that this one month was a kind of respite, a pause, that my freedom and independence would not continue, but the first "duty" I wrote down for myself in my diary was: "I shall always be happy."

Mania came to visit us in Berlin, glamorous and very pretty, caught up in the swirl of the "roaring twenties" in Paris. She managed to work, to earn her living and to have lots of fun. As usual I felt rather dowdy and dull in comparison to her.

We sailed from Stettin and Jim Somerville accompanied us to the pier. While waiting for our small steamer, we saw off the very same S.S. "Herbert Horn" which had brought us to Germany. It was leaving with a transport of Russian prisoners of war returning to Russia. We waved and shouted greetings to each other. They were rejoicing to go home. I did not have the heart to discourage them and sincerely wished them Godspeed.

I am a very poor sailor and the trip back was almost as unpleasant as the one we had taken in the opposite direction a

month earlier. But at the pier Iuri and Father were waiting
for us and the joy of our reunion was great.

* * *

Estonia was a charming small country, about the size of
Belgium, with a population of just over one million. It had
been part of the Russian empire since the 18th century but
became an independent republic in 1918. For two years war
with the USSR went on, in which the Russian North-Western
White Army of General Iudenich took part. The war ended
with the defeat of the White army, but the USSR gave up its
claim on Estonia in a peace treaty in February, 1920. Civil
war caused a violent epidemic of typhus. In some cities, like
Narva, for example, all the people in some parts of the town
had died. In 1921 I still saw entire streets of closed-down
houses that had been emptied by the epidemic and remained
uninhabited.

Estonians were the great majority of the population, speaking a language of the Finnish group, which has nothing in
common with any Germanic, Slavic or Romance language.
For several centuries Baltic Germans (descendants of Teut-
onic knights) were the ruling class of landowners. The Russian minority consisted of former Russian civil servants and
the Russian population at the eastern rim of the country.
All three languages were officially recognized.

In 1920 the population balance was upset by the results
of the civil war. Waves of refugees from Soviet Russia moved
in. The demobilized members of the North-Western White
Army roamed around, jobless and homeless, many of them
boys in their teens, with uncompleted schooling. The large
estates of the German landowners were nationalized, but the
owners were allowed to keep their homes and a minimal
quantity of land. The academic center of the country was
Tartu or Dorpat, with its ancient university, founded in 1632.
Narva was the center of the Russian minority and Reval, or
Tallinn, was the capital of the country.

The Estonians enthusiastically undertook the work of
building up their national state. There was an amazing lack

of chauvinism though tension existed between Estonians and the German barons. With some justification the latter considered that they had brought culture and civilization to the land, but they also treated Estonians as "natives" of a lower caste and their attitude was, of course, much resented. Curiously enough there was less resentment of Russians.

Reval is a picturesque medieval port town, originally one of the thirteenth-century Hanseatic League cities. Old streets and buildings clustered around the cathedral hill; in the center down below was the harbor with its flourishing export and import trade. At the edge of the town there was a beautiful park called Katherinenthal.

In 1920 Reval went through a critical shortage of housing. The city was crowded with new government institutions, foreign missions and new commercial enterprises. It was also invaded by Russian refugees and remnants of the Russian White Army.

This shortage of housing was our greatest difficulty during the first year. Father and Iuri lived in a large room in a dentist's apartment. Every time a patient rang the bell, the maid had to go through their room to open the door. They took one meal a day in a restaurant and ate sandwiches in the evening. During the first eight months Mother and I changed five furnished rooms that became available for short periods of time. We felt unbelievably lucky when we finally found an apartment into which all of us could move.

It was really a quaint little place, an old stone house in the backyard of a modern building, on one of the busiest Reval streets. Two or three old chestnut trees grew in the yard and gave the illusion that we were outside the city. The walls of the house were so thick that a staircase leading up in one straight flight to one of the rooms of our apartment was cut in the thickness of the wall. All three rooms were on different levels connected by steps. The dark and smelly kitchen had no window; it was a partitioned-off section of the middle room which we used as living and dining room. The second bedroom had a dormer window, so high up that you had to climb a ladder to get to it. There was also a dark closet, as large as a room. The middle room had wide, small-paned

windows, with window sills almost a yard wide. There was
no bathroom, but the ground floor must have been a laundry
originally and there were large wooden tubs on high feet,
where we could really bathe if we filled them with water that
could be heated on a small stove.

There was almost no furniture and the apartment, which
had been used as a workshop by a dental technician, was
full of trash. My mother and I cleaned and scrubbed it for
days. We bought very cheap wallpaper, with hideous flowers,
and put it wrong side on, so that the rooms were papered in
light grey. We put some pots with greenery and flowers on
the wide window sills and made cheesecloth curtains and dyed
them orange. There was a second-hand dining table, a sofa,
and four beds which we purchased from the American Red
Cross. Bookcases and shelves were made out of wooden
crates. We felt we were in a castle.

For each one of us the two years we spent in Reval was
a significant period.

My father's consultant job evaporated very soon. He was
kept somewhat busy by writing for the local Russian newspaper and preparing his memoirs, which were published after
his death. I am sorry to say that I learned to appreciate them
only much later. Even now as I reread them, I am amazed at
the wisdom, objectivity and vision he had in those early years,
immediately after the Revolution. He was really a broken
man, approaching his end, yet his thinking was much more
realistic and clear than that of most Russian émigré politi-
cians. I am afraid that Iuri and I only saw that my father had
nothing to do, that he brought home from the Russian Club
old volumes of an encyclopedia and spent hours reading them
and went to the movies several times a week. The things he
talked about or wrote about seemed uninteresting to us. I
still remember with pain how once, as I was rushing from
one of my so terribly important-seeming jobs to another, I
met my father in the street. "Say, Sonia," he called out, "what
about going to a movie with me?" He offered it to me as a
treat — the way it would have been only a short time before
"Papa, I cannot! I really cannot! I have no time. I am so busy!"
"All right, all right," he said. "I just thought it might be

fun." And he walked on looking weary. We miss so much in life and realize it too late.

Those two years were very different for my mother. At the age of forty-eight (and it seemed very old to me then) she put all her will and all her energy into becoming a "professional." At first it was simply her concern to earn a living. It went against her grain to build our life on the sale of her remaining jewelry or occasional dribbles of assistance, and hope that in a few months "everything would be over" and we would get our fortune back. Circumstances prodded her into becoming a teacher of English. She was invited to give lessons of English at the YW and YMCA, then at an Estonian school for girls, the at the German Realschule for boys. She gave as many as forty lessons a week and in addition translated books. She liked teaching and enjoyed adult students who wanted to learn. But she was quite unprepared to deal with large classes of teen-age boys. And to those youngsters, used to a German type of formal discipline, what a wonderful target she was — an elderly, badly dressed "lady," so unprofessional looking, so unsure of herself, carrying her notebooks in a market bag, speaking old-fashioned German . . . The principal was horrified because she said "you" to all the boys, instead of the customary German "thou." What a wonderful time the boys had at her expense, and how I raged when I saw her coming home, utterly exhausted and humiliated, on the verge of a breakdown. Yet even there she had a favorite, a twelve-year-old boy, Kruse, who got in trouble almost every day and looked like a blue-eyed angel. The principal earnestly spoke of him as "the black spot of the school."

She liked her Estonian girls' school much better and appreciated the courtesy of the staff to her, a Russian whom they might have resented. One day, as my mother came to a faculty meeting, the principal looked round the table and said: "I believe we all understand Russian and Frau (Mrs.) Shidlovsky speaks no Estonian. We shall continue the meeting in Russian." This impressed my mother so much that the very next day she bought an Estonian textbook and began learning the language.

As if this load of work was insufficient, my mother got involved, soon after our arrival, in relief work. The situation of the Russian refugees in Estonia was distressing. A whole section of the Russian population of the adjacent Pskov area of the USSR moved into Estonia. There was no housing for them, no work, no means of existence. The wartime type of activities run by the American Red Cross and the YMCA was being closed down. My mother brought together a group of Russian women who started a drive for clothes and food supplies for refugee children. The work snowballed, volunteers joined, money was contributed, our windowless closet became a storage place for all kinds of supplies distributed by the "Women's Committee." I think those two years in Estonia were a truly creative period for my mother, so much younger than I considered her.

For Iuri this period was a fight to regain health, to regain normality, and a hard fight it was. When we came to Reval he was so conscious of his appearance, his inflamed red skin covered with sores, his baldness (a side-effect of X-ray treatments from which he fortunately recovered), that he never went out in daytime, to avoid people looking at him. My father arranged for a tutor to work with him daily to enable him to graduate from high school, but this did not solve any of Iuri's problems. He fell in love with a pretty young German girl in a bakery and dared not approach her. He was eighteen years old, confused, insecure, unstable and discouraged, and in an attempt to commit suicide he swallowed twenty sleeping tablets. Fortunately my father came home early that day and found Iuri unconscious with an empty box of the veronal pills. He called an ambulance, Iuri was taken to the hospital, and in forty-eight hours he was out of danger. My father spoke to him sternly and said that unless Iuri gave his word of honor never to do this again, he would be taken from the hospital to an institution for the insane. Iuri sulkily promised. Then my mother spoke to him of life and death from a Christian point of view. He got badly scared and still remained unsure. At last it was my turn. I did not say anything, but Iuri whispered, "Sonia, you will help me to meet her?" I nodded my head, and Iuri cheered up.

The months that followed were not easy. Iuri still frequently wanted to end his life. We felt that he was, in a sense, "holding it over our heads" as a threat, and we did not know how to deal with it. For his own sake it did not seem wise to let him manipulate us. I knew that my friendship with him was special, that I had more influence with him than my parents, but I did not know what to do. Gradually life took its course. Very slowly his physical condition improved. After a second summer spent in Arensburg he was able to take a job, as interpreter for Edwin Wright, the YMCA secretary in Narva. There was a Russian High School in Narva and Iuri could prepare himself to take his graduation exams in the spring of 1922. I think it did him good to leave home, to become independent and active and make friends on his own.

Thanks to the letters from our American friends in Berlin I was given a secretarial job in the YMCA office in Reval. I became very much involved in more than just secretarial work and it meant more to me than a job to earn a salary.

As I look back at that time, I realize how the small local situation in Reval reflected much of a confrontation of two worlds that took place in many countries. There was Estonia, the new-born country, with its tri-lingual culture, eager for progress and growth. There were the human derelicts of the Russian tragedy, uprooted, shaken up, yet within the stream of a great spiritual tradition. And there were these zealous, idealistic missionaries like the kindly, yet culturally limited, Herbert S. Gott, Senior "Y" secretary in Estonia. They were missionaries of "the American way of life," innocently fervent in their faith in a "world made safe for democracy," believing in the constant progress of human society, and so lacking in knowledge of any culture except their own small-town American one.

We came to Estonia at a time when the YMCA wartime activities were being converted into regular peacetime work, a Christian service within a peacetime community. Orphanages and schools for Russian refugee children were being closed, work for the prisoners of war was over, and relief work was to be replaced by regular YMCA boys' clubs, gym classes, Bible study groups, educational courses, etc.

All this was new to me. After the years of destruction we had lived through, it appealed to our sense of responsibility and of participation in building up a new type of society. I vaguely felt that somewhere there was a discrepancy between the world-view on which all these activities were based and our own Orthodox concept of life, but I was young enough to be carried away by the naive optimism of the conviction that all evils can be straightened by our own efforts and a sufficient amount of good activities.

I was not the only one to be carried away by this concept of service. Soon quite a number of us, Russian young people in their late teens and early twenties, formed a pretty cohesive group. Most of the boys had the experience of civil war behind them, and all of us had gone through hardships. We were eager to think things through, to try ourselves out, to find answers to our questions. We had good times together too: we went skiing, we started a club, we ran a Sunday School for refugee children, we listened to lectures and discussed them, we even produced a manuscript magazine. The YMCA provided rooms for our activities, although we never quite fitted into the local secretary's idea of a program. For one thing we utterly rejected the idea of being divided by sex. Several Russians of the older generation showed a remarkably humble interest in our group and were willing to give us their time. I remember very interesting lectures on character growth by a psychology professor who must have been one of the assistants of Pavlov, the famous Russian psychologist. My father gave us several lectures in Russian history. The dean of the Russian Orthodox cathedral, Father John Bogoyavlensky, who later became a bishop, took us under his wing. Not only did he take the trouble to sit courteously, attentively and silently through the adult Bible classes taught by Mr. Gott, but he seemed to remain completely unshaken by our weird discussions. I remember that one day we set up a so-called "Literary Court of Justice," based on the story "Judas Iscariot" by Leonid Andreev, and somehow, to our own horror, finished up with a verdict of "not guilty." Father John's trust in us, his refusal to condemn us as heretics, or preach at us, was amazing. Even now I am not sure on what it was based.

A highlight of the American YMCA work for Russians in Estonia was a conference held in the fall of 1921 for teachers of all the YMCA-run orphanages and schools. It was held in Narva and the main speaker was Frank Ritchie, who was on a lecture trip through Europe. The conference set-up was quite original: the teachers were asked to imagine themselves a "normal community" and plan a program of activities and social work for such a community. Over one hundred people attended and they became increasingly interested. Certain aspects of the way the conference was run were rather funny. Mr. Gott had no idea that "Robert's Rules of Order" are completely unknown in Russia and every time he wanted someone to "move" a "motion" and then someone else to "second" it, people just looked blank and remained silent, though everyone was willing to raise a hand in a straight vote of "yes" or "no."

My own trouble was that a lecture was planned on sex education for boys, with a strong emphasis on the danger of venereal diseases. All lectures were given in English, which, of course, no one in the audience understood and I, a girl of seventeen, was the only interpreter provided. To have a young girl speak to an all-male audience on a subject which at that time was taboo, and the Russian vocabulary for which was practically unknown to most laymen (and especially to me), was pretty awkward. Herbert Gott thought he would help matters by giving me the contents of his lecture in private, but, having listened to him, I hated the idea even more. We gathered next morning in the big auditorium: the lecturers, secretaries, and a very miserable-feeling interpreter at a table in front; the attentive listeners on rows of benches. All kinds of unpleasant-looking charts and anatomical pictures were put up on stands. Suddenly Frank Ritchie got up, walked over to my place and said quietly: "I think you don't like interpreting this lecture. Please don't worry. The lecture is off." At that moment he gained my eternal affection.

Less funny was another incident which took place at the same conference. As I said, schools run by the YMCA for refugee children were being closed, and teachers were discharged. A Russian priest, who was on the staff of one such school, decided there was nothing left for him to do but return to his own parish on the other side of the frontier, in the USSR. Now news came that he had been executed there. When this was reported to Herbert Gott, he asked that the news be held back until the end of the conference, "not to affect its spirit." For any Orthodox Christian, the only possible reaction to such news would have been for the whole conference to have a service of prayer for the dead, and I was bewildered at realizing the difference between the two Christian mentalities.

Yet, thanks to Ritchie, "the spirit of the conference" really did reach unexpected heights. This man had vision and the capacity to understand other people's visions, to recognize what was really meaningful to them. On the last day of the conference he asked to be taken to the Russian frontier. It was marked by rows of barbed wire dividing a field and military guards on the road crossing it. As I stood, seeing Russia again, and feeling so desperately homesick, I asked the Russian guard to pick me a few flowers from his side of the field. He did it willingly, and we both stretched our arms through the several strands of barbed wire and he gave me this little bunch of "Russian" flowers. It was difficult for me to tear myself away from looking at the Russian roads, fields and sky.

That evening the conference closed with a banquet served to all participants. At the end of it Ritchie stood up to make his final address. He was an elderly, tall, somewhat heavy man, with a good speaking voice. "This morning," he said, "I looked at Russia together with one of you. As we were leaving this member of our conference said: 'The sky is different over there...'" It was as if an electric shock went through the audience! Now, after more than fifty years, I do not remember what Ritchie said in his speech, but I know that he touched our most sensitive spot, that what he said was relevant to all we had gone through, to the life we lived. He saw what was in our hearts and showed that he valued it. When he finished everyone stood up and the thunderous applause went on for a long time. After Ritchie had left, people stayed in the hall, talking and exchanging impressions until the small hours of the night.

Next day a very different but equally moving farewell took place. Ernest C. Ropes, a war-time "Y" secretary who had run the schools and orphanages, was being recalled to the States. A small farewell party was given him by his Russian co-workers. Russians love verbose expressions of affection and respect, and the party went on and on. At last it was time for Ropes to make his speech. He had spent his boyhood in Russia and spoke Russian well. He stood up: his tall, lean figure, his uniform, his twinkling glasses and humorous face — all so very American. He began in Russian: "To say one word of thanks is not enough . . ." He stopped. Complete silence reigned in the room. A minute went by. Suddenly Ropes turned on his heel and walked out. The silence continued and then we all heard the treble voice of little John, his six-year-old son: "Father, why are you crying?"

I must mention here another American who impressed me deeply with his sensitive perception of other people's experience. Hugh Fullerton was a young attaché at the American Consulate. He made friends with us on Easter night in 1921. Many Americans came to the Russian Cathedral for the Easter midnight service. They watched the traditional procession around the church, they listened admiringly to the Russian choir and after about an hour they left (as many Russians do too). The congregation stayed on, of course, for the whole long service and we were somewhat surprised to see Fullerton remain to the very end. My mother invited him to join us for our breakfast — the traditional Easter night meal with all its famous special foods and cakes — and he seemed pleased to do so. What did this young American think of our queer little apartment, of our obvious poverty, of the very strangeness of us as a class of people? He stayed quite long and it was getting light when I was sent to see him out into the street, with the heavy, almost medieval key to open the door. Birds were twittering in the old chestnut trees, the sky was a soft grey, tinted pink and yellow in the east. It was Easter morning, the time which always reminds me of the women hurrying to the grave on the first Easter. Fullerton

suddenly stopped. "Are you very happy?" he asked me. I
suppose, taking everything into consideration, that it was a
strange question for a well-off young American to ask. "Very,
very happy!" I exclaimed spontaneously, for who is not happy
on Easter night! But I was somewhat surprised at the almost
wistful way in which he asked his question.

Next Christmas Fullerton invited me to bring three of my
Sunday School children to his private Christmas party. I chose
the children carefully — one from the very poorest family,
one well-behaved little girl who spoke German and thus
could communicate with Fullerton, and one adorable little
boy who bubbled over with energy and had a knack of getting
in trouble. I was amazed at the way Fullerton received us.
It was not philanthropy. Everything looked as if he were expecting the most distinguished guests: snow-white table cloth,
beautiful silverware, elegant dishes. The meal was served by
a maid and the children behaved beautifully. Iura, the boy,
did nothing worse than drop a fork on the floor. Then the
Christmas tree was lit and there were presents for everybody.

I never saw Fullerton in later years. I believe he remained
in the diplomatic service and I am sure he must have been one
of the best representatives abroad of that quality of American
character that is truly precious.

The two years in Reval were a period of great inner turmoil for me. Before leaving Russia, after the failure of our
first attempt to escape, I experienced a period of something
that might be called "spiritual uplift," but in a sense our experience in Russia was a struggle for existence rather than
life. In Reval I felt suddenly exposed to new possibilities,
new challenges, new relationships, new conflicts. As I look
through my diary of those days I can see how funny and
pathetic was my belief that I can and must organize all of
my life. Over and over again all my duties are carefully listed
under separate headings: God, family, self, work. I was so
sure that if I conscientiously cooked for the family, washed
dishes, attended Bible classes, and studied shorthand, was
on time at the office, remembered to say my prayers, and left
X minutes a day for "family relationships," I would attain
a Kingdom of Heaven on earth. All those good intentions

and plans failed at pretty regular intervals and I finished up frustrated and desperate. Our youth group was my first experience of living as a member of a group outside my family, of sharing my thoughts and feelings with others on my own, as an independent person. For the first time in my life, too, I was in love, and though the boy who gave me his first love was as frantically puritanical and idealistic as I, our unexpressed love was no less real for that. Growing more mature, however unconsciously, I inevitably grew apart from the exclusive intimacy I had with my mother, and, quite unconsciously too, she was jealous of my new interests and my new friendships. She did not disapprove of them, but she wanted me to share everything with her, whereas for me the essence of my new experience was that it was my own.

My mother was going through a difficult time. Without any of us realizing it, my father at sixty-one was drawing close to the end of his life. A kind of invisible wall of indifference and weariness separated him from his family. My mother, at forty-nine, had to accept the loss of almost everything that was meaningful to her: the kind of life she had lived in Russia, her relationship with my father and her family as an entity, a unit. She had a tender, passionate, and vulnerable nature, and all her love, a rather possessive love, centered on me, her last child remaining with her.

Iuri had grown independent too, but for him I remained a "core" of the family, a kind of root which made him feel secure, and so he also resented my new loyalties.

As time went on I began to suffer more and more from my lack of education. I don't quite know what made it so painful. It was not a thirst for knowledge as such, or an intellectual curiosity in some special field. I think I felt that an "educated" person was quite different from an "uneducated" one. I felt a real hunger and thirst to become this kind of bigger person. Remaining "uneducated" was equivalent to giving up part of my growth and of life, like being crippled. Perhaps it was a matter of rather false self-esteem (*samoliubye*). Anyway it was my hurt ego that triggered off one of the hardest efforts I had ever made. One evening we were playing "charades" in our youth group. Most of the other

boys and girls were high school students. We were supposed
to present a lesson given in a classroom. The boy who acted
the part of the teacher asked an elementary question in trigonometry. I was playing the part of the good pupil who knows
all the answers. To my mortification I had to say that I had
never studied trigonometry. I shrugged it off laughingly, but
at night, when I came home and went to bed, I wept bitterly
and long. Then and there I decided I would complete a high
school course, whatever effort it cost me.

The European high school ("Gymnasium") has an eight-
year program. In 1918 I had completed the first four grades
of it. Now in 1921 I undertook to cram into one year the
remaining four years of study and pass my final exam (*abitu-
rium*) in the spring of 1922. I planned to do this without
giving up my full-time job and without causing any expense
to my parents. I brushed off the additional difficulty of lack
of textbooks by asking the members of our youth group to
lend me theirs when they were not using them. My boy friend
undertook to coach me in mathematics. Now my daily schedule
and list of duties were again revised: work at the office from
8 to 5:30. During the lunch period I earned additional money
by taking three little German boys on an "English walk."
All my home chores were done from 6 to 9, and then I settled
down to my studies and worked until midnight. I got up early
and studied from 6 to 8 A.M. There were some circumstances
to my advantage. My knowledge of foreign languages was
more than sufficient to pass examinations without preliminary
work. I had also read extensively enough not to worry about
Russian literature and history. But the Russian "Gymnasium"
program had a far greater number of subjects than the American high school. We had to pass both oral and written examinations in mathematics (algebra and trigonometry), physics, chemistry, cosmography, Russian history, world history,
Russian language and literature, French, German, Latin, law,
psychology, logic, and, of course, religious instruction. I "did"
the physics course during my summer vacation in Arensburg,
and this subject, which I studied while relaxed and rested, remained my favorite. Mathematics was the hardest, for I
could barely assimilate the theory and had little time for

solving problems. The other subjects were just a matter of memorizing a textbook for each one of them.

All in all I progressed slowly but surely. The load was a heavy one and in December I got sick. The doctor said I had overstrained my heart and insisted on a fortnight's complete rest. I spent two very happy weeks at Kumna, the home of our friends the Meyendorffs, related to us by the marriage of one of my cousins. Old Baroness Meyendorff was a delightfully wise and very intelligent woman, her middle-aged daughter Maya energetically carried on the farm work on the remnants of their old estate, and the three lovely grandchildren were a joy to watch. I came back rested and refreshed and went on with my work.

Then, just as I thought I had things pretty well under control, came the sudden need to make a very painful decision, one of the hardest decisions I had ever had to make. A letter came from the American YWCA, in which they offered me a full scholarship that involved going to the United States, attending a college there, and training to become a YWCA secretary. All expenses would be paid, including the trip, and I would have to go in a few weeks.

For me, such as I was then, it was like a gate opening to heaven, like being released from prison, like having the most wonderful and exciting road open up before me. I literally felt as if I had been dying from thirst and someone brought me water. Yet I knew, too, that accepting this offer would hurt others. It would leave my parents alone, and I realized all too clearly what it would mean to my mother. At this point all my newly acquired "American Protestant" beliefs in the Godgiven right to pursue happiness, my belief in my own freedom and personal rights, came into a violent clash with my deeper Orthodox world view.

I was hurrying up the street on my way to the office when I met Father John Bogoyavlensky. On a sudden impulse I stopped and asked him whether I could come to talk to him about my difficulty, briefly outlining it. Father John was silent for a moment, and then peering at me thoughtfully through his glasses, he asked: "Are you ready for a *podvig*?" This is an almost untranslatable Russian word which means both "heroism," "heroic feat" and "ascetic toil." In that instant I knew what his advice would be and I knew that I would follow it.

I am quoting a paragraph from the letter I wrote to Miss Marcia Dunham, Senior YWCA Secretary, our good friend, who stood behind the offer.

I thought and thought on the matter. I turned it over in my mind, and the more I think about it, the more I see that under present circumstances, and as far as I can see for many years to come, it is quite impossible. I do not think that even you will realize how hard it is to refuse for good and the reason I am writing is partly that I want to feel that my decision is good and solid and there is no way back. I don't even know whether, after all, I will have the courage to send the letter off . . . I feel as if I was cutting myself off from *the* ambition of my life, from all that I used to dream about for these two years, everything which seemed to make life bright and gave an object to it. Well, the object must be found in a different direction and I am sure I will find it. I am sorry if this letter is not clear enough, but it was so awfully hard to write.

The weeks that followed my decision were really difficult for me. I had tried to keep the whole matter and my decision secret from my parents, but my mother received a note from the YWCA office asking her to cable whether I would be leaving with a certain boat on a certain date. My parents simply could not imagine that I might even want to go and considered the whole plan quite ridiculous. I believed that it was my duty not to let them feel that I wanted to go and tried to hide from them how hard it was for me to refuse. Somewhere, somehow, I had a childish hope that if my parents discovered how much I suffered without my telling them, they would insist on my accepting the offer. It was the very innocence of their assumption that I could not possibly consider an acceptance that made things so hard. My loneliness was great, for the boy with whom I was in love had left in the fall to study in a university in Germany. My brother Iuri saw well enough through my pretense of carrying on as usual, and resented my "making a victim of myself," but he was quite unable to understand how I could want so badly to become "a bespectacled YWCA secretary." In his letters he tried to comfort me by saying how unhappy I would be in America and how good it was that we would all remain together. I found as little comfort in this as he had in visualizing me as a "bespectacled YWCA secretary." I can see now that he was right in some ways. There was a lot of unwholesome arrogance in my "self-sacrifing" attitude, in my insistence on feeling responsible for the family. My refusal to take things easy was part of a self-righteous image. All this is probably true, but at the time I was sincere in my efforts and sincere in my pain.

The person whose understanding and sympathetic attitude helped me a lot was the old German doctor whom I went to see on my own, because my heart condition bothered me again. His kindliness was a good medication. Time went on, my unhappiness became less acute, the examinations were approaching, and all my thoughts turned to them.

How often in years to come I gratefully remembered Father John's advice. Everything I dreamed of came to me in its own good time, when, I think, I was better prepared for it. How much I would have missed if I had accepted the offer then.

My father's health was deteriorating. His heart condition was growing worse. He often had to spend the night in an armchair because he could not breathe if he lay down. But both he and my mother insisted that I need not worry and that I could leave them for a fortnight to take my exams in Narva. The examinations were taking place there at the émigré Russian High School, because Estonian was not a required subject there as it was at the Russian High School in Reval, which was part of the public school system. The sixteen examinations were to be given over a period of one month but since I could not ask for such a long leave of absence at the office, I was granted permission to go through all of them in two weeks.

Iuri found a room for me in the same house where he lived. It belonged to a charming family of four old people, two brothers and two sisters in their seventies. The house was old, too. The walls in my room were covered with quaint frescoes of a dark greenish tint, dating back to the early nineteenth century, representing interiors of masonic temples. A glass door led out on to a balcony from which I could see and hear the river Narova boiling up as it approached the Narova rapids. Trees and flowered shrubs pressed in on all sides.

Iuri and I had good times together. His elderly house-owners adored him and received me with open arms. I found Iuri as indifferent to his clothes, his personal cleanliness, and the condition of his room as any hippy in the sixties. However I gradually bested him: took all the dirty clothes I found lying around to the laundry, repaired and ironed them, and one morning, while he was still asleep, threw out the dirty and tattered underwear he had been wearing. I brought to his room a big tub, soap, towels and plenty of hot water and then woke him up. I can still see him standing in the door-way, hiding behind an opened umbrella and roaring with in-dignation. But in a short while I heard him singing as he splashed around and soaped and rinsed himself and finally came out to be admired by all of us.

It was a relief to be able to concentrate only on my stud-ies, and Iuri's attitude to the examinations helped to relieve my tension. It is true that he had had two years to prepare himself as against my one and that the first year and a half he was not working and had a tutor coaching him regularly, but on the whole we were pretty equal. One night, on the eve of the chemistry examination, which was one of the dif-ficult ones, Iuri and I settled to work in our separate rooms, each one with a candle. The night before had been a sleepless one for Iuri; he went by train to meet the girl he was in love with at a station she would be passing through at two A.M., just to see her for a few minutes. Now he was full of good intentions to catch up on his studies. I was deep in my chemis-try book when I heard the flip-flop of bare feet in the next room. The door opened and there was Iuri in his underwear, his candle in one hand and a Gospel book in the other. "Sonia," he announced, "I just opened the Gospel and it fell open right at the words about Peter and how when he became afraid he began to sink! Good night; I am going to bed!"

The day I arrived and registered at the school, I was taken into a classroom where the oral examination in Russian history was going on. I was so scared, and tense that for the first few minutes everything swam before my eyes and I could not take in anything. I was sure I would fail, I was sure I would never, never pass those wretched exams. Gradually my mind cleared. I began to take in my surrounding and listen to what was going on. The boy who was answering seemed unsure of himself. He hemmed and hawed and had difficulty in bringing out the words. Used as I was in my childhood to our private tutoring at home, when we were expected to know our lessons perfectly and answer fluently, smoothly and without hesitations, I began to feel concerned for the boy. "Do you think they'll pass him?" I whispered to the girl sitting next to me. She looked surprised. "Of course they will! He knows all the answers!" That *was* a relief. I knew I could do better than this.

Much later I learned that I need not have worried so much about the whole matter of examinations. Most of the boys graduating that year had been volunteers in the White Army and their education had been interrupted by the civil war. The faculty was told to be lenient and let them get their high school diplomas even if they were weak in some subject. Those whom it was impossible not to fail were given a chance to retake the failed examination in a few weeks. I had expected higher standards and as result received very good grades — fourteen "Fives" and three "Fours" (in algebra, trigonometry and chemistry). In Russian schools five means excellent, four — good, three — satisfactory, two — unsatisfactory, one — failing.

I remember very clearly my last night in Narva. All the difficult exams were over and I was sure I would have no trouble with my last one next day. Still, I stayed up late reviewing the textbook and it was almost daylight when I stepped out on to the balcony before going to bed. My heart was full of happiness and gratitude. During the past year I had so often felt discouraged, almost hopeless. I knew that if I failed I would never have the courage to try again. And now it was all over. It was a heady and exhilarating feeling and I was sure that this was not a dead end. A road would open up before me.

My parents have been writing me regularly — cheerful, encouraging, loving letters, humorously describing their attempts at independence and some of their failures. Only in the very last one my mother wrote sadly that my father was not getting any better and that it might be well if Iuri came home too after the examinations. As soon as the last examination was over I called up the YMCA building in Reval. We had agreed that I would leave a message there, since we had no phone at home. The Estonian janitor answered my call. Yes, he was glad to get my good news and he would pass it on. But he was sorry he had bad news to give me. My father was dying; I should take the earliest train home.

My father died four weeks later. For a few days my success and my return home cheered him up and he seemed to improve; then he continued slipping. It was a painful death. He suffocated if he lay down, but was too weak to sit up. His feet were so water-logged and swollen that the skin split, and sores opened up. Morphine had to be injected several times a day to relieve his suffering and he grew confused. Day and night my mother and I took turns nursing him. Iuri came for a few days, but had to go back to his work in Narva. Having been absent from the office for two weeks, I could not take time off again and continued to work until the day before Father died. During the night either my mother or I sat up on the sofa next to him, supporting him. We divided the night so that each one of us could get a few hours of sleep. I remember well the last night I sat up with father. I do not know how conscious he was. Suddenly, uncertainly, his hand groped for mine. Feebly he carried it to his lips and kissed it. Did he think I was Mother? Or was this his last gesture of tenderness and love for me? What did he want to say? I choked, I tried to comfort him. And then I sat on. I knew my mother would come to relieve me at 4 A.M.

I remember how I fought my drowsiness, how I looked at the clock counting the hours and then . . . I don't know how it happened, but when my mother came in, a whole hour earlier than she was supposed to, she found me in the next room, on the bed, covered with a blanket and sound asleep. I must have dozed off while sitting with my father and in my sleep I got up, climbed the steps into the other room and lay down. Fortunately my father was well propped up by pillows and did not fall.

I am glad that I faced my first death under old-world conditions, with no funeral parlors, no beautifications, no cosmetics, no artificiality. We who loved him did all that was necessary, bathed and clothed him, laid him out and prayed. He was taken to the Russian cathedral directly from our home.

At that time in Reval my father must have been something of a public figure. Perhaps the Russians there *wanted* to consider him prominent; they felt the need to demonstrate their Russian unity and loyalty. My father's funeral became a solemn occasion. The cathedral was crowded; the funeral procession went on foot through the whole city to the Russian cemetery. On the way a short requiem service was held at the foot of the monument to Peter the Great. The Russian newspaper came out with a wide black border. When I called to pay for the funeral expenses I was told everything had already been paid.

The letter my sister Mania wrote from Paris was almost childlike in its sorrow. I believe that for her this was the real break with all her ties to our past, the end of her feeling that somewhere she had a family that was a real entity, to which she was linked, however independent she might be.

A few weeks went by. One day our friend Paul Anderson and another "Y" secretary arrived from Berlin. They came to see us and spent the evening with us. Seeing Paul reminded me of the conversation we had had when we had just escaped from Russia, when I was so full of hope and energy. Now I was feeling tired, somewhat depressed and very old — the way you can feel sometimes when you are eighteen years old.

Next morning I came to the office as usual. The only

people there were my friend and colleague, an Estonian girl of my age, and Maurice Ross, the elderly instructor in physical education of whom we were all very fond. "You know, girls, what I heard yesterday?" announced Ross. "MacNaughten and Anderson were talking about their visit to your home, Sophie, and they said you and your brother would both be getting scholarships to study in a university in Germany." "What? . . ." I gasped. "It can't be true!" "Oh, yes, it's true! I heard Paul Anderson say: 'This winter she'll be at the University in Berlin.'" I hugged Mr. Ross and went out into the big auditorium, a former ballroom, that had large windows at both ends. The green leaves of huge chestnut trees filtered the sunlight streaming in. Breathless, I walked up and down the room. I was so happy I could not speak. My dream had come true. Indeed these two years had not led me into a dead end. The road was opening up.

* * *

We left Reval in October 1922 and all our friends gave us a wonderful and warm send-off. At the pier the bright blue uniform caps of the girls from the Estonian school looked like a puddle of water reflecting the sky. The boys of the German school had argued with the headmaster because whole classes wanted to see my mother off, but he insisted that two boys from each class would be sufficient. However, the young boy Kruse remained true to himself. He did not go back to school when the other boys did and I saw him jumping up and down on the pier as our boat began to move. "The black spot of the school" must have earned another demerit that day.

Our country home in Voltchy.

*The "birch avenue,"
one of Alexandrovka's
several avenues.*

*COVER PHOTOGRAPH:
The author and members of her
family on the steps of the old
cottage in La Séguinière.*

*On the lawn of Alexandrovka, the country home
of my grandparents Sabouroff. Included in the
group are my grandmother, my Aunt Mary, and
other relatives.*

Myself at age 6.

My brother Andrei, 1915.

Myself at Voltchy, 1914.

*My sister and I with our governe
at Voltch*

My father in his study in our
St. Petersburg home.

A Sunday evening reception at my grandparents' St. Petersburg home.
Seated on the far right is my grandmother; directly behind is
the Grand Duke Constantine Constantinovich.

The Temporary Executive Committee of the Duma, as pictured on a postcard sold on the streets of Petrograd in 1917. My father is seated second from the right. Standing second to the right is Kerensky, who soon was to head the Provisional Government.

My brother Yuri and I,
Tallinn, 1921.

Gania and
her husband Peter.

Conference of the Russian Student Christian Movement, Argeronne, 1924. Seated in the first row, from left to right: Evdokimov, Zander, Fr. Kalashnikov, Fr. Bulgakov, Kartashev, Zenkovsky.

Berdyaev with a group from the Russian Student Christian Movement.

My first Sunday School, Tallinn, 1921.

*My husband and I
on our honeymoon, 1932.*

*Baby Elizabeth kissing Metropolitan Evlogy's
panaghia in our home, 1933.*

*My mother shortly before her
death, with little Elizabeth.*

*Xenia, myself with baby George,
Olga and Elizabeth.*

On the eve of our departure for America: Nikita, his brother
Yaroslav, myself, Olga, Elizabeth, "my Aunt Mary" and George,
Xenia and "Nikita's Aunt Mary."

Our home in Nyack.

As a member of the St. Vladimir's Seminary faculty.

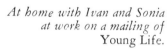
*At home with Ivan and Sonia
at work on a mailing of
Young Life.*

As grandmother and teacher, with Alex, Sonia and Ivan, 1974.

CHAPTER FOUR

We were back in Berlin again. It was a cold and drizzly October that somehow suited the pompous, heavy, well-ordered city. My mother went on to Paris to stay with my sister Mania until Christmas, and I settled down in a boarding house where a Russian family my mother knew was already staying. We three students: my brother Iuri, my friend George Lunin, to whom I had become unofficially engaged, and I, felt very free and without a care in the world. Our scholarships amounted to ten dollars a month for each one of us, but with the deflation of the German currency, we were much better off than most of the German students. Our first goal was to gain admission to the schools of our choice. Iuri decided to apply at the School of Agriculture, which he thought would give him a practical profession without involving mathematics, which he hated. The "Landwirtschaftliche Hochschule" in Berlin had no vacancies and on their advice Iuri enrolled in a provincial school with the prospect of transferring to Berlin later on.

Berlin-Paris, 1922-1926

I decided that getting a scholarship was much too good an opportunity to be wasted on practical training in some profession. Surely my knowledge of languages, typing, and shorthand would always provide me with a bread-and-butter job. Now I had the chance to study for the fun of it ("for the soul" according to a Russian expression). I wanted to enroll in the Department of Philosophy of the Kaiser Wilhelm University in Berlin, choosing history as my major and philosophy and history of art as my two minor subjects. The real difficulty was getting admitted at the university. Academically my certificate of matriculation from the Russian Gymnasium in Narva was sufficient, but in these post-war years all universities were overcrowded and there was a limit to the number of foreign students that could be admitted. However, my wonderful luck held and the road opened up before me in a very unexpected way. Somehow we met in Berlin a man who used to be my older brothers' German tutor. He was now completing his medical studies in Berlin and welcomed us as if we were his long lost family. He *happened* to have an uncle, an old German professor, who had been the president (*rector*) of the Berlin University, and the old German professor *happened* to have been a student at the University of Dorpat when my grandfather was president of its board of trustees (*curator*). So the old German professor told his nephew to have me call on him. How my German stood up to the trial I do not know, but I do remember that we talked about Russia and the Revolution, about my experiences there during the difficult years and what these experiences had meant for me. We spoke about Tolstoy and Dostoevsky and why the latter seemed more meaningful today. Suddenly I saw a tear rolling down the old gentleman's wrinkled face. He patted my cheek and gave me a card to the President of the University asking him to accept me as a student. This proved successful, and I was enrolled without any further difficulty.

The nice old professor and his wife did not lose sight of me. They invited me to their home and because of them an oil portrait was made of me by Franz Triebsch, seemingly a fashionable artist of the time, who felt that he had too many portraits of generals and elderly members of the German imperial family for his next exhibition and wanted to paint a young girl. I loved his old-world manners: he called on my mother to ask for her permission to paint me, and every time I came to sit for him, his wife stayed with us and poured tea for us. At the end of our sittings he brought me a present, a Russian book of poetry which I still have and use for the Russian lessons I give to my grandchildren.

German university life was very different from that of colleges in America or in England. There were no faculty advisors, no guidance offices, no supervision of student life, no dormitories. Students lived wherever they wanted, and the university bore no responsibility for their way of life. You could register for as many or as few courses as you wanted, as long as at least one of them was in your major field of studies. The courses registered for were listed in the student's booklet and on this basis the student paid his fees. The lecturers affixed their signature at the beginning and the end of the semester. Attendance was not checked. There were no examinations during the first three years. After three years of such freely chosen studies you could present yourself for the State Examination, or decide to work for your doctorate, at which time you had to choose the theme of your thesis, involving some kind of original research. I suppose that from then on you worked more closely with some professor until the time when the thesis was accepted and had to be defended. If you studied philosophy you did not get a textbook which presents the teachings of various philosophers, but were expected to read the original works and draw your conclusions. As someone summed it up, university studies did not put a roof on the house of your education; you were expected to have that done before you came to a university. University education meant adding a tower to your house.

I can see the advantages of such independence, but I must say that coming as a foreigner, with very insufficient knowledge of German, I felt rather at sea and my first semester served merely as an orientation period. I do not know what I would have done without George Lunin, a second-year student, to help me.

I remember choosing a course in German history, quite naively, for the very reason that I knew so little about it and thought it would be a good idea to learn more. It was a great mistake. For a whole hour I listened as well as I could and understood only one word "Herodotus," and even then I could not understand what the fourth-century B.C. Greek historian had to do with German history.

However, I did understand and was really interested in

a course entitled "Introduction to Philosophy," taught by Prof. Wertheimer. Gradually I learned to select courses and seminars where my poor German did not handicap me so much. I really profited a lot from a seminar in Russian history taught by Professor Stehlin, where all the sources were in Russian. Nor have I ever forgotten a course in the history of early Italian Renaissance art, which Professor Hildebrand taught us in a dark auditorium, teaching us by means of slides to recognize schools and painters, showing all the details, the handling of textures, of hair, as well as the composition.

As soon as I could be admitted to a seminar my relationships with the other students and my professor got closer. I worked in the seminar of Professor Stehlin on the history of the Russian revolutionary movements. The seminar library was well stocked, the theme was interesting, and I studied and wrote papers willingly. I am afraid I was still the least academically minded of the seminar members, but they were very friendly to me. One of the students was Serge Yacobson, who later was in charge of the Russian section at the Library of Congress in Washington, D.C., and he was very helpful. I remember the cozy little Christmas party we had in the dark old seminar, with a candle-lit tree, the smell of the singed pine needles overcoming the somewhat musty atmosphere.

During lectures students expressed their opinions and feelings in an impersonal but very effective manner. If they approved a professor's statement — usually it was the expression of some patriotic feeling or thought — they stamped their feet. If they disapproved, they shuffled. One day, a generally popular professor objected to the presence of a dog in his class. A student stood up and explained that it was a blind student's "seeing-eye dog," but the professor still looked dissatisfied and mumbled something about dogs not being admitted. The whole auditorium shuffled, and how! The dog remained, although in a less obvious place.

None of us knew of Hitler in those days, but the stage was being prepared for future events. The German nation was painfully recovering from the war. The humiliations of defeat were deeply resented, the economic hardships were real, and thus the soil was ready to receive the seeds of any teaching or movement that appealed to national pride. Foreigners were disliked at the university. Deflation gave them the opportunity of living better than their German colleagues, and in German eyes they were "vultures," profiting by the country's disaster — "war profiteers." Of course I sensed this enmity, but could sympathize with its causes. As I look back at this period, however, I also remember very vividly the warm friendliness that we experienced a number of times during our stay in Germany.

My mother returned from Paris around Christmas time. In Berlin she was given work, teaching English at the Correspondence School organized by the American YMCA for former Russian prisoners of war still interned in German camps. Those who had stayed did not want to return to Soviet Russia and it was important for them to get vocational training before being released to look for jobs in some foreign country. There was no suitable textbook for the English course and my mother was asked to write a "self-teaching manual of English." The book proved very successful and thirty years later, when displaced persons started to arrive in the U.S.A., many of them were studying English using the "Shidlovsky manual." She thus had an interesting full-time job and could do most of the work at home.

We found clean and decent furnished rooms in Wartenburg Strasse, a quiet street a few blocks behind Anhalter Bahnhof. Later, when Iuri transferred to Berlin, a third room was made available. Our widowed landlady, Frau Kühn, was very pleasant and undertook to cook our evening meal for us if we did the shopping. She had little Trüdchen to help her, a tiny, good-natured and very willing eighteen-year-old orphan. Trüdchen's whole family died during the food shortages of wartime, when they tried to enrich their diet by gathering mushrooms and ate some poisonous ones.

Berlin landladies were not known for their pleasant attitude, and in the first months we had known some real dragons. The Russian philosopher Berdyaev, who came to Berlin at about this time, told us once that he had never experienced as pure a feeling of hatred as he did for his landlady, who insisted that he take turns daily sitting on opposite ends of the sofa in his room, so that it would not sag at one place. With Frau Kühn we were really lucky; she was always friendly, conscientious, scrupulously clean and honest. The only point of disagreement between us was some of her cooking. One day my mother asked her to cook some macaroni with cheese for our evening meal — I bought what I thought was necessary — ½lb of macaroni, grated cheese, a little butter. Next day Frau Kühn proudly served us a panfull of a glutinous, watery mess. "How did you cook the macaroni?" asked my mother somewhat surprised, although she had never been able to learn to cook herself. "Oh, I cooked it real properly," said Frau Kühn proudly. "I soaked them in water overnight and then cooked them for a good hour!" After this we decided to keep to the German "cuisine," and since even in our capacity of "profiteering foreigners," we could not afford steaks or roasts, we did pretty well with sausages, potatoes, and fruitsoups.

On Christmas Eve, that wonderful German feast of feasts, Frau Kühn invited us all to her little Christmas tree party. Her son, an engineer, came too. Trüdchen brought her little brother from the orphanage, the only other surviving member of her family. There were presents for everybody, there were cakes and cookies, the tree glittered with its many candles, we sang German carols and, best of all, there was a truly Christmas atmosphere, joyful and close, of a small group of people who, however different their backgrounds, had lived through hard times and could still be happy.

Another time my mother and I were brought into contact with a very different kind of German life style. Years before, in Petersburg, my mother had made friends with a rather popular philosopher and writer of German Baltic origin, Graf Herman Keyserling. He came to see us quite frequently. We children did not care for him, although the only reason for this that I can remember was that, as he talked of mysticism and the power of spiritual experience over material ones, he ate with great gusto, smacking his rather full red lips. Now, in 1923, when he met my mother in Berlin, Graf Keyserling proved to be a loyal friend. He sent us tickets to his lecture, and I remember him speaking with great warmth of his Russian friends and what they had gone through. Keyserling was married to Bismarck's granddaughter, and some time later we received an invitation from Fürstin Bismarck, widow of the chancellor's son Herbert, to spend a weekend at their country place.

This was the only time in my life that I was a guest in this type of home — at a beautiful big country house, imbedded in the almost feudal traditions of the West European "ancien regime," so different from the informality of the Russian country homes of my childhood. It must have been the beginning of the hunting season, for on Sunday a mounted cavalcade of hunters rode up to the house to salute the Bismarcks. They sang some folk songs appropriate to the occasion, and I still remember my feeling of homelessness and rootlessness, that sense of "not-belonging" that must always be part of the émigré life. The old Fürstin Bismarck was very gracious and kind, her young son was a kindly and patient host, showing me the countryside while our mothers talked. It was an enjoyable and interesting occasion, but somehow quite separate, quite strange to the way of life we had to follow, the road we had to discover for ourselves.

The pleasantest personal contacts we made in Germany were with a charming family, so remotely related to us that I have to go two generations back to explain the relationship. My maternal grandfather had an older brother, Pierre Sabouroff. During his service at the Russian Imperial Embassy in Berlin he met young Leontine von Fitztum, a member of an aristocratic German Roman Catholic family. They fell in love, became engaged, and my grandparents came to Germany to attend the wedding. Almost on the eve of the wedding Pierre shared his misgivings with his brother and sister-in-law. He was not sure of his love; he felt the marriage to be a mistake. My romantic grandmother thought it was better to call everything off, however late, but my grandfather felt it would be dishonorable to do so. Pierre tried to speak to his fiancée, saying he was unworthy of her, but she threw herself in his arms and said she loved him as he was. Pierre spoke to Leontine's mother, but she thought things had gone too far with all the wedding arrangements. "All the cakes are baked!" my grandmother quoted her in disgust — rather unfairly, I thought.

The wedding took place. Very soon Leontine was expecting her first son. Pierre brought her to Russia, to his parents' country home Alexandrovka, a lovely old place in our eyes, but very disorderly and uncivilized from a West European point of view. I do not know how old the baby was when Pierre finally abandoned his young wife and asked for a divorce. My grandmother, my mother and her sister learned to love Leontine and did their best to comfort her, but finally it seemed best to have her return to her family with her little son Alick. Loyally Leontine made sure that her son learned to speak Russian and asked her sisters-in-law to find a Russian nurse for him.

Years went by. Pierre's career progressed and he was appointed to a position in the foreign service where it was indispensable for him to be married and have a wife act as hostess. Neither he nor Leontine had remarried, so their divorce was annulled and their marriage patched up. They had another son, Peter, many years younger than his elder brother.

I remember both of them in their old age: Uncle Pierre, a handsome, good-natured octogenarian, walking around with a cane, and Aunt Leontine, an invalid, with a bad heart condition, always breathless, always easily upset, all her love and life centered on her second bachelor son. They both died before the Revolution; Uncle Alick, made governor of Moscow, was executed in the first months after the October Revolution. His wife and children perished in Russia.

It would seem that Aunt Leontine's German family had little reason to like their Russian relatives by marriage, but, curious as it may seem, very friendly personal relations were maintained all through the years and visits were exchanged. Now in Berlin we came in touch with the young von Metzch branch of the family. They received us as affectionately as if we had been closely related, using right away the German "Du" (*Thou*). I especially appreciated their kindness and informal hospitality while my mother was in Paris and I was alone in Berlin. Alick v. Metzch (named in honor of Aunt

Leontine's eldest son) was a very young man in 1914, engaged to be married to an American girl, Gertrud Steinway, of the Steinway piano family. When war was declared they got married immediately and a day later he left for the front. Gertrud saw him next when he was barely alive, with, I believe, 16 wounds in his body. He was still slightly crippled in 1923 and could not use his arm. Gertrud told me he might never completely get over the wound. They had three lovely children, a very attractive home and Alick held a good position in a bank. I suppose the Steinway background must have helped too. With them I felt really comfortable and at home, and I am sorry that in later years we lost track of each other.

During the first year of our stay in Berlin an event took place which exercised an important influence on the intellectual and spiritual growth of the Russian emigration. More than this, it probably greatly affected the impact of Eastern Christian thought on the western world and in recent years became an important factor in the movement of religious reawakening in Soviet Russia. In November 1922, in a moment of rather inexplicable liberalization of its policies, the Soviet government deported a group of eminent Russian philosophers and scientists: Nicholas Berdyaev, Fr. Sergius Bulgakov, S. L. Frank, L. P. Karsavin, I. A. Ilyin, B. P. Vysheslavtzev, and a number of others. They were the elite of the Russian religious revival of the early twentieth century, most of them rediscovering Christianity, and more specifically Orthodoxy, after being deeply involved in the materialistic thought of the earlier period. They came to Berlin a few weeks after our arrival and quite soon founded there the so-called Religious Philosophic Academy. Because their writings and their influence was so generally important, I allow myself to relate in some detail how I personally was affected by my contact with them. I am very unacademic and untheological by nature, not very inclined to abstract thinking, and for this very reason it may be interesting to see how the arrival of this group of learned men affected my life.

Soon after the "professors'" arrival a public meeting was organized in the auditorium rented for the occasion. Several hundred people attended and, of course, George Lunin and

I went too. If I am not mistaken, Berdyaev, Frank and Karsavin spoke that night and it was Karsavin who impressed me most, probably because he touched a theme to which I was most sensitive. He spoke about the contrast between the comfortable, tidy, safe life in Berlin, and the hardships and fears of life in Russia. "And yet," he said, "I already miss it. There is a quality of life there, that seems missing here, something 'is' there, which 'is not' here." Every word of his echoed in my mind. I knew what he was saying was true and it hurt me.

Regular classes of the Religious Philosophical Academy were held in the evenings at the French High School in Berlin. I attended the very interesting course taught by S. L. Frank on the history of philosophy, which rounded out my university studies and gave them a better sense of perspective. The course that held me spellbound, however, was the one taught by Ivan Alexandrovich Ilyin, entitled "Our Worldview and Our Personality." Ilyin was quite different from the rest, more of a religious psychologist than a religious philosopher. I realize now that he was not as great a person as Berdyaev, nor as original a thinker. Politically he identified himself fully with the "White" Russian movement which history proved to be something of a dead end. But his thoughts were very enlightening for me; they seemed to relate more to my own personal experience. He was a brilliant speaker, with a keen sense of humor, sometimes quite sarcastic. In a sense all this made him a better teacher of young people. I was carried away by his insights into the meaning of being an "autonomous person" as opposed to a "heteronomous" one, of finding in oneself the touchstone that makes one recognize and accept the right values. Berdyaev's lectures were harder to follow, partly because of his physical defect (a nervous tic that twisted his face and his tongue), partly because of the round-about logical structure of his sentences. Yet I think that all of us who came in contact with his writings and his lectures did absorb one basic concept that became an integral part of our worldview: man's freedom under God, man's freedom as part of God's vision for the creation of man, the inner freedom that no slavery can destroy.

What amazes me now, as I look back at the time, is the interest all these men showed in us young Russians they met abroad. They were willing to give us so much of their time and attention, and they gave it so generously. Ilyin came to our house and had me come and visit him and his wife and talked to me at length. I thought quite a lot about going back to Russia and he tried to convince me that it would be a wrong decision. Berdyaev learned that several of us met on a regular basis at our house and offered to come and talk to us. We enjoyed the evening immensely, and he was very good-natured and I think amused by some of our reactions. A cousin of mine, a general's daughter, was amazed that the Berdyaevs had served as officers in the crack guards' regiment of the "Chevaliers Garde" and that one of them had taken part in the famous battle of Borodino in 1812. Berdyaev was friendly to me personally because I was chosen several times to act as interpreter for him when he met with American visitors. He had never spoken through an interpreter before and I think felt that it was my personal "gift of tongues," so that for several years, at the international conferences we attended, he insisted on using me as his interpreter. The hardest nut I had to crack was when the American Baptist minister Sherwood Eddy asked Berdyaev to give him a one-sentence definition of how Orthodoxy differed from both Roman Catholicism and Protestantism. In my English translation Berdyaev's answer ran: "Orthodoxy is the fulfillment, the perfection, of freedom in and through the fulfillment of communion, fellowship." For this last term Berdyaev used the untranslatable Russian word "sobornost," for which "catholicity" is the more accurate term than "fellowship" or "communion," but I was afraid that in a Baptist preacher's mind the word "catholicity" would not convey the meaning that Berdyaev intended.

A certain "lordliness" was part of Berdyaev's temper. At one of the regular discussion meetings that took place at his house an incident happened that might serve as an illustration. Berdyaev's wife was a Roman Catholic. The twenty or thirty attending the meeting were crowded around a long dining table and Mrs. Berdyaev poured tea. This particular meeting was well attended because our guest was the Russian Orthodox Archbishop from Paris, Metropolitan Evlogy, who was appointed by Patriarch Tikhon to head the Russian church in Western Europe. I do not remember the topic of the general discussion, but in the midst of it, S., a rather arrogant young man, began to speak with violent hostility against the Roman Catholic Church. He went on for some time and Mrs. Berdyaev got up quietly and left the room. Metropolitan Evlogy must have sensed the tension, for when his turn to speak came, he did it with even more than his customary kindliness and affbility, saying how the Orthodox Church must be like a sun, warming everyone with its rays, bringing all people together.

We crowded into the hall to see the Metropolitan off. As soon as the door closed behind him, Berdyaev raised his hand and asked us to stay. He began to speak, saying that as long as any non-Orthodox person attended our meetings he would not permit anyone to speak inimically and insultingly of other faiths. He was really angry now, his eyes flashed and he roared like a lion, in the good old Russian tradition of someone "bawling out" a subordinate. He finished by demanding that S. apologize to his wife. Mrs. Berdyaev came in, S. apologized abjectly and kissed her hand, and then Mrs. Berdyaev kissed him on the forehead and said that she saw in him her brother in Christ . . . For a long time the incident caused a lot of talk among us. I think S. rather fancied himself as a martyr for the Orthodox faith.

The year 1923 saw the birth of a movement within the Russian emigration, a movement that fifty years later proved to be the strongest bridge for contacts with the spiritual awakening taking place in Russia. Small groups of young Russian émigrés, many of whom a year or two before had been fighting in the White Army, came together in most European countries of the Russian Dispersion, searching to make sense of what they had lived through. They had to discover what values really stood the wash of war, revolution, and exile. They were disenchanted with political creeds, blind loyalty to the past did not seem to be the answer and democracy sounded like a naive American cure-all. The presence in émigré circles of such people as the exiled professors and others who joined them greatly stimulated the thinking of this younger Russian generation, adding depth and scope to it. A rather unexpected third element which played an important role in giving the movement structure were representatives of Protestant Christian organizations, especially a few men of real vision and understanding. They contributed financial assistance, organizational cohesion, and leadership training. With their help a conference was called at Pserov, Czechoslovakia, in 1923. Rather naturally it was planned according to the usual type of such conferences in Protestant organizations, with Protestant services of worship, and Protestant-oriented Russian speakers from the pre-revolutionary Christian Student Movement. But the people who came to attend were very different from the pre-revolutionary type of membership.

Father Sergius Bulgakov proposed that each day begin with an early Divine Liturgy and end with Vespers. For some of the students such a participation in the liturgical life of the church was a completely new experience. Even for those who were already fully within the Orthodox tradition this experience of fellowship was enriching and vital. At the end of the week the conference became a retreat. Everyone went to confession and received communion. Strangely enough the non-Russian, non-Orthodox organizers of the conference were deeply impressed too. They had the humility and the vision to recognize and accept that a Russian religious movement and Russian religious needs are different from American, German, or British ones, and they worked quite dedicatedly to help it.

I was not among those who attended the Pserov Conference. Our Berlin group took part in the second one in Falkenberg, Germany, in July 1924, when the Orthodox conference pattern was already established and all the lectures were given by people like Berdyaev and others of his group. But one of my very good friends, Katia, later Menshikov, attended Pserov and I think her story is characteristic. Katia was a medical student in Russia, and was now continuing her work in France. "At the end of the week," she told me, "I made up my mind to go to confession and receive communion. Father

Sergius was hearing confessions. I stood silent, unsure how to start. 'When did you go to confession last?' he asked me. I had to answer, 'Seven years ago.' Suddenly this seemed so horrible to me, that for seven years I had refused to accept the Church, that I couldn't say a word. I just stood there and cried, and cried . . . And Father Sergius cried with me. Not a word more was said. Then he placed his epitrachelion on my head and read the prayer of absolution."

I believe that a large number of the people who attended those first conferences became deeply involved in church life and most of the Orthodox church leaders outside of Russia were to a certain extent its product. Personally I was deeply influenced and shaped by what I received there.

* * *

In 1924 my maternal grandmother, Elizabeth Sabouroff, and Aunt Mary Sabouroff, my mother's unmarried sister, whom we left in Moscow, came to visit us in Berlin. It was the period of liberalization in Soviet Russia, known as the New Economic Policy (NEP), and they had no great difficulty in obtaining this permission. They stayed with us for a month and then went back. Observing our life in Berlin, they felt they had more security in Russia. My aunt, then fifty-five years old, held a steady office job in Russia, but was afraid that she would not find employment in Germany. Even my grandmother, eighty years old, was often invited as a consultant in sorting out old diaries, letters and manuscripts at the Literary Museum of Moscow and was paid for this work, which she enjoyed. Their apartment was crowded, it is true, but the people were congenial: two old maiden cousins, Grandmother's former maid, now married to a Communist, but still devoted to Grandmama, and the former teacher of the Alexandrovka village school. Soon after they returned Aunt Mary was arrested, imprisoned and later exiled for two years.

The currency devaluation in Germany reached catastrophic dimensions. Smallest expenses were counted in millions. I remember watching an old woman who came to the bakery

to buy a loaf of bread. Her market bag was crammed full with
bills which she could not even attempt to count as she emptied
her bag on the counter. The saleswoman was horrified. "Isn't
it enough?" stammered the old woman.

I do not remember the order in which political events took
place which brought Marshal Hindenburg to the post of president. The recovery of Germany gained impetus, a currency
reform was introduced and a new stable Reichsmark replaced
the millions of inflation. The "vultures" could not profiteer
any more. Our ten-dollars-a-month scholarships were part of
the profiteering and the bubble of our security burst. We held
a family council. My studies being of a strictly impractical
nature could be easily interrupted any time, but Iuri had one
more year to go to get his degree in agriculture, which we
hoped would open the doors of a profession for him. We
decided that by pooling both our scholarships he would be
able to finish and that my mother and I would move to Paris,
which was rapidly becoming the center of Russian émigré
life. The camps for Russian ex-prisoners of war in Germany
were closing and the YMCA was moving its headquarters to
Paris; thus my mother would still have a small part-time job
there in the Correspondence School which it was decided
would continue. I was sure I would find some job, and perhaps
an opportunity to continue my studies would present itself
later.

* * *

The next two years were my true apprenticeship in the way
of life, the struggle for existence, of émigrés. Our two years
in Estonia had been very much part of what used to be Russia.
The student days in Berlin were a carefree time, with all our
modest needs taken care of by our scholarships, but now my
mother and I were truly on our own. We had to discover our
"market value" in the competitive economic world of a highly
civilized country. And the situation of foreigners like ourselves in France was not always easy. France was very open to
foreigners: tourists, wealthy visitors, even artists and students. French people were very tolerant about the strange
ways of foreign people and never imposed their own moral

and social standards on them. But French homes, French family life (at least until World War II) remained closed to strangers. Wealthy and important foreign visitors might be invited at the level of formal receptions, or the top level of the Paris cosmopolitan society, but we were a new brand of foreigners — poor, undesirable economically. We had come to stay, we competed for jobs, we tried to penetrate into respectable professions, we were not "good customers." On the other hand we belonged to no identifiable social class of people. The French social structure of those days was very crystallized. The owner of a small grocery store, who served his customers himself, was in a quite different social class from the owner of a larger store with five salesmen. The least important civil servant was in quite a different class from a factory worker. The old aristocratic families were a mysterious world of their own.

We could not identify ourselves with any French social class; at least our great majority could not. In our work in shops and offices, as taxidrivers and factory hands, we moved in one type of social hierarchy and established our relationships with our colleagues within it. Very often our background, our education, our experience of life, and our values did not fit into this pattern. They looked down on us as "those crazy Russians" (quite often with some justification) and we looked down on them as limited dull "petit bourgeois" materialists. During the first twenty years of our life in Paris, I was invited to partake of food in a French home just twice. This is not a criticism, and during and after World War II we learned to make close friendships and to know France much more intimately. But this explains to a certain extent why the Russian émigrés in France became such a "state within the state."

There were anywhere from sixty to ninety thousand Russian émigrés in Paris, according to various estimates. Most of them were either former members of the Russian army, or had belonged to the so-called "intelligentsia" or to the former upper classes. Their life in Paris was a strange fusion of their former status and former attitudes with their present work and economic condition. Certain professions in Paris, like taxidrivers, were practically monopolized by Russians. Those who had a little money tried to start businesses of their own: "maisons de mode," tea-rooms, restaurants, delicatessen stores, antique and Russian crafts shops, boarding houses, etc., and these gave employment to quite a few Russians. The Citroen and Renault automobile works absorbed very many Russians capable of becoming workmen. During the twenties a number of Russian institutions were created in Paris and the suburbs: a fully accredited high school, several boarding schools, two kindergartens, the well-known St. Sergius Theological Seminary, a Russian Theater, a Russian Opera, two daily and several weekly newspapers, over fifteen Russian Orthodox churches and numerous societies, clubs and organizations of all kinds. Social life bloomed with endless charity balls, concerts, parties and lectures, and just plain friendly informal gatherings with wine, singing and dancing, and a very good time. The younger generation went through French schools and colleges, taking for granted the need for a university level of education, which was not at all characteristic of the French tradition for the social class on the level of which their parents and older brothers and sisters worked.

When my mother and I arrived in Paris in September 1924 we landed in the lap of a very hospitable and friendly clan of relatives and friends. For two weeks we stayed at the home of the Tatistchevs, old friends whose parents were our neighbors in the country in Russia, and their student son Alyosha showed me Paris and climbed the Eiffel Tower with me. Then we shared a furnished apartment with a young Russian couple. Mania stayed with us for a while, but this did not last long. She was one of the few Russians who found her place not in the Russian émigré community, but in the cosmopolitan society of Paris. She shared with the rest of us our complete economic insecurity; she earned her living working in an American bank on the Place Vendome, but she refused to be "a poor refugee." With her attractiveness, charm, considerable intelligence and great ingenuity she gaily overcame the difficulty of sharing the good times of people who had all the security of wealth and position.

During these whirlpool years Mania developed lung trouble. The head of her bank arranged for her to be sent to a sanatorium in Switzerland. After a year or two there she recovered completely and moved to England, where she made her home for the rest of her life.

The first job my mother and I found in Paris was at the Berlitz School of Languages on the Boulevard des Italiens. The school advertised widely that all languages were taught by natives of corresponding foreign countries, but they had a shortage of English teachers. I had *never* been in England and my mother just once for a very short while, yet we were engaged and assigned to teach English and were even given English names. I was christened "Miss Gordon", while my mother chose the name of "Miss MacIntosh," because Connie MacIntosh had been her much loved governess and she felt sure Connie would not have minded her using this name. Even our pay checks were made out to these names. I must say, however, that we were the only ones in such a position; the other English teachers were real Britishers.

The Berlitz system is very strict: from the very first lesson only the language being learned is used. No word can ever be translated. The classrooms were little cubicles opening on a long corridor and the doors were purposely kept open during lessons so that Mr. Beard, the school inspector, would hear us and make sure that we followed the method. If we ran into difficulties he came to our assistance, but teachers who failed too often were discharged. The teachers' pay was miserable. Students paid twenty francs for an hour's private lesson, and out of this the teacher received three and a half francs. Even worse was the fact that the teacher had no fixed time-table. When you left in the evening, you looked up your name on a chart where it was indicated at what time you were to come for your first lesson next day. It might be at 9 A.M., but on coming in the morning you would discover that you were to give one lesson from 9 to 10, another at noon, at 5 P.M. and at 8 P.M. Thus your day would be taken up from 9 A.M. to 9 P.M., but you'd be paid for 4 hours only. In those "good old days" there were no "minimum pay" laws, no social security, no health insurance, no paid vacations.

English was the most popular language and the majority of teachers were English: elderly spinsters eking out an existence of genteel poverty, or lonely women stranded for some reason in Paris. There was a dark and shabby teachers' room with a gas ring where we made ourselves endless cups of tea. It was a strange company and the arrogant attitude of many Englishwomen of those days to anything foreign contrasted with the shabbiness, the frustrations and the difficulties of the situation in which they found themselves. The real Englishwomen could have easily resented my mother's and my presence there under false pretenses (though not of our making), but on the whole they were very friendly and kind. Sometimes there were scenes with arguments and tears, when a teacher's schedule was such that she earned almost nothing.

I rather enjoyed the work. Besides the English lessons I had two pupils for Russian. One was a very attractive American girl, Elizabeth Burgess. I believe she came from an old and wealthy American family and she was in France with her mother, trying to obtain the chance of a singing engagement at the Opera. She did have a beautiful voice, but I understood that it took powerful influence to be allowed to perform even once. Elizabeth and her mother made friends with us and we saw quite a bit of them outside the school. The other student of Russian was an elderly French colonel and I enjoyed him too. I always had a taste for teaching and the Berlitz method made it fun to explain things by acting out words. One drawback however was that you taught a different class every time. Officially the reason was that students should not get accustomed to the accent of one teacher only, but I think that the real one was to prevent students and teachers getting acquainted and discovering that it would be more advantageous to all of them to switch to private lessons outside the school.

I looked on my job as a transient one. Very soon after arriving I realized that in order to get a good secretarial job I had to know French shorthand and registered at a commercial school for a daily two-hours course. The Berlitz School agreed to give me no classes from 2 to 5, which was a quiet time anyway. In my spare time between the lessons I could practice my shorthand homework. My mother used the spare hours to correct the work of her Correspondence School students. Each one of us managed to earn an average of five hundred francs a month. This was not enough to pay our way fully — it cost us about fifteen hundred francs a month — but still it was a great help. The hours were really tiring: we left home at 8:30 A.M. and returned at 9:30 P.M., and there were no free Saturday afternoons. My mother's health was beginning to feel the strain and her heart was giving her trouble. I worried more and more about getting off this treadmill.

As soon as I completed my basic shorthand course and before even acquiring the necessary speed, I began to look for a new job. Finally, through an ad in the newspapers I obtained an interview with an Italian engineer who had a small office of his own and needed a secretary. My French and English were good enough for his needs, my typing was satisfactory, but when he tried me out in dictating letters, I fumbled, was too slow and could not reread what he had dictated. Feeling very small indeed I apologized for taking up his time, explained that I had not really completed my shorthand training, and prepared to leave. The kind old man stopped me: "How much time would it take you to complete your training?" he asked. "We might try to get along without shorthand at first." Then and there he offered to give me the job for a salary of nine hundred and fifty francs.

I was elated by this unexpected success. My mother and I figured out that with such a salary, and with what she made at the Correspondence School, she could reduce her workload at Berlitz, giving up the evening lessons. This would make it much less tiring for her. I asked for an appointment with Monsieur Matthieu, director of the Paris Berlitz School, to give him my resignation and ask for shorter hours for my mother. But Monsieur Matthieu, an elderly Frenchman with a square black beard, saw it differently.

"You seem to have it all worked out," he said, as I rather naively explained to him all my plans. "But this does not suit the school. You are young and seem to have a knack for teaching. The school prefers young teachers because they are more popular with the students and have not acquired teaching habits that contradict the Berlitz method. Your mother is elderly (she was fifty-five years old) and now *you* want to leave and you want us to make special conditions for your mother. Evening hours are our prime time. I am sorry, but if you leave, your mother will have to leave too."

This was a blow to all my plans. I asked Monsieur Matthieu for time to think it over during the weekend. Nine hundred and fifty francs was not enough for us to live on. Could we risk making the jump, in the hope that my salary would be increased? Or that my mother would get additional private lessons or translations? Would it work out any better for my mother's health, or would it put an even heavier load on her shoulders? After thinking over our problems and trying to examine all possibilities, we decided that unless I left Berlitz School, I would never get a better job, and I would rather take a risk than stay there indefinitely. On Monday I returned to Monsieur Matthieu and told him I had made up my mind. I hoped he would find it possible to let my mother stay, dispensing with her work in the morning hours, which were less busy ones for the school, and that in a few months I thought she would retire. Monsieur Matthieu hesitated for a while, but somehow looked more benevolent. "You really seem to have a head for planning," he said. There was a moment's silence and I prepared to leave the office.

"Miss Gordon, or rather Mademoiselle Shidlovsky, wait a moment! Since you really made up your mind to leave us, you might as well do it for something worthwhile. Here is a card, please call at this address. They are looking for a translator and I have recommended you to them."

The card bore the name of Georges Valensi, Engineer, Executive Secretary of "Comité Consultatif International de Communications Telephonique à Grande Distance." When I called there I found it was an international research center for long distance telephones with a staff as small as its name was long. It was located in a very elegant house on the Avenue de Messine, quite close to the Parc Monceau. Monsieur Valensi engaged me as a translator from English and German into French, at a salary of twelve hundred francs, with Saturday afternoons off, and a month's holiday in summer. It appears that Monsieur Matthieu had spoken to him about me, even while he was still trying his best to force me to stay at Berlitz. I remained in this office, with two very kind and pleasant colleagues: M. Lavoignat, a chubby middle-aged postal employee, and Mademoiselle Felix, the secretary, for two years, and left only when I left France.

We began to settle down in Paris with a little more sense of permanence than we had before. Of course we did not have a really permanent home, and during the first year moved seven times from furnished rooms to furnished rooms. But the last one was a tiny furnished two-room apartment, in a very small old house, on a crooked little street near the Eglise d'Auteil. It looked like an old country house. There was no bathroom and just one open fireplace for heat, so we had to buy a "Salamandre," a coalburning room stove, to keep warm. The small rooms were crowded with stuffed furniture, fussy little ornaments, antimacassars, and pictures of ancestors. The landlady was fussy too, but we carefully packed up in all her precious "bibelots," mirrors and portraits in cartons before we broke any of them, and the place began to feel really cozy. Iuri graduated from his School of Agriculture in Germany and joined us for several months while looking for a job. A room was found for him on another landing.

Office hours were from nine to six in France, with a two-hour break for lunch. Many people went home for a big meal, but cooking was really not my mother's strong point. By now she had interesting translation work (including articles by Berdyaev). The only thing she knew how to cook was a cheese omelette — very good indeed when she put her mind to it. But when I turned up at home at 12:30, more often than not she would either guiltily jump up from her work table saying it wouldn't take her a minute to cook lunch, or the acrid smell of something burning and blue smoke billowed out as I opened the door. I discovered a pleasanter way of spending my lunch time. If the weather was fine, I bought bread and cheese and a chocolate bar and settled down with a book on one of the benches in the lovely Parc Monceau. Sometimes I had rather unusual company. The Russian church on the rue Daru was quite close, on the other side of the Parc Monceau. The Russian Archbishop, Metropolitan Evlogy, who lived there, was ordered by his doctor to take daily constitutionals, so we sometimes met in the park and would take a little walk together. He always reminded me of an elephant — bulky, wise, with a twinkling sense of humor in his eyes and endless kindliness.

Another pleasant alternative was "Chez Biron" — a little French restaurant close to rue Daru. Several friends met there daily: my Uncle Kolia (my father's older brother), who worked as treasurer and accountant at the Diocesan Office, and several of my cousins and friends, some of whom worked close by at the "Maison de Mode" of Countess Orlov-Davydov. I figured out a menu that was really inexpensive and yet delicious: "boeuf gros sel" — a piece of boiled beef with a few vegetables, bread, the wonderful French bread, and a cup of coffee, and I always ordered it. What made lunches at Biron's so pleasant was our comfortable fellowship: we were so ourselves, we were together in our past and in our present, we were all of the same kind. There was no need for explanations; the background and experiences of all of us were of the same kind. It was a good-natured relaxed relationship. Our jokes and our frustrations were so very much our own, shared by all of us.

One conversation touched me deeply. One of our group, whenever he could afford to come, was Count George Sheremetev, called "Goga" by his friends. A former "chevalier garde" officer, he must have been in his forties, married and father of two young children. Always good-natured and cheerful, he worked as a janitor at the Maison de Mode. One day, when our other companions had already left and I was gathering up my books, he began speaking to me. Spontaneously, as simply as he always did everything, he spoke of spiritual life, of the "Jesus Prayer," of the dangers and pitfalls of unguided spiritual efforts, of asceticism. "Why? Why? How do you know I am thinking of this? . . ." I stammered. "Oh, that's pretty obvious," he said breezily. I never forgot what he said to me. Later he came to visit my mother and me and spent a long evening with us, telling us some of the things his family and he went through. There was not a word said about religion, but both of us felt as if we had been in the presence of a very pure light. Later on George Sheremetev became a priest and died in London in his eighties.

I must say that at that time I felt rather as if I was trying to live in two different worlds at the same time, or perhaps suffering from a split personality. On the one hand I was drawn to the Russian family clan, the Russian society in Paris. I felt my common roots with them. The young people of my age were attractive; they had the gift of having good times, of enjoying themselves, of being young. I envied them their unpretentious simplicity, their youth of spirit. I would have liked to be part of it all. On the other hand, my involvement with the type of people who formed the Russian Student Christian Movement pulled me in a different direction. It stimulated me intellectually, it opened new horizons, new concepts of the meaning of life, of Russia's past and Russia's future. It introduced one to a different kind of church life than just going to church on Sundays and "making one's devotions" once a year. Having once tasted of all this, I could not disregard it, could not give up my new vision. Yet somehow, for some reason, I always had a difficulty identifying myself completely with a "cause," a "movement." It always seemed to me that there exists a different point of view, another side to the question that is valid, too. In some ways, very often, I felt neither fish nor fowl — a "blue stocking" in the eyes of some people, and something of a "snob" in the eyes of others.

The most interesting development in which I took part during those two years was our growing closeness to the Anglo-Catholic movement. It started with a few members of our Russian student movement attending a conference in England of the British Student Christian Movement. There we met a few Anglo-Catholics, who were as distinct from the other people there as we Orthodox. Most of us had never heard of this movement within the Anglican church and it was like meeting in a strange country unknown members of one's own family. Later on, a Fellowship of St. Alban and St. Sergius was founded and we met at yearly conferences that were very meaningful to all participants. Most lectures were given by outstanding theologians — Father Sergius Bulgakov was the leading personality on the Russian side — but the younger generation also participated very actively. The liturgical life of both Orthodox and Anglicans was as full as possible and allowed us to discover each other in our fullness. And of course all this took place in an atmosphere of growing personal friendships, mutual curiosity, interest and young enthusiasm. Many personal visits to our friends' homes and their visits to us in France followed up the conferences. I am sorry to say I have forgotten by now most of the names, but even within the last decade I would sometimes come across a reference in the newspaper to some Anglican bishop or dignitary or author and would recognize the name of one of our friends from the early days of the Fellowship.

My role of interpreter continued. I remember especially well two occasions. One was a public meeting at which the Archbishop of Canterbury and Metropolitan Evlogy exchanged opinions on Anglican-Orthodox relations and the question of their "rapprochement." I translated from English into Russian and from Russian into English for the benefit of those who spoke only one of the two languages. It was quite an experience to be something like a wire along which a powerful electric charge was transmitted.

The other occasion was a private and very intimate conversation between two men of deep spirituality. One was Father Sergius Chetverikov, a remarkable Russian priest, very different from Father Bulgakov. Quiet and humble, very reserved, he was not a brilliant speaker, but rather a traditional Russian Orthodox priest, who had not gone through the spiritual upheavals of the "Neo-Orthodox" who returned to their faith from atheism and Marxism. His power lay in something for which I can find no other word than the spirit of holiness, a serene and simple sobriety of thought and an ability to come in touch with others, never condemning anyone, never getting upset.

The Anglican priest, Father Elwood, if I am not mistaken, had been a missionary in India; he believed that Hindu spirituality and Christian mysticism have much in common, that Christianity can become acceptable in India only if it is completely divorced from its Western pattern. He had lived in an ashram in India, trying to follow the Indian way of life.

The two of them went for a walk, asking me to interpret
for them. In a few minutes I was quite out of my depth, and
continued to translate word by word, without attempting to
understand what it all meant. But neither of them had any
trouble understanding each other when they spoke of "mental
prayer" and whether it was this or the other part of the heart
that was involved in it.

* * *

During this time of my life I thought that major changes
always took place every two years. There was our life in
Moscow, the two years in Estonia, the two years in Berlin,
and now two years in France. One major change had already
taken place: I broke off my engagement to George Lunin.
We had been virtually engaged for almost four years. Both
of us grew and developed and gradually changed. It was very
painful and distressing to discover that somehow everything
had become different between us. I believe that we both suffered at the time, but as I look back I can only be grateful
for the good quality of our relationship while it lasted. I know
that our young friendship enriched my life.

Another major change was approaching. I have already
mentioned how men like Paul B. Anderson, Gustave Kullman, Ralph Hollinger and others changed the policy of the
YMCA for its work among Russians abroad. Instead of orga-
nizing regular YMCA activities in various centers of Russian
dispersion, they sought to give help in projects that the Russian
Orthodox people could recognize as authentically valuable
and relate to their own Christian experience. The three major
projects in which they helped were the St. Sergius Theological
Orthodox Institute created in Paris, the Russian Student Christian Movement, and the creation of the YMCA Press in Paris,
the only publishing house that printed Russian religious and
theological works outside of Russia. Now the YMCA obtained
a grant from John D. Rockefeller which included a scholarship for a Russian Orthodox student with leadership ability
to come to the United States and study American methods of
social work, youth work, and religious education. Candidates

for the scholarship should be able to see, understand, appreciate and assimilate whatever they found valuable in American Christianity and also to remain true to their own Russian Orthodox heritage and be acceptable within their own community upon their return. I understand that the selection of the first student to go was made jointly by Paul B. Anderson and Metropolitan Evlogy. Their choice fell on me.

Gustave Kullman was the first one to speak to me about this plan. I was impressed, flattered, excited at the idea. My only concern was how my mother would take it. I realized that her feelings for me were somewhat unusual. She not only loved me but was completely dependent on me. She felt that our close relationship was the only thing that kept her alive. The idea of losing me for a year, just as she thought we were settling down for a peaceful and comfortable life together, would be unbearable to her. Gustave, who was very fond of my mother, said he knew he would be able to persuade her to agree.

My misgivings proved to be true. Gustave spoke to my mother, and at first she angrily rejected any idea of my going away for a whole year. The separation would be unbearable, she said. I did not want to push her. Somehow Gustave found a different level in my mother's thoughts and feelings at which he was able to reach her. He knew that her love for the church was sincere and deep, that she had a strong sense of duty. He came to see her again and finally succeeded in persuading her not to oppose the project.

It really was a hard time for my mother. Iuri had at last landed a job, but it involved a contract for three years in the coffee plantations in the Belgian Congo in Africa. He left in July and letters took nine weeks to be exchanged, for there was no airmail in those days and only one boat a month. My departure was scheduled for the beginning of September. We gave up our cozy apartment in Auteil. During my absence my mother would live in a hotel on the Boulevard Exelmans, where a Russian family, distant cousins of hers, were already living. We spent a wonderful vacation in Juan-les-Pins, then a little-known sea-side hamlet. Then came a few days of last minute shopping and packing, during which my mother cried

most of the time, and on Septmber 21 I sailed on the S.S.
"Leviathan" for my year's adventure. It shaped my vocation
for the rest of my life.

CHAPTER FIVE

When I began writing these reminiscences I came across a package containing letters which I wrote to my mother during my stay in the United States. I believe that they give a better picture of my life during that year, of what I thought and felt, than what I could write now, fifty years later.

September 28, 1926

Letters from America, 1926-1927

Thirty hours have gone by since I arrived. It is nine o'clock in the evening and I am sitting in my own room, on the eighth floor of International House on Riverside Drive. I have unpacked everything and everything is in its place: the icon in the corner, the photos and the candlestick you gave me on my desk. My desk is at the window — and out of it there is an endless view of New York, thousands of buildings standing like huge children's blocks. International House stands high above the Hudson River and there are wonderful views everywhere, but my window faces the city, not the river. It is quite dark, it is raining and I can only see the endless city lights, like jewels.

My life here is being organized with lightning speed. I left the docks at two P.M. yesterday, but I am already settled in my room here, and all the financial arrangements are straightened out. I attended a lecture at Teachers' College, saw several professors for whose courses I want to register,

125

have almost completed all the registration procedures, saw Miss Dunham and her two friends, and have learned to find my way around. In my mailbox there is a notice for another medical checkup (my sixth one during the last two weeks!), and invitations to attend two meetings tomorrow night. When I came home in the evening there were beautiful flowers in my room, from Paul and Margaret (Anderson) for my names-day. And all of this sandwiched in between being introduced to "bright and helpful" people who were trying to make me feel at home. I am not saying this ironically; they are really very touching and try so hard to be hospitable and do every-thing for you, but sometimes it is a little overdone, especially for me who like to be by myself. So far I have not succeeded in eating a single meal by myself without someone coming up: "Are you all alone?"

I want to reassure you about my finances. My tuition and my stay at the International House are all paid for and I am getting fifty dollars a month for my food and personal ex-penses. My food fits easily into $1 a day (breakfast 15¢, lunch 30¢ and dinner 30¢). There are facilities at Interna-tional House where I can do my own laundry.

October 1

Decidedly I am suffering from moral indigestion. Only two days have gone since I started college life, but there are so many new impressions that I have no chance to sort them out, or even just to draw my breath. Every conversation, every lecture, every book-page seems like a confrontation with a completely different world and quite unconsciously I am straining all the time to understand their point of view and to try and make them see mine. This constant tension is really quite exhausting. I have not met anyone yet with whom I could talk heart-to-heart, as we say. There is no inimical misunderstanding; on the contrary it is impossible to be friendlier than they are, but I find myself all the time in the limelight, and you can't imagine how tiring it can get. I always feel the need to digest such conversation, to analyze

whether I said anything I shouldn't have. My third morning
in America I had four lectures. The first one on "Principles
of Religious Eudcation" turned into a class discussion. At
the end I just sat there, open-mounthed, and couldn't even
think. It seemed to me that I had arrived from a different
planet, that what *they* call religion here has nothing in common with what *we* call religion. One of the students said
that "the best way to teach religion is to teach that which all
great religions have in common — Buddhism, Judaism, Christianity, Mohammedanism . . ." And yet in the morning, when
I attended Chapel at Union Theological Seminary, it was such
beautiful Christian worship that I was really moved. What is
my place in such a discussion group? It's no use to speak about
what we believe, it will be strange to them, and I'll just make
a fool of myself. After all I have not been sent here to preach
Orthodoxy!

Three other lectures followed on teaching methods and
psychology — they were all right. Nothing special to digest,
except perhaps that the teaching methods described seem to
be based on the same principles in kindergarten, in high
school and at the university. Went back and for dinner was
joined by three nice girl students.

Next morning attended Chapel again. Fosdick spoke and
spoke really well. What impressed me, though, was the beauty
of the service, especially the singing. They have a beautiful
choir that enters and leaves in procession and the closing
hymn was beautiful, both the music and the meaning of the
words — it might have been part of an Orthodox liturgy.
So they *do* have this vision, they *have* experienced this, it
must be alive somewhere in their depths, so we *can* come to
understand each other.

At lunchtime there was a conversation that needed to be
morally digested. He was a Canadian, was ordained a priest
sixteen years ago, but had never actually served as a priest.
Again our conversation turned to Russia. He is a Christian
socialist and for him everything is "the great experiment."
We spoke about love for mankind. He said you have to love
men in order to find God; I said you cannot really love men
unless you love God. At this point our neighbor could not

stand it any more and joined in, more or less supporting me. But I was displeased with myself. Why do I speak so much, why am I so vehement?

Settled down to my reading assignments, and whatever I read it seemed to stir up my thinking, to bring new ideas. I'd like to have time to think it all through.

October 4

It is now eight days that I have been here. My work here is pure delight, in the full sense of the word. I am absorbed in my reading, in the luxury of reading, I am bathing in reading, gorging on mental food. Just to sit in the library for hours, to look up things, to think . . . My favorite teacher is Dr. Coe — the one in whose class I got upset by the religious ideas expressed there. I am taking his course on Principles of Religious Education and my major term paper will be for him. ("Meaning of Worship in Orthodox Religious Education.") Dr. Coe is quite an old man, over seventy, and is retiring at the end of the semester. If he were not an American Protestant, I'd say that he looks ascetic. He is the founder of the new trend in religious education, but he never "flirts" with his "progressive ideas" and never tries to make himself popular (both of which I think Fosdick does). His basic idea is that religious education is an education for freedom, for authenticity and for creativity, so he refuses to subscribe to any theology. In his class I feel rather like a Christian facing sixty hungry lions, because I think theology is not something you can simply discard. Much of the time in his class is spent in discussion and with my feeling that to remain silent is kind of cowardly, and my lack of qualifications to defend Christian theology, I face the lions rather nervously.

About Dr. Coe himself I am sure that when he will get to heaven, he will find it a very different place from what he expects it to be, but he will be one of the first persons to get there! I am really having fun because I am the only Russian here, and more than that, the only Russian anyone of them has ever seen. It *is* rather fun.

And on top of this — no drudgery, no drudgery at all.
Everything is so comfortable and everything I have to do is
interesting.

The thing that really bothers me is what people think and
feel and say about Russia. Ninety-nine per cent of the people
here know nothing, *nothing at all*, about Russia, but they are
interested and eager to know. And then you have men like
Sherwood Eddy who visit Russia and come back and tell them
what to think. The day before yesterday I went to his lecture.
It was the same old "rigamarole": with his own eyes he saw
thousands of young men standing in line before the simple
tomb under the walls of Kremlin to get a glimpse of the body
of their dead leader, dead more than two years ago. He had
witnessed himself "the passionate, burning love for humanity
consuming those men that call themselves atheists, a passion
for humanity that must shame our Christian government.
The government is atheist, of course, but we must not forget
that the only religion they have come in contact with was the
bureaucratic, old-regime, czarist church." And he says all this
eloquently, sincerely and I have to sit and listen and know that
all his listeners, who know nothing at all, absorb whatever he
says as dry sponges absorb water.

After listening to his lecture I went up to Sherwood Eddy
and told him that I thought he was giving an unfair picture
of what is happening in Russia. He was very nice to me and
asked me to come and speak to him when my classes were
over. When I came he was already waiting in the empty lecture hall, and we talked for almost an hour. I tried to find the
best words I could to show him what I thought he was missing
in his reports on Russia. He answered: "I have no interest
in Russia, I am interested in saving America, for I believe it
is beginning to commit the same mistakes the czarist regime
committed in Russia. I am using my visit to Russia as a weap-
on to this end — to awaken, to sting the American public
to see its faults." I tried to point out that it seems unfair for
a Christian who visits Russia today to see all he saw in Lenin
and not to say a single word about Patriarch Tikhon, but he
answered: "I admit I do not render justice to the Orthodox
Church. I do not understand it. I do not respect the Patriarch

(I do not mean that I despise him); he is a good, kindly, meek Christian old man ..."

And Sherwood Eddy is not alone. Scores of lecturers and speakers repeat the same stuff.

Gradually I met a few Russians and was made welcome by the Korotnevs, a very nice Russian family where I always felt as though I was touching home ground. Gradually real friendships emerged from my contacts with American students. My best friends were Thornton Merriam and Celia Ann Moyer, whose room was across the hall from mine. Dr. Ernest C. Scott and his wife, both of them from Scotland, really adopted me. Mrs. Scott mothered me, making me presents of woolen stocking, snowboots, etc. and feeding me as if she suspected that I was starving. Dr. Scott was the only man to whom I could talk about Russian literature and history and who was intelligently interested in the subject. Their only daughter Nora was in college in England and I must have been a "daughter figure" to dear Mrs. Scott.

October 10, 1926

Thornton Merriam, a fellow student, and I went to the Metropolitan Art Museum and in the evening he invited me to attend the Young People's Society in his church (which is Dr. Fosdick's church). He said an interesting man, Bill Simpson, was to speak. Bill Simpson is something like what we would call a "holy fool" — a "holy fool" in modern America! He had graduated with honors from Union Theological Seminary before the war, became a minister, then gave it up. He went through a difficult time and then "discovered" the life of Saint Francis of Assisi. He sold all he had, became a beggar, worked in a factory without accepting pay, ate the food and wore the clothes that people gave him. He went around, often barefoot and in tatters, preaching at the crossroads and sometimes in churches. In old Russia he would have probably become a monk and a pilgrim, but in American society there is just no niche for him. And he was to speak at the Young People's Society on Park Avenue.

The meeting began at 6 o'clock. A young girl in a sky-blue dress and hair tied up with a sky-blue ribbon "meowed" a song — I think even I could not have done worse, and I'm sure I could not have matched her simpering. While she was still singing the door opened quietly and Bill Simpson entered. He looked like a poor working man, and a working man who had not put on his Sunday best. His face is attractive and sensitive. He looked very much out of place in this Park Avenue setting, but he sat down and listened. When the sky-blue young lady finished, another one, very plump and dressed in a young child's dress, recited the poem "Christopher Robin says his prayers..." This lasted quite some time and then the chairman of the Society got up, two fiddles and a piano began playing, and everyone sang a hymn very lustily. The chairman announced that he had the pleasure of presenting Mr. Bill Simpson, who would give us a talk.

Simpson got up, rather unwillingly. Without stepping up to the podium, he stopped, but did not raise his head. He just stood there and there was a deep silence. They have very beautiful chimes in this church and in the silence we suddenly heard them. I really liked Simpson at this moment. He was trying to bring himself under control, his face had a kind of spiritual aloofness and the contrast with the whole setting was really strong. The silence continued and without raising his head he began to speak very quietly: "I cannot speak. You have come to be amused and I am a number on your entertainment. For me it is all. Religion is all. You give up your father and mother for it, you love it more than anything else, more than your life. I cannot speak about it here." You know, I think I have never seen anything so tragic. This dead silence, the scared chairman jumping up and trying to smooth things over, and again the silence and the chimes. I think Simpson also felt that the tension was too great for the people there. He said: "Let us sit a moment in silence!"

Now began the comedy. The only thing that would have been realistic would be to sit in silence for a few minutes and then get up and go home. But do you know what happened?

After a correct and decent minute of silence the chairman asked Mr. So-and-So to lead us in prayer. Then he announced the next number on the program, a violin solo by Mr. X. Mr. X. played a minuet, then there was another performance, and people began to move and get up. Simpson was leaving. But some of the youngsters could not stand it. A young girl spoke up, obviously very sincerely and asked Simpson to stay and speak to them. Others joined her. Simpson said that he was really unable to speak right then, that he would go and stay alone in church for a while and try to come back. In his absence announcements were made, they sang another hymn, and then somebody ran down to the church and brought Simpson back. I was sorry he came back. When he said that he could not speak it was a moment of real religious experience, when "realness" collided with "unrealness." He could say nothing that would be stronger than this. His speech lasted for some seven minutes. He spoke with a degree of exaltation, about love and joy, and non-violence and peace. There was a little hysteria in all this. Just once I felt elated again: "Foolishness? ... Yes, foolishness, foolishness ... grace ..." Let him stay in good health for many years for being able to say these words, the way he said them, a modern American in America today.

The effect of it all on the Young People's Society reminded me of an anthill that somebody poked with a stick. As we were crowding in the doors to leave, I heard a girl say to her mother plaintively: "I came up to him after his talk and said to him that I enjoyed it very much. And you know what he answered me? 'You did not understand it, you did not get it at all.' Isn't it strange? After all wasn't it only decent to tell him that I had enjoyed his talk?" I am exhausted from too much talk, too much misunderstanding. When I reached my room, Celia Ann, the girl from the room across the hall from mine, asked me to drop in. She is really very nice — older than I am, and just plain sensible. She gets fed up with all these organized efforts to establish friendly relations and calls them "tommy-rot." She is very much alive to things, senses what is false and what is true. She told me a lot about herself and when I finally got to my room I felt much more at peace.

October 18

Today I was invited to have lunch with Boris Bakhmetev, the last Russian ambassador here. You know, few people have ever talked to me as well as he did, so kindly and wisely, leaving me with such a good feeling. He asked me to tell him about the Russians my age in France, about the Student Movement, about the young girl from Soviet Russia who joined us. He already knows so much that it is not difficult to speak to him. And very observant — noticed that I had no cream in my coffee and realized it was a fast day. He listened critically and understood so well the "rightness" and the "falsity" that are involved in the things we were talking about. Then he began speaking about the things that I must not miss in America, the goodness that is to be discovered here. And he spoke so well that his words really penetrated into me. When we had finished and were about to leave he looked at me attentively and said very seriously in a manner that I think would have pleased you: "I know that you are independent and have seen a lot. But you are very young and you are alone in a strange country. Perhaps some things will go hard with you, maybe you will have difficulties, maybe you will not know what to do, or how to act. Maybe you will be just lonely. I'd like you to know, really know and remember, that I will be always ready to help you, morally and materially, in whatever way I can. In other words, if you ever need help, let me know."

You know, there are ways and ways of saying such things and the way he said it warmed the cockles of my heart and made me feel that the world is a much more comfortable place to live in than I had felt these days.

October 26

You know, I met Frank Ritchie — you remember, the one who lectured in Narva in Estonia and for whom I interpreted? He was very nice and invited me to spend the weekend at their home in New Jersey. It was very enjoyable; I loafed the whole weekend and they drove me around all over New Jersey. It was funny to see Ritchie at home, wiping dishes for Mrs. Ritchie who was washing them. Very different from Narva . . . and very likeable, too. I was not at all disappointed in him and you remember how he impressed me in Narva.

October 20

Gradually I learn to be less impatient and not to knock my head against the walls. I begin to learn the meaning behind the words that people use and when someone says "democratic fellowship with God" I realize that he is trying to express something of what we mean when we say "sobornost." I think I also am beginning to sort out people and funnily enough it is often those who *say* quite impossible things which probably make all our ancestors turn over in their graves, that really are reaching out to understand what you want to show them. I am really learning to be unshockable.

November 2

It is election day — no classess and I had my first experience of what they call a "hike". We took the ferry boat to cross the Hudson River and went to the Palisades — a solid wall of cliffs on the other side of the river. Americans are really good at picnics! We built a fire and cooked our lunch, played baseball, climbed the cliffs. They really let themselves go having fun! And it was such a gorgeous fall day, with a very blue sky, windy, marvelous colors and space, space, space! It was fun feeling part of it, being just one of them, and not "representing" Russia, or the Orthodox church or what else!

Now it is evening and I am sitting at my desk in my cozy little room. It was a wonderful day, but for some reason I am heavy-hearted. I don't know how to explain it. I never envy them, their wealth, their freedom, their comfortable life. I really would not care to have any of it in exchange for my life.

But *this* — their "joie de vivre," their "youngness," almost childlikeness, their "unbrokenness." Thank God that they are so unbroken and they share it so generously with me. But we — we just cannot emit this unbroken sound any more. It is not that I am bitter and I can feel very happy with them. You understand it is somewhat like Voltchy: None of us are bitter about it, but if suddenly something touches that spot, you know how it hurts.

November 8

I am taking a course with Dr. Goodwin Watson on educational psychology. A short paper has to be prepared every week. It is one of my favorite courses — has nothing to do with Russia or religion. I have never met Watson personally and am just one of the 150 students in his class. He always puts all the corrected papers on a table at the door and last Saturday I was surprised not to find mine. This Saturday I began looking for my papers and found both of them, marked I and II (I is the highest grade). The first paper had to give an illustration of a case of psychological adjustment and I used an example from our life in Moscow, putting it in the third person, of course. On the paper, next to the grade I saw written: "See case of Wanda Neumann." I was really non-plussed and for the whole hour wracked my brains about what it could possible mean, and even began to worry. During the intermission I went to Watson to ask him. Just as I began saying: "You see, this is a false name under which I escaped from Russia, six years ago . . ." he interrupted me very coolly "Oh yes, I know it." I gaped. "You see, I am a good friend of Keeny's. I hope it did not worry you." Even now I am somewhat at a loss. Even if Keeny told him about us, how did he recognize me among all the others, how did he remember the names involved? So here is the end of feeling so nicely anonymous in this class . . .

November 10

Last Saturday night I went to Vigil to 125th Street and, can you imagine it? There was Dr. Coe, standing among the people in the dark church. During our last class sessions we were discussing worship and the place of worship in religious education, and I simply could not get across what church worship means to us and why we feel that our children are not excluded. So I guess he came to look for himself.

After some time I went up to him and said it would be perfectly all right for him to sit down — after all, he must be close to seventy! But he did not want to sit down and stood right through to the end.

When the question of worship came up in the next session of our class, Coe said that he realized that a ritualistic type of worship could be very meaningful "I was deeply impressed attending one," he actually said, "but . . ." and then he went on with his usual arguments.

Another pleasant thing happened this week. We had a test today in my course on General Psychology for Students in Education. Generally speaking I don't like tests as they are given here with lots of "true" or "false" choices. Somehow a statement never seems to me completely false or completely true and I'd like to say something about it. But this particular test was really well prepared and really tested your knowledge and it was fun doing it. It lasted almost two hours, but at the end Watson showed us how to score the results ourselves. The majority of the 100 students who took it scored from 70 to 80 points. The eight best students scored between 95 and 99 and I was the one who had 99! I know this is not very important but I am terribly pleased. Does it give you pleasure too? Americans are really wonderful — all the girls on my floor are as pleased as if they were my family.

December 13

It was so nice to see Aliosha Tatistcheff. He brought me

a letter from Metropolitan Evlogy addressed to Metropolitan Platon. But the really nice part was to have someone here with whom I could feel so comfortable.

Yesterday I spent the evening with Miss Dunham and her two friends. They also are people who are thoroughly good, through and through. I think I have learned, since I am here, to appreciate this living goodness more than people being "interesting." So often I am in conflict with the opinions and the thinking of people here, but I *have* learned to love my Americans, to love people like Miss Dunham and her two old-maid friends, and Thornton Merriam, and Sam Keeny, and Celia Ann, and many others. I love them for what they stand for and in them I feel the "holiness" of America. Yes, I feel it so much more in people than in lectures, or books, or all their theories.

December 18

Today I saw Jerome Davis — you remember him from Moscow? He lectures a lot about Russia here and is even more in sympathy with the Soviet regime than Sherwood Eddy. I feel almost worse about him, because he *was* our friend in those difficult days and should have been able to sense what was taking place. I told him that I felt pretty bitter about what they both were doing. Still our conversation was quite friendly and he asked me to give you his greetings and ask you to forgive him his many sins.

December 24, 10 A.M.

I feel as if I were in a fairy tale. I am sitting in a Pullman car and the winter views on the right and left are like a travelogue in the movies. The official purpose of the trip is to attend a huge YMCA conference in Milwaukee on Dec. 27th and 28th, but I am going to spend Christmas with the Wrights, our friends from the Narva YMCA days. They simply would not hear of my being in the States and not coming to visit

them and sent me money so that I could interrupt my journey
and spend two days with them.

Everything is snowed in. I have not seen snow like this
since Russia. I am all by myself and it feels like being in a
book, and I'll remain on this train until tomorrow at two P.M.
I love that feeling of traveling in a completely unknown
country, all by myself!

I received all kinds of Christmas presents before I left:
a fruit basket for the trip, a reproduction of Giotto's St. Francis of Assisi from Celia Ann, stationery from Miss Dunham,
but the most fun was a huge box of Elizabeth Arden cosmetics
from this funny little Russian-Persian fellow I met at the
Korotnevs, Prince Ruknedin Mirza Kodjar, to give his full
title. He works at Elizabeth Arden's and he really sent me the
works — soaps, liquids, powders, rouge, creams, eye shadows,
lipsticks, bath salts and things I don't even know how to use.
But I tried *everything* — it was really such fun!

                                              10 P.M. same day

My train fairy-story continues. Because of the heavy snow
our train is delayed. Of course everyone is a little upset because it is the American Christmas Eve and everyone is expected somewhere. So people began talking to each other and
my neighbor proved to be a quite old chubby gentleman. Again,
as we exchanged friendly gossip, everything I could say about
who I am and from where I come and what I am doing here,
is so impossibly unusual from his point of view that he could
not remain indifferent and he asked and asked questions, and
however much I tried to play down my answers, I felt that
I was getting more and more glamorous in his eyes. He invited me to have dinner with him in the train diner and I
could not resist it. After all, it was Christmas Eve, and I had
only three sandwiches to last until 2 P.M. next day, which
now would be even later (in addition to the fruit basket, of
course). So we had a marvelous dinner with all the Christmas
trimmings. When we came back the poor old gentleman got
quite touchingly pathetic and told me he would like to adopt

me! Really, he said it quite seriously! I had some difficulty convincing him that it would not do.

I will be back in New York on Russian Christmas Eve in time to go to church. After church I'll come back to my room, will light the vigil light before my ikon and will settle down to read your letters that will have come by then and open your Christmas parcel. On Christmas Day I am invited by Metropolitan Platon for tea.

I am so glad I feel like Christmas already, and I know that this letter will reach you on Christmas. Even our two calendars have come in usefully this year.

January 7, 1927

... It is Christmas Day today. Last night I received your letter, but none of your parcels. This morning, I skipped the classes and went to church and received Communion. When I came out I felt so festive that I decided to continue my celebration and went to a good restaurant and had a wonderful lunch, with fried chicken and everything. Since I thought that your parcels would not come that day, I decided to go shopping and imagine that you are with me and buying me presents. I had a wonderful time and bought lots of things at the 5 & 10: a fat red candle to fit your candlestick, a lampshade for my room, and two frames for photos on my desk. But when I got home I found two packages from you: a sweater and your photograph and a Christmas telegram from the Wrights. Your photograph, my dear, is marvelous — every time I look at it I can see how you will look at my funeral. But you look so sweet that I don't really mind being dead! My darling, I love you so much; every present from you is like a little part of you.

I dined at the Scotts. They are darlings and had a special party for me with three professors. One of them had been in Russia, as a young man, in the year of our Lord 1877! Unanimously they decided that it was a shame that "a brilliant girl like me throws herself away on such a thing as religious education, when I could devote myself to real science — Greek, or theology, or archeology."

January 25, 1927

Last days of examinations and I am working very hard. Keeny, whom I see quite often, has spoken to me about plans for my work after I return to Paris. I always enjoy Keeny's teasing, though he does tell me that I have the most unhealthy, introverted and twisted mind he ever saw. We are very fond of each other and it is so pleasant to talk to someone who does not take you too seriously. Well, he spoke to me about my future work, the somewhat difficult relationships between the Russian Student movement and the YMCA, and what my role should be and how I should plan whatever I am to do, and what my relationships should be with the other people working there. I must say I did not agree with him. I don't think I can plan what *I* will do to improve matters. First of all I must become really a part of whatever is being done already, identify myself with it, and not attempt to "teach" people.

Next day Dr. Coe gave one of his last lectures and it was so good, that I suddenly decided to ask for his advice regarding the right way to approach my work in France. We had a very good talk and he was extremely helpful. At the end of the talk I mentioned my "day-dream" of perhaps some day being able to work in Russia, and to this he responded with such warmth and understanding that I was amazed. I felt that he really saw what it means to me and somehow shared my feeling.

It was getting dark when I went home, everything covered with snow and the snow still clean. Big ice-floes moved slowly down the Hudson and electric signs were lighting up along the Palisades on the other shore. I felt as if I had seen a miracle: there is this old man, Coe, with generations and generations of Americans behind him, with their struggles and searchings, their own kind of holiness, and there am I, and all the generations behind me, and Voltchy, and all the past, back to our ancestor Solomonida Sabouroff [St. Solomonida, a 15th-century Russian princess], and never have these generations had anything in common, but suddenly now our paths cross, and I can go on again my separate way somehow enriched by old Dr. Coe, having received something from him. I think the sense of the miraculous comes when you see the "bigness' of life and time and how this bigness penetrates your "littleness."

February 2

Exams are all over now and today is the first day of the new semester, just about half-time of my stay here. Last night we had a farewell dinner for Dr. Coe, who is retiring. He made a very good speech, the point of which was that we should never go around a difficulty we meet in life, but go right through it. The other point he made was that religious faith must not remain on the defensive, but should always take the offensive action. Then he went on telling us how he plans to spend his retirement, and this was almost best of all. He spoke of the log cabin he has in the woods, where everything has been built by himself, of his boat called "School's Out," of his fishing and hunting and the long nights spent in the woods. Coe says he is no mystic, but his feeling for nature and for beauty comes very close to mysticism.

One thing gave me pleasure: Coe said that the greatest of all compliments paid him was when a few days ago a student came to see him. "The student," said Coe, "disagreed with almost all I taught, but wanted my advice." I think he was referring to our conversation, though I had not stated so baldly that I disagreed with him. Anyway the evening gave a good start to the new semester.

February 21

On Sunday the weather was as miserable as my mood. I had a headache too. I had promised to take to the Russian

church a group of children whom my fellow student Celia
Ann teaches in Sunday School. Celia Ann had told them about
worship in the Old Testament, altars and burnt offerings, and
mentioned that there are churches today where candles are
part of worship. So they decided they'd go to the Russian
church.

The weather was so bad that to my relief Celia Ann decided to postpone the visit. Half an hour later, there she was
with the four nine-year-old kids, who simply refused to give
up the visit. They were really amazing. Neither Celia Ann
nor I had told them anything about how they should behave
in church, but during the whole time they were there, they
did not let me go for a second, whispering questions in both
my ears: questions about icons, about communion, about
prayer. Not a single question that was not to the point or
irreverent. I went to put up a candle to give them a chance to
look closer at the icons, but I noticed that they stopped at a
little distance. The little girl said afterwards: "You know,
I don't know why, but I just could not come any nearer and
look, it was something at which you should not stare." The
youngest little boy was completely overwhelmed. He stood
without asking anything and his eyes grew rounder and rounder. The best thing happened at the end. The church warden,
seeing this small group of American children, gave them a
prosphora [holy bread]. When they returned to their school,
Janet, the older little girl, said: "I think we must eat it with
very much respect and carefully." The other little girl added:
"I would like to take a little bit to my brother at home; he
is sick." Of course then the others decided they'd have to
take bits home too. And these were American children, 100%
Protestant! They did exactly the same thing, instinctively,
that Orthodox children would have done. The children's behavior really lifted up my spirits. Of such is the Kingdom of
Heaven.

February 26

Well, I think the ghosts of father and grandfather were

helping me today! I hope that they approved of my public speaking. This is what happened.

There is an organization here which is called "Reconciliation Trips," and its purpose is to arrange trips to various centers of community life in New York. I was asked to speak during today's trip, which dealt with Russia. The first meeting took place in the "Russian Club" organized by the Russian émigrés and the theme was "Many Good Things About Old Russia." After the talk the group went to attend a service in the Russian church. The next day a meeting was to take place at the editorial offices of a Russian-Jewish newspaper where they would listen to a talk given by the editor: "A Revolutionary Speaking of the Old Regime." The third session was to take place at a Communist group — "Achievements of the Soviet Government." I was invited to give the first lecture and my first reaction was to refuse. It seemed such a crazy combination of people and themes. I finally decided one had no right to refuse although it would be difficult to give the first address in such a way that the two later ones would not destroy any impression I could produce. I did have one advantage — my age, because the other two speakers were both elderly men, so that even if, at twenty-three, I spoke of Russia's past only, I would still be "the voice of the younger generation."

I prepared myself very carefully, because I wanted to leave an impression of objectivity. I left out anything that could sound emotional. I was supposed to talk for half an hour and then for another half-hour answer questions. I felt that something of Father's gift of public speaking found its way into me. There were about a hundred and thirty people, more than they had expected, so that quite a few had to stand. I said that Russia, like any country, is going through stages of development, and these stages can only be understood in the eyes of one's love for the country. We cannot understand the stage it is going through now, nor its future development, unless we look with a loving interest at the stages it went through in the past. Neither can you understand the past unless you love Russia today and unless you are thinking of its future. I spoke of the difference in the social structure of old Russia — peasants, intelligentsia, "upper ten thousand."

Then I went to speak of what Russian culture stood for, its literature especially. And I ended up trying to give an image of the Orthodox faith and what the Church meant in the life of the people. I mentioned many things which I thought were wrong in old Russia — it was important, it seemed to me, to recognize them.

During the question period the first to jump up was an elderly Russian Jew, quite antagonistic, though I think he was not a Communist. He spoke with a heavy accent and his three questions were really attempts to attack what I had said. The chairman had to ask him to put them in the form of questions. Then he said "Well, you spoke of Dostoevsky, but is it not true that the old regime condemned Dostoevsky to forced labor?" "Yes, it is true," I answered, "and I have already stated that there were many dark sides to life in old Russia which I don't want to whitewash. But I think that what matters most is what Dostoevsky wrote and said and thought *after* he had known forced labor." The audience applauded my answer, so it seemed to have been sufficiently convincing. The other questions were asked by Americans and were just factual ones. There was a woman professor in the audience who had been in Russia before the war. She came up to me when the others had left and said: "You have really done a patriotic work, in the *world* sense of patriotism, and you have completely won the audience." She was not a gushing kind of person so her comment gave me real pleasure. She asked me to let her know when I'll be lecturing again or having a "symposium." And I have not the slightest idea what a "symposium" is! And, Mama, me, a "lecturer"? She said it as if she did not see what a joke it was.

March 1

I have learned now how the rest of the trip went. The socialist who spoke to them in the editorial offices of the newspaper did very well, with no enmity towards Russia, though he had spent many years in prison, and he was definitely anti-Communist. The Communist speaker made a rather poor impression. "He sounded so very much on the top of the world, had no perspective and seemed to have such a party spirit and see only one side of it," said a teacher who attended. "It was statistics, statistics, all the way through and we know well how statistics can prove anything." The best thing came during the question period. One of the people attending asked: "You say there is perfect freedom in Soviet Russia, but we have just listened to two presentations by people who impressed us very much and both of them cannot return to Russia and would not be free there. How do you explain this?" The poor Communist found nothing better to answer than say "There *is* perfect freedom, but not for everybody!" And the audience roared with laughter!

The old gentleman of the Pullman car turned up. He invited me to dinner and ordered a whole roast duck for the two of us in a restaurant where roast duck is a specialty. It was so good that I stuffed and stuffed myself and was more dead than alive when I came home and borrowed a hot-water bottle from Celia Ann. And then, two days later, he sent me *three* boxes of candy — and Great Lent starting at that. I quickly ate the fruit candy and sorrowfully gave the other boxes with chocolate to the girls on my floor.

March 19

... Spent a very nice evening at the Keenys'. You know well enough that my greatest trouble is my tendency to show off. Keeny asked me once: "How many volumes of your autobiography have you written around tea tables?" Yesterday Keeny said: "Don't you realize how much more interesting in is to get a person to show him or herself to you, than to show yourself to a person? Try it out, just as a sort of game, see how much you can find out and understand about every person you talk to." This may sound somewhat silly, but it really impressed me and I tried it out the very next day and the results just took my breath away ... First of all it relieves the inflammation of your "ego". And then, I always thought that I spoke so much about myself, because that was what people wanted from me and I was amazed to discover that if you start the right way about it, they are even much more willing to talk about themselves. And, thirdly, you discover in people around you, whom you thought quite dull, a gold mine of interesting things. There is a fellow here, Fred Shoemaker, whom I always thought a rather nice, but very ordinary person, and that the only possibility of talking to him, was *telling* him about something. Well, I tried the new method, and, you know, before fifteen minutes were over, he became more interesting than a book. His parents were German émigrés and when he spoke about how they celebrated Christmas, about their old kitchen, and how, when he, twenty-three years old, went to Germany and in a little village found his uncle with whom he could barely speak, but could see his likeness to his dead father whom he missed so badly — why, it meant to him what Voltchy means to us.

I really want to continue this game.

March 13

This is my Easter letter to you: Christ is risen! my darling, my love.

You will never be able to imagine what a heavenly place I am in just now. I am staying at a convent and everything is blessedly peaceful and quiet. The room reminds me of the rooms in Alexandrovka, there is complete silence all around since it is their Holy Week, and this letter will reach you for our Easter. Christ is risen, my darling!

I feel as if I am living in a dream. I am not sure whether I am living today, or yesterday or fifteen years ago. It is spring and I am full of spring and I feel spring all around and spring inside myself. Yesterday I went to the post office to pick up your Easter package, and even the old postmaster must have been feeling the spring; he was so nice and asked me about you. I took the parcel to the restroom at Teachers' College and opened it there: the dress is just lovely, it is perfect, and the embroidery around the neck is the last touch of loveliness. Everyone admires it: even the old lady who was the only other person in the restroom to whom I *had* to show it; I put it on the same day after ironing it and there is really some magic in it. The cashier handling my bills suddenly stopped and said: "Pardon me, but what a perfectly lovely dress you have on!" The Jewish Rabbi in my class admired it too and asked me many questions about you.

April 25, Easter Monday

Christ is risen!

I'd like to write a long letter, but am so sleepy that I think it will be a short one.

Our Russian Holy Week was so good. I was able to attend services I always missed because of working in the day time.

On Saturday I bought a little paskha and kulich in a Russian store for the breakfast Alyosha and I had planned. The Korotnevs were having a big party with American friends immediately after Matins and were not staying for Divine Liturgy, but Alyosha and I wanted to stay for the whole service and receive Communion. Alyosha has an uncle living alone in New York and he got his permission for us to have our Easter breakfast at his flat. The uncle said he'd join us. When Alyosha and I arrived at three A.M. there was no trace of the uncle, but there were some parcels with very good things to eat obviously planned for the breakfast. So we tidied up the room, laid the table and telephoned the Korotnevs. Sergei Sergeievich Buturlin said he'd have much more fun with us and left the party to come and join us. We really had a very good time and at five o'clock Alyosha went to finish the night at the Korotnevs and Sergei Sergeievich took me back to International House. I am very fond of him!

And now I have to prepare myself for another speech — at the retreat of Union Theological students, where my address is sandwiched in between two professors. I think this is more frightening than the Reconciliation Trip.

May 17

I am thinking more and more of my return to Paris, not because I am homesick or tired of things here, but because I am so eager to start my work there.

It is quite difficult to explain just what I feel about my future work. You know, you can live year after year and then come up against something and suddenly feel that this is *the* thing, this is the thing you have been looking for all your life, this is what you have been thinking about, this is where all the different circumstances of your life were leading you. I guess what I mean is that I have discovered my vocation, just as a painter or a musician might. Even if for the rest of my life I have to pound away at typewriters in fifteen different offices, I know that I will always work with children and for children. Children are my vocation, I suppose. My head is bursting with ideas of all I want to do, and even of the books, or at least *a* book I want to write, a book on church worship for children. After all, this is not *that* impossible.

I have also another feeling or idea about my future work. I think I can never approach a job with a worked-out plan of all *I* want to do, however good it seems to me. I have first to learn to understand what is *already* being done, of how it is being done, of what the people who are already working feel and want to do. I have to become one of them, part of their work, and only when this becomes our common experience, when some of my conceited ideas have been knocked off, and I have learned to understand their ideas, only then can something new start growing.

The more I have learned here, the more I have to learn when I come back.

I came back to Paris in July 1927. My mother had found an apartment, very charming, newly decorated and newly furnished in a kind of French rustic style, at 39 rue Lafontaine, in Auteuil. It was the nicest home we've had — two rooms joined by an arch, a kitchen and a bathroom. A new chapter in my life began which was to last for five years.

♦

When I came back to France in July, 1927, I found two important changes in my life there. For the first time since we left Russia we had a very pleasant and attractive home, where we were quite on our own. And for the first time in my life I was being paid a salary for doing what I really wanted to do. My vocation became my salaried job. More than this —

Building
A New Life,
1927-1939

I did not step into a well-defined position that existed before I came, where someone else had been doing the work that I was to carry on. My task was to create my own job, to build up the religious educational work of the Russian Student Christian Movement among émigré children. My own understanding of my task was influenced by my training in America; I was convinced that it was more important to learn to understand a situation, see its needs, appreciate what was already being done by others and only then begin to build up what would be an answer to a "felt need." In this way, I felt, the work would grow organically, would not become something imposed. I was also influenced by the years of my past secretarial experience: I believed in giving my work set hours daily, in keeping files and accounting in order, in making reports, and in answering letters without delay.

It is somewhat difficult to understand today the exact nature of our fervor and inspiration in the Student Movement. We were very conscious that religion and spiritual values were being destroyed in Russia. Loyalty to them in Soviet

149

Russia involved martyrdom. We abroad, having shared in the tragedy of Russia, but being free now, were responsible for preserving these values *for Russia*. Thus the religious and national elements were very closely interwoven. We realized that the formal pre-revolutionary religious education in Russia was very defective, yet we had no new manuals, no new programs, no new methods to guide us in our new circumstances. We were conscious that what really mattered was not the information we gave, or the lessons we taught, but the life we lived, the corporate life of our school and our youth groups, and that our children had to be involved in this corporate life creatively, in their own way.

Gradually my work expanded. In response to parents' requests I started instruction by correspondence for Russian families scattered all over France and North Africa — on isolated farms, in small factory towns. In a committee of priests and theologians we worked on preparing a new curriculum for Orthodox church schools. But the biggest responsibility added to my work was running our summer camps for girls, of which I was appointed director.

We had no camp ground of our own and every year I had to scout around all over France for a suitable place to rent. To start with, we had practically no camp equipment and everything had to be acquired gradually. A large percentage of our girls could not afford the full camp fees, and "camp stipends" had to be established. Money had to be raised for all this. Counselors had to be trained, programs carefully prepared.

Our first camp was situated in the tiny old Breton village of Le Logeau — in the lovely and peaceful bay of Morbihan. For our campground we had two old stone school buildings, dating back to the 18th century, each one of them consisting of a single, large, brick-floored room with an open hearth on the ground floor and an attic above. The two houses were joined by a large yard, and a meadow we could use for games adjoined the property. A little cowshed could be converted into a chapel. The beach, a lovely empty space used only by us, was a couple of hundred feet down. I planned that the ground-floor room of the smaller house would serve as our kitchen and the one in the larger house as our refectory and game room in bad weather. The two attics and two small tents would serve as sleeping quarters for the 45 girls and six leaders we were expecting. The cook and I arrived a few days ahead to prepare the camp site. As we were stuffing the straw bags that were to serve as camp beds, I realized that in my inexperience I had underestimated the space we would need for them. We would not be able to place more than 24 bags in the larger attic and 12 in the smaller one. Desperately I telegraphed our office in Paris, asking them to stop enrollments and to stagger the arrival of the already enrolled girls. But on the eve of the day camp was to start I received a brief telegraphic answer: ARRIVING 56 GIRLS AND 4 LEADERS. I really do not know how we squeezed them all in the two rooms we had, but we managed.

The camp ran up quite a big deficit but neither then nor later could I make myself regret it. Most of the children came from very needy homes, where plentiful and wholesome food was still a problem. Our food supplies were stored in the dining room, and between meals the children gorged themselves on "tartines beurrées" of the good village bread and the fresh local butter. Our Russian cook loved to bake huge Breton prune tarts and in the evenings passed generous helpings through a hole in the kitchen ceiling to the dormitory in the attic. Bowls and bowls of milk were absorbed by the campers whenever they felt like it and all the children put on several pounds. Being overweight was not a problem among our refugee children.

The camp was run in a way that was very demanding on the leaders. We spent all our time, 24 hours a day and 7 days a week, with the girls, with no privacy or rest for ourselves and we took very much to heart our responsibility for the program as a whole and for each child individually. Curiously enough our program in that camp fifty years ago involved more of the children's participation and responsibility than I have seen in modern camps here; it must have been Dr. Coe's influence on my educational philosophy. We held a general meeting on the first day of camp, at which the campers volunteered to participate in this or that committee that

was responsible for some aspect of the program: entertainment, educational activities, church services, sports, overnight
hikes etc. There was an adult leader on each committee, but
a lot of the planning and of the work was done by the girls.
The church committee, for example, cleaned the cowshed,
whitewashed it, and with sheets and greenery arranged the
traditional icon screen. They baked the bread for the Divine
Liturgy, they ordered the wine, they sold the candles and
cleaned the chapel after services.

Our first chaplain was the unforgettable Father Sergius
Chetverikov, who had just been appointed spiritual adviser
and chaplain of the Russian Student Christian Movement.
He arrived a few days later than we did. We had not met him
before and expected someone exceptional and impressive
who would drop words of wisdom to which we would listen.
The elderly priest who arrived that day, reserved and almost
shy, with a very quiet and unobtrusive manner and an icon-
like face, was very different from my expectations. On the
first evening, after supper, we all moved to the adjoining
meadow, where we used to play informal traditional Russian
games — *gorelki, kolduny*, or just plain tag. Father Sergius
stood quietly watching us and never moved from his corner.
As it grew dark and we turned in, he approached me: "Sofia
Sergeievna, you know there is a hole in the ground there;
it must have been made for a post. It is quite dangerous,
someone could break a foot running. Tonight I stood in the
hole while you were playing, so it did not matter, but I think
it should be filled by tomorrow."

The first church service was quite an adventure. In our
inexperience we thought that it was sufficient to have a few
girls and a leader who could sing to make a small church
choir. Father Sergius brought with him a seminarian, Dima
Klepinin who, we thought, could conduct a choir. The evening
church service is less well known by lay people than the Sunday
Liturgy, and the melodies and the words are different each
week. The service was a disaster. Dima was inexperienced at
conducting and the girls knew nothing of church music. False
starts were made over and over again, and finally in despera-
tion the choir would wade through a hymn in complete dis-

harmony. The campers gathered in the chapel quite reverently, but as the service went on, they began to titter and gigle. When the service was at last over Mania Zernov, always the sensitive one, exploded: "This is impossible! We cannot have a service tomorrow! It is sheer blasphemy! Let's wait until we have trained a choir." Rather sheepishly we were inclined to agree with her when our youngest camper, Irina Vishniakova, rushed up excitedly: "Isn't it wonderful? Isn't it marvelous? It's my birthday tomorrow, and now we have a church and a priest and we will have a service, and I will be able to receive Communion at our very first service, on my own birthday." Mania Zernov looked distressed: "Well, I guess there is nothing else to do but go ahead and have a service tomorrow" she said mournfully. "How can we disappoint her?"

Dima chose five girls, two of whom came from a Russian orphanage where they had sung in a church choir. They went far away on the beach and for two hours I could hear, if I listened carefully, strange noises coming from there that sounded like cats mewing. But in the morning a small choir performed quite creditably and Irina shone with joy as she received Communion.

During our first summer camps we had either Fr. Sergius Chetverikov or Fr. Alexander Elchavinov for chaplains. In those days we had no tradition of Orthodox camps and we solved problems as they came up. We naturally had morning and evening prayers and Divine Liturgy on Sunday. But how far should attendance be compulsory? I remember how one of the nicest older girls spoke to me very earnestly: "Please, please, do not make church services compulsory. For six years I have been in a Russian boarding school in Yugoslavia with compulsory church attendance, and I hated it. Now, for the first time, church services begin to mean something for me. It will all be spoiled if you make them compulsory."

We brought the question to Father Sergius. He thought for a while and said: "Attending church services is the duty of every Orthodox Christian and should be recognized as such. But compulsion — with disciplinary measures for non-attendance — that's not doing any good." So "obligatory but not compulsory" remained our basic principle from then on.

Another tradition established in our early summer camps was confession and communion for everyone at the end of all summer. In those days the general practice had been to go to confession and communion only once a year, during Great Lent. I especially remember how this new practice took place in our summer camp at Soulac-sur-Mer, in a pine forest on the Atlantic coast. We had a hundred and twenty girls from eight to eighteen and a staff of some twenty people. Because of the principle of "non-compulsion," the girls were quite free to go to confession or not, and as usual there were a lot of decisions taken at the last moment on the basis of friendship. "Will you go?" "Yes, I will . . ." "Well, then I think I want to go too."

Confessions started at four P.M. They were interrupted by the church service at seven P.M. and then went on again. At ten P.M. we realized that it might take Father Sergius all night to confess all those who were waiting, so we sent the girls to bed, promising to wake them up when their turn came. It must have seemed rather like the Last Judgment, with someone shaking you awake in the darkness of the night: "Get up, get up! It's time to go to confession!" Father Sergius confessed all night, except for a half-hour break, continuing right up to the Divine Liturgy and even a few late stragglers during the service. I remember he told me that he was using the stole that had been given him by the Optino "starets" Father Amvrossi and that he liked using it because it was so light. I had never thought that the weight of a stole could make a difference.

Now, almost fifty years later, I realize how many of these children and young people who attended our camps became active in the life of the Russian church, both in Russia and abroad.

All of us who worked in the Student Movement were involved in the effort to raise money for our work. I remember particularly the two weeks I spent one winter in Nice, helping Mrs. Elizabeth Skobtsova to raise money for the work she wanted to start among Russian émigrés scattered in provincial factory towns and mining centers. Most of them were

former members of the Russian White Army who had come
to France with contracts as laborers. Separated from the main
stream of émigré life in the larger cities, unable to become
assimilated in the world of French factory workers, many became disheartened, and reverted to drink as their only solace.
Mrs. Skobtsova proposed to visit these small communities,
organize clubs, lectures, courses, help the men to better themselves vocationally, and establish contacts with the larger
Russian centers. In later years Mrs. Skobtsova became very
well-known as "Mother Mary," the Russian nun who died a
martyr's death in Ravensbruck because of her efforts to help
Jews during the German occupation.

Mrs. Skobtsova was one of the most fascinating and most
exasperating persons I had ever known. Before the days when
her appearance was dignified and improved by a nun's habit,
she dressed and looked like a typical nineteenth century
"nihilist" in worndown men's shoes, badly washed and un-
ironed hand-me-down clothes, a pince-nez either insecurely
perched on the bridge of her nose or dangling down on a
black cord, her hair pinned up in a bun with large metal
hairpins, with wisps of hair escaping untidily. The secret of
her hat she confided to me proudly: she worked as a cleaning
woman in a millinery shop, and every day she had to sweep
out lots of felt snippets. These she collected, cut up and
braided in multicolored strips. She then wound the braid into
a kind of beehive shape with a wide brim. She had a round
and ruddy face and was rather near-sighted. I must admit
that in the daytime, as we rang people's doorbells, I often
felt quite embarrassed by her appearance.

But then came the evenings. A Russian family allowed
us to stay in two little "maids' rooms" in the attic of their
house. Even in Nice, winter nights are chilly in unheated
rooms, but in my room there was a gas-ring on which we
could boil water for endless cups of tea. The room would get
comfortably warm and Mrs. Skobtsova and I, wrapped up in
our blankets, talked until the small hours of the night. What
a conversationalist she was! What a brilliant mind she had,
what sensitive perception! She wrote poetry and could recite
poems by the hour. She managed to draw out of me my in-

nermost dreams and imaginings without ever letting me experience the embarrassment one so often feels after having
talked too much and too openly.

We were poles apart. My vocation was definitely motherhood although I was still unmarried. She was a woman twice
married with both marriages broken, mother of four children
of whom she had already lost two, but her vocation was social action. She was a socialist who had turned to Orthodoxy.
She belonged to the intellectual elite of the Russian "intelligentsia," with her roots in the "silver age" of Russian literature. I was the product of the Russian aristocracy, who
always felt uncomfortable with the "intelligentsia." But how
I enjoyed our evenings! How absorbing were all the stories
she told me! I am glad to say that our money-raising campaign was successful and started her off on her career of
serving "the humiliated and the injured" of the Russian
emigration.

Mrs. Skobtsova's fifteen-year-old daughter Gayana attended our summer camps. She was an over-sensitive, tense
child, obviously suffering from the neglect which was almost
unavoidable. She was always badly and insufficiently equipped
for camp, her things were not clean enough. The family's
poverty was extreme. Mrs. Skobtsova was a poor provider
and was too involved in other interests and activities. I will
always remember Gayana's assumed bravado when letters
were distributed to children and she pretended not to expect
any. Gayana was eighteen or nineteen, when she decided to
return to Soviet Russia, influenced by the Soviet author Alexei
Tolstoy who was staying in Paris. In Russia she married and
was quite happy, but in a few months news came of her
sudden illness and death. I went to attend a memorial service
for Gayana at the chapel of the settlement founded by Mother
Mary, the former Mrs. Skobtsova. All through the service
Mother Mary remained prostrated on the floor of the chapel,
a motionless figure in her black habit. If she had ever failed
Gayana, I am sure the bitterness of it seared her heart.

My work in the Russian Student Christian Movement
lasted for almost seven years. The only interruption was a
two-month stay in 1930 at St. Christopher's College in Eng-

land. It was a Church of England college, training missionaries, supervisors, and directors for the educational work of
the Church. Miss Catherine Newby, who was in charge of
the college, was a remarkable woman. The whole atmosphere
of the place was of course very different from Teachers'
College and Union Theological Seminary in New York,
much less sophisticated and radical, rooted in Christian church
tradition. The English manner of understatement, of respect-
ing each other's privacy and of a certain reserve in the
expression of one's opinions was very refreshing. The courses
I took were very helpful in a practical way, and the friendships I made remained lasting. Towards the end of my stay
Mary Duke, our senior student, asked me to speak to the student body on a Saturday night, when rather informal gatherings took place twice a month. She said that the students
wanted the factual story of *my* life. They felt that any lecture
about something would not be the same as getting the taste
of the thing itself.

I was hesitant about the wisdom of getting so personal
and carefully prepared my story, avoiding dramatization and
sentimentality in relating our experiences. When it was over,
the students remained silent and then spontaneously rose and
went to the chapel. I purposely stayed in chapel for a long
time, hoping everyone would have left by then, but Miss
Newby was waiting at the door outside the chapel. In an
unusual gesture she hugged me and said: "My dear, the way
you told it they all feel that it is a story with a happy ending,
but I know that you have not reached a happy ending yet."
I stammered trying to explain that I was afraid my talk was
too personal, which is always a bad thing. "Don't worry,"
she said, "you were completely selfless."

The friendship and affection showered on me at St. Christopher's was heartwarming. I was given an affectionate nickname "Trotsky", because they said it was easier to pronounce
than Shidlovsky. The day I was leaving, before the end of
the term, they signalled the letter "T" in Morse code over the
fire alarm system and the whole college poured out to see
me off.

In 1928 my grandmother Elizabeth Sabouroff and my

mother's sister Mary Sabouroff were able to leave Soviet Russia and join us in Paris. Aunt Mary had been arrested in 1925, spent several months in prison and then two years in exile. She was now allowed to leave Russia accompanying her invalid mother, aged well over eighty. We were able to find rooms for them in the same house in which we lived and later settled together in an apartment at 13 Avenue de Versailles. This was another big step in the process of our resettlement. For the first time we rented an unfurnished apartment and became owners of furniture — second-hand furniture bought at auctions, but now our own property. For the first time all our belongings could not be packed into a few suitcases.

Granny was beloved by all the family and by her many friends. Those last three years in Paris, where seventy years earlier she had spent a part of her happy childhood, were a peaceful sunset to a remarkable life. She was a person of great charm, combining wonderful "joie de vivre" with sincere humility and deep spirituality. A "great lady" of St. Petersburg society, in the best sense of this word, she was well known as the hostess of Sunday receptions, reputed for the high quality of music played there and the interesting and outstanding people who gathered to listen to it.

Her husband Andrei Sabouroff distinguished himself as an active statesman during the period of the "great reforms" in the second half of the nineteenth century, especially in the field of the legal reform of the courts. He was then appointed Minister of Education, but lost this position after the murder of Czar Alexander II, because he was considered too liberal. He became a member of the State Council and died in 1915. I was eleven years old at the time, but curiously enough I never forgot a counsel he gave me. Grandpa was teaching me to play chess and showing me various movements of the chess figures. Suddenly he interrupted himself and, illustrating his words with one of the chess figures said, "You know, there is a saying 'One man on a battlefield is no soldier' and they usually take it to mean that there is nothing just one man can do. But I understand this saying differently. A man in a battlefield never remains just one man. If only one man comes forward, he is sure to be followed by others. Never be afraid of remaining alone, never give up because of this."

In her personal life Granny had known sorrow. She lost three of her five children: her charming, beautiful and gifted eldest daughter Sophie died of tuberculosis at the age of sixteen; a few months later the delightful little tomboy Xenia died from diphtheria on her fifth birthday. Another baby died from scarlet fever.

At the time of the revolution the entire world Granny knew collapsed around her. I remember her in Moscow, well over seventy years old, in her unheated room, wrapped up in her old and now shabby fur coat, eating some boiled potatoes with her little silver fork. "You know, I have always *so* loved potatoes," she said. "It is really my favorite food. I wonder whether it is not a sin to be so fond of food?" She never complained, she was always cheerful. During Aunt Mary's imprisonment and exile, she began to suffer from a nervous eczema of the hands and because of loving but unskilled care lost all power to move her fingers. She also lost almost all of her eyesight, but her capacity to enjoy life remained undimmed. She enjoyed everything: people, friends, thoughts, food, pretty clothes, and her sympathy for other people's experience was boundless.

Aunt Mary, two years older than my mother, unmarried and completely selfless, had always been a second mother to us. In later years she became the firm cornerstone in my own family and I shall often have occasion to speak of her.

My brother Iuri had by the end of the twenties settled in Western Africa, first in what was then called the Belgian Congo and later in the French Congo. The tropical climate was exhausting and life on the coffee plantations lonely, but it seemed to suit Iuri, who called himself "the cat that walked by itself." So much of our Russian émigré life abroad irritated him; so much of it seemed to him artificial and unreal. He resented my absorption in my work in the Student Movement, in my friendships there, in my interests. Was it my fault? I can well imagine that I had become something of a "woman with a cause" and this can be pretty exasperating. But I also can see that Iuri's ill health during his childhood and youth

had left its mark on him, had caused a certain aloofness. Because of the very depth of our closeness and affection for each
other through our childhood and adolescence, he resented and
was jealous of the interests and influences that led me away
on paths of my own.

In the early thirties Iuri went through a very difficult time.
Agents sent from European headquarters had overestimated
the potential of the coffee plantations recently acquired, probably to cause a good impression. The actual harvests were
lower than predicted and the local black labor force was
blamed for this. Supervisors were instructed to introduce
harsh disciplinary measures. My brother refused to punish his
workers, conflicts arose, and he was dismissed. He took the
blow very much to heart and although he remained in Africa
for another five years and finally after an endless trial received
an indemnity from his firm, the satisfaction in his work
was gone.

By the year 1930 I felt at a crossroads. I did feel a vocation
for working with children, but I also felt an even deeper
vocation for family life and motherhood. My feelings in this
respect had not changed in the ten years since I said to my
Soviet colleagues that most of all I wanted to be a mother.
I was twenty-seven years old. I had been half in love several
times and had been honored by the love of excellent and outstanding men. Several times I had been informally engaged,
but for some reason I could not understand, I always had
doubts at the last moment and backed out. The idea of becoming a spinster doing good works frightened me. Somehow
I could see only two alternatives for a way of life, either
getting married and having a family, or becoming a nun. I
began to think quite seriously of the second way. In the year
1931 everything changed suddenly when Nikita Koulomzin
entered my life again.

Our friendship with Nikita went back to our early childhood. We were not relatives but my father's brother, Uncle
Kolia, had married Nikita's father's sister, Aunt Katia, so
that their children were our first cousins, both Nikita's and
mine. Nikita's parents were much younger than mine. I was
the youngest of five children and he the eldest of six. The

same old lady-doctor delivered us both and, since she had first committed herself to attend my mother, Nikita's parents were very anxious that the two happy events would not coincide. I was born fifteen days earlier than Nikita and my parents sent them a message "Green light!" When Nikita was born one of the two mothers commented: "And here is a fiancé for Sonia!"

The Koulomzins lived summer and winter at their country place, Kornilovo, not far from Kostroma on the Volga, but they always came to Petersburg for a few months when a new baby was to be born. Three brothers and two sisters followed Nikita, so that these visits were pretty regular and were used to catch up on the older two boys' education, which was happily ignored during the rest of the time. Nikita's charming and always cheerful mother was very sensitive to her children's talents and she did all she could to encourage Nikita's interest in mathematics, physics and mechanics and to develop his inventor's mind. Yet in comparison to the strict educational routine which my mother had established for us, the Koulomzin children grew up in a blissful ignorance of the three R's. Sometimes during their stays in Petersburg, Iuri, I, Nikita and his next brother Fedor, were taught by the same teacher and they also joined some special classes, like gymnastics or art, held at our house. Nikita was a very handsome little boy, with large brown eyes and a mop of curly hair. Very good-natured, he always tried to stop any quarrel or fight that might arise and we gave him the nickname of "peacemaker." Fedor, three years his junior, was the business man and manager of the family. He always knew at what time they had to leave, and their plans for the next day, and the telephone number that had to be called.

From this period of our childhood I remember an incident that was very typical of the Koulomzin boys. One winter we were joined for some of our lessons by two little girls. They arrived once with two beautiful balloons they had just bought. "Don't touch our balloons!" they cried. "Don't touch, they might burst!" Iuri and I looked somewhat wistfully at the balloons, but obediently left them alone. Next year our classmates were Nikita and Fedor, and one day *they* arrived with two balloons. "Sonia, Iuri!" they yelled as they came in. "Look at the balloons we brought! Let's play with them." And the four of us had a glorious time with the balloons, until they burst with a satisfactory bang. I don't know how many times I told this story to my children when they were small and to my grandchildren later on, always pointing out the same moral at the end: "And we never saw the two little girls again, but Nikita and Fedor remained our friends all our life and Nikita married Sonia and they were happy ever after."

After the Revolution of 1917, we saw the Koulomzins for the last time in Moscow in 1918, where they were waiting for their last son, Yaroslav, to be born. They left then for the country place of their maternal grandmother, Baroness Meyendorff, not far from Kiev. For some strange reason she was convinced they would be safer there than in any large city and she persuaded several of her married children to bring their families to "Babushkin Hutor," her country estate.

We met with the Koulomzins again in France, the year before I left for the United States for my year's study there. My mother and I had heard, of course, of the tragic events that had taken place in our friends' life, but that summer of 1926 when my mother and I were spending our vacation in Juan-les-Pins, at that time still a little-known sea-side village on the Mediterranean coast, we came across Olga Koulomzin and her children living in Cannes. The two younger ones, thirteen-year-old Elizabeth and eight-year-old Yaroslav, were living at the Russian orphanage in Cannes, and Mrs. Koulomzin was employed there too, mending linen, I believe. Nikita and Fedor were scholarship students at the Sorbonne in Paris, but during the summer holidays they found jobs in Cannes. Mrs. Koulomzin invited us for lunch.

The whole family shared a tiny room in the lodge at the entrance to the main house. Extreme poverty was obvious, but the meal served on a table in the corner of the orphanage garden was a truly joyous celebration. The centerpiece was a large juicy watermelon, expertly chosen and bought by Fedor. We then went on a long walk in the surrounding hills. The boys and I went on ahead, but our mothers tired soon and settled for a rest on a low stone wall on the way. It was there that Olga Koulomzin told my mother all about what they had gone through.

In 1920 the country place Babushkin Hutor was within the area of civil war. The White Army was advancing, the "Reds" retreating, and in the no-man's land area the "Green" troops of Makhno were pillaging and murdering on their own.

A band of "Makhno-men" came to Babushkin Hutor. They arrested Nikita's father and took him to their headquarters. Olga insisted on coming too. At the last moment, when she realized her husband would be executed, she heard him say: "Olga, the children! Go home!" She jumped out of the window and ran home. Her husband was shot immediately. Olga's two brothers, Iuri and Lev, were both officers in the White Army. As their section drew close to their mother's country home, they decided to visit it, since their families were staying there. It is believed that a peasant, who saw them crossing the bridge, signalled to them to warn them of the danger, but they did not hear him. They fell right into the hands of the Makhno men, who took them to the same headquarters. The manner in which they were killed was gruesome: they were beaten and stamped on until the brothers were barely alive. At that moment Makhno entered the room. Iuri was able to lift his head and he begged Makhno to have them shot. Makhno frowned and said: "Finish them off, someone! You hear!" "Too bad to waste a cartridge on them!" answered one of the men, but he took a heavy wooden laundry roller and hit them on their heads. In a minute all was over.

Lev had a wife and three children. Iuri was a widower and father of four. Before his ordeal began he asked to be allowed to write a letter to his children. Now, one of the men said with a smirk: "Let's see what he has scribbled there!" and he began to read the note aloud. Iuri wrote:

My very dear children,
Perhaps we shall not see each other again in this life. Forgive me, my darlings, I wanted to give you pleasure by visiting you, but the way it worked out I am depriving you of your father for ever. Let's accept God's will . . . Do not

grieve for me, bear your sorrow patiently, and may your lives increase goodness and truth on earth. Never try to revenge my death, neither in deed nor even in thought. God allowed it. Pray to Him that He forgive me all my transgressions. I am not afraid of death and I am going to my Lord to answer for my life in the living hope that He will accept me. I am asking Granny to take care of you. Be good grandchildren to her; comfort her in her sorrow. I bless you. God keep you and God guide you in all that's good.

Your father.

There was an awkward silence and the man who read the letter stuffed it in his pocket.

All these details were known from a young student who had been arrested together with the brothers Meyendorff and witnessed the whole scene. He was released later.

Curiously enough the man who read the letter did bring it to old Baroness Meyendorff. He advised her to leave the place immediately and when she answered that all their horses had been requisitioned, he promised to send a horse next day. He did not get a chance to do this, because that night the White Army advanced and liberated the whole area.

Olga Koulomzin immediately began looking for the bodies of her husband and her brothers. Her little son Seraphim, then five years old, was the one to find them. "Look, it's Uncle Iuri!" he cried scooping up earth from one of the bodies buried in a shallow trench. All three, and others who were executed with them, were given a church burial in the nearby town of Uman.

Nikita was sixteen when his father was killed. In later years he told me that his father had a clear premonition of his death, several years before it actually happened.

Occasionally, as time went on, he would refer to it. He'd say to his wife: "Oh, Olga, can't you leave the diapers for a while. We have so little time left!" A week before his death he went to confession and received Holy Communion at the village church. The priest must have told him not to become superstitious, for from that day on he did not speak of his death. But he did call Nikita and spoke to him, privately and at some length. "I know I will not be long with you. You are my oldest one, you must take care of your mother when I am gone and help her bring up the children. God will help you." Nikita had a feeling that his father had had a vision, in some way connected with St. Seraphim, and that it had happened many years earlier, but he did not really know.

Most of this tragic story my mother learned from Olga Koulomzin on that sunny afternoon in Cannes. My mother and I went back to Juan-les-Pins taking the little local train. They waved us off, but Nikita bought a ticket that gave him access to the platform and saw us off to the car. "This is when I realized that he had fallen in love with you," my mother-in-law told me much later. "We were so poor at the moment that his spending a few pennies for the access to the platform meant a great deal."

A year or two later Mrs. Koulomzin and the two younger children moved to Paris. They found a modest apartment in an old house in Sevres and there the five of them lived on the scholarships received by the two boys (fifteen dollars a month for each of them) and the very irregular earnings of Mrs. Koulomzin for painting porcelain. Their diet consisted exclusively of vegetable soup and rice, though a steak was always bought for Yaroslav "because he had to grow," and butter was bought as the cheapest source of nutritional value. Day in, day out, the meals did not vary, but to my amazement all through our later life, rice remained my husband's favourite food. The home was always cheerful; no one in the family was ever poverty-conscious; the "hierarchy of values" was unquestioned: church came first, then education, food was admitted as a necessity, all the rest was non-essential and you were just grateful for whatever came your way.

In the fall of 1930, when I came back from running the summer camp, I found Nikita waiting for me. There was some trouble with the children's luggage that was routed to the wrong station; parents got upset and children were excited. I was hoping to leave for my vacation next day, and the whole day was spent in trying to untangle the confusion. The whole day Nikita helped me to look for the wretched suitcases, until at last they were all found and properly delivered. When my mother and I left for our vacation I knew quite definitely one thing: I was not sure whether I loved Nikita or not but feeling as I did about him, I had no right to make any other decision. Now that Nikita was through with his studies I would be seeing him and matters would clear up. But the very day I came back from my vacation, I met Nikita's sister and learned that Nikita had found a job in geophysical research to be carried on in the Sahara and had left for Africa, He would stay there at least a year, perhaps longer! Lilenka thought it was just like her brother to go and look for water in Sahara!

Nikita is not much of a correspondent and during the whole year I received only one letter from him, asking me for information about certain conditions in Soviet Russia. Years later I learned that this one letter was the result of prodding by Aunt Katia, the very much loved aunt we had in common.

Fortunately for me the Geophysical Research Society ran into financial difficulties and abandoned its project in the Sahara. Nikita came back and found a job very much to his taste, as assistant to an inventor in the then new field of electronics.

Now we met every day. Nikita would call for me at 10 Boulevard Montparnasse, headquarters the Russian Christian Student Movement. We would walk home together, a matter of some forty minutes. One Sunday, on November eighth, as we arrived at the door of our house, Nikita said: "Sonia, you know, I want to speak to you ... Let's have a good, long, unhurried talk. Let's talk somewhere where no one will disturb us. Let's talk quietly, unhurriedly ..." Somehow, doing it unhurriedly seemed very important to Nikita. "Well, tomorrow evening I have to attend a committee. What about the day after?" I said this in a very business-like way, though my heart thumped. "No," answered Nikita, "That day I am tutoring Andrei Meyendorff." "All right then, let's meet on Wednesday after work."

However, poor Andrei Meyendorff got no help in math that week! Nikita turned up at 10 Boulevard Montparnasse on the dot of 6 P.M. and we started off on foot for our walk home. Somewhere under the elevated metro line near the La

Motte Picket — Grenelle station, everything was decided and when Aunt Mary opened the door, we went straight to my mother's room to ask her to give us her blessing.

Everyone was very happy at our engagement. My mother's love for me was rather possessive, but giving me away in marriage to a husband whom she could trust and love was something for which she had always prepared herself. She was aware of Nikita's absolute kindness and complete self-lessness. I am happy to say that for the few years that remained before her death, our relations with her, as part of our family living with us, were completely harmonious and unclouded. With Nikita I felt a security I had never felt before, a trust that no hurt, no harsh and angry judgment would come to me from him. In my relationship with him, for the first time in my life I felt completely unafraid. And at the same time I felt that we both completely and utterly trusted each other's sense of values. If Nikita felt something was wrong, I knew it was wrong; if he felt something was right I could trust it to be right. Recently I found a letter which I wrote to my sister Mania at the time of our engagement:

> I think that Nikita and I are so well attuned to each other, are so much inwardly in harmony with each other, that I cannot even call it being "in love." Somehow I think that, as years go by, this being in tune with each other will grow stronger and stronger.

Forty-five years later I can only confirm what I felt then.

Our engagement was short, and we seemed to be carried on a wave of everyone's affection and good wishes. Letters and presents came from my old nurse Gania, Nicholas Berdyaev, my parents' friends of old St. Petersburg days, Father Bulgakov, friends in America, members of the family scattered in all the continents of the world, parents of the children I worked with. A very special letter came, of course, from Iuri in Africa:

December 12, 1931

My dear Sonia,

The next mail boat will not be leaving for quite a time
but I am using this very first free minute to write to you, to
give you my good wishes and to bless you, my loyal armor-
bearer, at the beginning of the new road on which you start.
I write these words "to bless you" and you cannot imagine
how ironic they sound to me, in the midst of our life here,
life that is so coarse and black that you would all be horrified
if you knew more about it. I can well imagine the entire family
ceremonial parade that surrounds you these days, with all
the uncles and aunts, and congratulations and prayer-services
and everything — everything that seems to me so far away
and so long ago that I doubt whether it really ever existed.
I feel both ashamed and afraid. Ashamed, because who am I
to give you my blessing, and afraid because while the whole
family ceremonial follows its pattern, with each one in his
or her right place, playing the right tune, I feel like a singer
who has lost his voice and can neither sing nor play.

I am convinced that what has now happened to you is
your reward for being the only one who "kept the home fires
burning," for everything you did for mother, and for everything you bore from all of us. Quite truly, not just because it
happened this way, but objectively speaking this is the very
best thing that could have happened to you — to marry "normally," in harmony with all the spiritual and material com-
ponents of your life.

For heaven's sake, my dear, don't complicate matters now
and tie them up in knots. May God grant you power to rightly
solve the cloud of problems that will be sure to arise. I hug
you and kiss you and bless you for your task — to create the
family that none of us older ones was able to create.

Yours always,
Iuri

P. S. If you are again leading me by the nose and your
engagement is off — please consider this letter cancelled.

Instinctively I left all the practical arrangements to my mother, feeling that she found comfort and happiness in them. My "trousseau" was not of the most practical kind. On one hand my mother was guided by the requirements of olden days, with dresses and frocks for all occasions; on the other hand there was obviously no money to spend. My wedding dress came as a present from one of mother's friends, the lace veil was a family heirloom, passed on from bride to bride in our family, but all the other clothes were second-hand. A week's honeymoon trip was arranged to Cannes, to stay at a hotel, where a friend could get special rates, the third class ticket was even cheaper than usual because of a special fare arranged by the Russian Red Cross. Aunt Mary prepared a basket with cold chicken, fruit, and wine to take for the journey. An old friend of grandmother's, who quite unexpectedly had become a wealthy banker in Paris, contributed his elegant car and chauffeur for the wedding. Nikita wore a borrowed morning suit and looked very well in it. No one saw that having forgotten to provide either a belt or suspenders, he used a piece of string to hold up the pants.

Yet the wedding was beautiful, really beautiful. It was celebrated by the two Fathers Sergius — Bulgakov and Chetverikov — and Metropolitan Evlogy insisted on officiating himself at a special service of thanksgiving after the wedding ceremony. The St. Sergius choir sang as well as it always did, omitting operatic flourishes and using ancient chant melodies. The Institute chapel, decorated in the old Byzantine style, was crowded. Two rows of my church school children lined up in the middle, holding white flowers. Nikita's icon was carried by little John Meyendorff, and mine by my small godson Nicholas Mozhaisky. There are always many small children attending Russian weddings and in our pewless churches they tend to wander around. At our wedding one little three-year-old girl managed to escape from her mother and place herself right between Nikita and myself. Nikita bent down and gently moved her out of the way.

A friend of mine, Katia Menshikov, told me afterwards: "I saw Nikita close his eyes in prayer. I saw him nod his head slightly as if affirming something, as if he wanted to say: 'Yes,

yes, I accept everything, I accept her as she is, with all her
school children, with all her work'."

There was a small reception at our home afterwards,
with everything prepared and contributed by friends, even
the champagne. At eight o'clock in the evening we left for
the Gare de Lyon and took the train to Cannes. We were off
on our honeymoon and on our new life together.

* * *

"Sonia, it is perfectly wonderful!"
"Darling, I am sure it is exactly what you need!"
"Do tell us that we can take it. Can we?"
"I really think you should have a look at it."

My mother and Nikita's fourteen-year-old brother Yaroslav kept interrupting each other and they were both so excited I thought they would burst. I made a real effort to match
their enthusiasm, but I was so nauseated it came with an
effort.

To my great joy I was expecting my first baby and we
were looking for a permanent home in which my mother would
live with us and which we would furnish ourselves. Unfortunately I proved to be just as bad a sailor in pregnancy as
I was on any kind of boat.

My mother and Yaroslav undertook to look for a house.
The "jewel of a house" in Chaville which they found was
really exactly what we wanted. Chaville was within twenty
minutes by train from the center of Paris, surrounded by beautiful woods. A few Russian families had already settled there
and there was a small Orthodox church installed in a garage.
The house was inexpensive, but it had four rooms, a kitchen,
a bathroom and a large closet. Behind the house there was a
little garden with young trees. The rooms were sunny and
pleasant, though not large. Nikita and I did not need to be
persuaded and on July 15th we signed the lease for our beloved 17 avenue Gaston Boissier where we lived for seventeen years, where three of our four children were born and
two members of the family died. In later years it proved to

be our Ark through the flood days of war, occupation, famine and cold.

Towards the end of that summer camp period my mother wrote me from Paris that Granny was weakening and soon after that the news came of her end. It was a peaceful sunset to all her remarkable life.

As I think back of the years 1933-1937 the major theme of our life during this period seems to have been the growth of our family and the need for both of us to work in order to support it.

Our first daughter, Elizabeth, was born on February 14, 1933. She was only five months old when I realized for the first time the inescapable conflict between my work and my own motherhood. I realized quite well that I could not conduct a full scale summer camp sharing fully in its life with a baby in my arms, but I thought it would not be so difficult to assume responsibility for a small group of young children, twenty-five of them from three to eight years old. They were lodged for the six weeks of summer camp in a small building adjacent to the large building of the girls' camp on the Mediterranean coast. My co-workers were George L. Romanov and his wife, and Mrs. Samarin, who cooked our meals. I had planned to rent a room for my mother and have Elizabeth stay there with her.

Things went wrong from the very beginning. During our train journey we discovered that one of the children had a bad case of flu. Upon our arrival we found out that our quarters were too small and very primitive. We could not isolate the sick children and in a few days we had a regular flu epidemic on our hands. The water supply was insufficient for the needs of the camp and after two or three days we could only get a few miserable drops from the pump. All water had now to be brought in pails from another pump which was quite a long distance away. Mrs. Romanov was recovering from major surgery, Mrs. Samarin had a heart condition, so the water-carrying chore fell on the shoulders of George Romanov and me. And you do need a lot of pails of water for twenty-five children. The beach was about half a mile away which was quite a walk for young children.

Baby Elizabeth was affected by the heat. She developed diarrhea, cried a lot, and could not sleep at night. To my dismay I found that it was quite impossible to rent a room for my mother, the way I had planned it — there were just none, only entire villas for hire. During the long night hours I would walk around the yard, with Elizabeth in my arms, trying to soothe her and not let her disturb the other children. It came to the point when I felt I'd better go home, but George Romanov pointed out quite reasonably that the whole situation was too bad for me to leave them in the lurch. At this difficult time the woman who owned a small cafe on the beach said to me after listening to my woes: "It is true that there are no rooms for rent here, only villas. But you know, several of these villas are owned by a very wealthy lady, Madame de. . . . She lives in one of them now. She is not a pleasant person and hard to deal with, but I heard that she can be quite kind when children are involved. She has two now and lost one a few years ago."

That same day, when the children were having their midday rest, I went to see the difficult lady, as usual carrying Elizabeth in my arms. The lady's villa was perfectly lovely, standing on a hillside in a pine grove, catching all the cool breezes from the sea. The lady was having coffee served to her on the patio. I explained my difficulty and my need of a room. Without saying a word she rang a little bell and when the man-servant appeared she told him to show me to the small villa next door, used for her domestic staff. I tried to thank her, but she interrupted me: "When it is a matter of a child's health there can be no question. Everything has to be done."

The room was lovely, clean, on the northern, cool side, with a tiled floor, running water and electric light. I sent a telegram to mother, she arrived next day, I borrowed a cot for her from the senior camp, Elizabeth had her portable crib, a box or two made excellent shelves and a table, and an alcohol lamp warmed up food and bottles for Elizabeth. My mother was happy to spend entire days with her grandchild. She recovered quickly and greeted me with smiles and gurgles when I came up from camp to nurse her and bring my mother's meals. At night I could sleep on the floor next to Elizabeth and give her her night nursing. The epidemic in camp subsided, the children were well and having a good time. "All is well that ends well!" I thought, but, good heavens, how tired I was. Towards the end of the camp Nikita came to join us for his vacation. He slept in a shed and his good-natured and willing help with all the camp chores was a great relief.

In the fall of 1933 my work for the Student Christian Movement ended. It was depression time in America and the financial support given to the overseas work of the YMCA was greatly reduced. The big house on Boulevard Montparnasse was sold and most of the salaried staff discharged. The Russian Student Movement acquired a modest house in a working-class section of Paris (rue Olivier de Serres, Paris 15). It began to rely more heavily on volunteer work and I am glad to say that it prospered and continued its work until the seventies when it was instrumental in assisting the dissidents' movement in Russia.

I had to look for a new job to help our family budget and this meant relying on my shorthand, my typing and my knowledge of four languages. Oddly enough, German, the language I knew least well, produced my first job for me. I am afraid it was impossible for me to write long letters in German without making any mistakes, so my first two jobs folded in a few months. I realized that for a foreigner to keep a job at that time he had to be much better qualified than the available French employees, and to be willing to accept a lower salary. By now I was expecting again and had trouble with phlebitis, so I gratefully worked through the summer on a part-time job for a lonely Englishman struggling against his hopelessly alcoholic condition. Then on November 1, 1934, our second daughter Olga was born.

I never wanted those outside jobs, never felt the need to be "liberated" from my domestic ones. The need for them was strictly financial: if we wanted to have more than one child, I had to be a second breadwinner. I tried to find part-time jobs, but times were hard and I had to take what I found. As I think of those days I am amazed not only at my

energy, but also at my obstinacy. While I was still nursing
Olga, I took on a full-time office job, which meant leaving
early in the morning and coming back for lunch during the
long French two-hour break at noon. I would race home,
making a change on the subway, catch a train for Chaville,
run home, nurse Olga for twenty minutes while Aunt Mary
fed me my lunch, and then reverse the whole process, running
all the way. I rather doubt that my breast feeding of the baby
under such circumstances was doing her much good.

Then suddenly Elizabeth became very ill with a kidney
infection. I gave up my full-time job and found a part-time
one which enabled me to stay home in the mornings. After
a few weeks Elizabeth recovered completely and I kept my
job for over two years. My mother was failing now and she
needed constant nursing. Aunt Mary, alone after Granny's
death, moved to Viroflay. We were able to rent her a small
one-room apartment nearby and she spent most of her time
at our house, looking after the children during my absence.

Through these years Nikita's work, though not very rewarding financially, absorbed his interest entirely. Constantine Chilowsky, the man for whom he worked, was an inventor, and this suited Nikita's tastes and interests completely. Time did not exist for them. The more difficult the
problem, the more interesting it was to find a solution. There
was no such thing as giving up a project because it did not
work. It was just a matter of trying a little harder. Sometimes
I felt that they were, true to the Russian proverb, "spend a
dollar to buy a penny," but, of course, I was no inventor.
Their field was the new and absorbingly interesting realm of
electronics and they were both carried away.

We were by now drawing to the end of the first period
of our married life. Before we could begin a new and eventful period in our lives, we had to take leave of two of those
who were closest to us.

In the fall of 1936 our kindly family doctor suggested
that we consult a specialist for my mother's condition. Quite
unexpectedly the specialist's diagnosis was cancer of the
spleen, very much advanced. My mother made up her mind
not to undergo an operation, which had little chance of suc-

cess. She failed rather fast after that, but fortunately she did not experience the severe pain that can accompany cancer. Only three or four weeks before her death she had a painful attack and asked for morphine. Soon after Easter she began to sink fast. By the day of Pentecost she seemed unconscious when I bent over her: "It is Pentecost, Mother. You remember: "Thou art our God, who doest wonders!' " These words, sung during the feast of Pentecost, had a special meaning for her. She had used them in giving her blessing to her sons in times of danger. Suddenly her beautiful eyes opened wide and it seemed to me that they were full of light. She whispered several times: "Thou art our God, who doest wonders!"

Once a visitor came with an armful of roses from her garden, still wet with dew. Since the old days in Voltchy Mother was always passionately fond of roses, and as I bent over her, bringing the fragrance close to her face, her beautiful luminous eyes opened again and I heard her murmur: "How beautiful! Oh, how beautiful!"

The agony of our loved ones always seems endless. But at last Aunt Mary and I standing at her bedside, realized the end was coming. I took the prayer book and began reading aloud the prayers for the departure of a soul. Mother was still breathing when I came to the end and I continued to read from another section of the prayer book. When I came to the Easter hymn "Christ is risen from the dead trampling down death by death . . ." Aunt Mary stopped me. "It is over, she said.

According to mother's wish she was buried in the small local cemetery, not the big Russian one of Ste. Geneviève des Bois. "I'd like the children to be able to come and play at my grave, plant flowers, water them . . . It is such a long trip to Ste. Geneviève . . ." Elizabeth was brought to church for the funeral. I thought it was important for her to experience, however childishly, the beautiful and solemn ending to her grandmother's life. She was very quiet, but when she noticed that I was crying she hugged me.

Two days later, when I came into the nursery in the morning Elizabeth sat up in her cot and announced very cheerfully: "You know, Mommy, 'Baba' came to see me!!"

"Yes, darling," I replied in the calm way mothers use in reacting to the most unexpected announcements of their young ones. "She told me that she was very pleased with me because I behaved so well in church. And you know, she said that God has given her a very comfortable bed, so comfortable that nothing hurts her any more. It is funny; she looked so young, so young, so beautiful. She sat on my bed and worked on her embroidery." My mother's wish was granted: there was no dark fear in Elizabeth's mind connected with her first experience of death.

I grieved for my mother but her end was so peaceful, her life so fulfilled that there was no bitterness in my grief. She had loved and suffered and toiled and had accepted it all and now she was at rest. Aunt Mary came to live with us so there was no need to worry about how to provide for her. When all the bills connected with my mother's sickness and death were paid, there remained a small sum from her savings which allowed us to settle our debts, pressing and unpleasant, however small. The relief of knowing that the milkman and the grocer and the coalman are all paid up and we did not have to juggle with the "urgent" and "less urgent" payments at the end of each month was very great. With great pleasure I gave notice to the insurance agent for whom I was working and with a sigh of relief prepared to become a full time housemother. But this was obviously not to be my fate. Before I even stopped working, I was offered the job of a private secretary to the new continental manager of Universal Pictures Co. in the handsome and luxurious new office on the Champs Elysees. The job was a full-time one, but the salary was three times as much as I was earning with my German-Jewish refugee insurance agent.

"Do you think I *have* to accept it?" I asked Nikita as we were talking it over.

"Sonia, I am afraid we have no choice," Nikita answered somewhat sadly. "Fedor's (his brother in Canada) logging business has fallen through. He is bankrupt and we will have to take over the care of my mother and Yaroslav.

The long years of privation and overwork had taken their toll. Nikita's mother had tuberculosis in a rapidly progressing form. She refused to be hospitalized, but scrupulously observed precautions against spreading contagion. Yaroslav came to live with us and we were lucky to find an elderly Russian nurse who was willing to live with my mother-in-law in a little cottage not far from the Russian Home for the Aged at Ste. Geneviève des Bois near Paris.

During the last months of her life my mother-in-law could not absorb any solid food. She was too weak to move around. She lost the use of her voice. She could scarcely hear and was very nearsighted. And yet she still preserved her joyous nature. As she lay in the garden on her chaise-longue, she watched a couple of swallows building their nest in the eaves of a barn. "Is it not wonderful?" she whispered to me almost inaudibly. "Everything is so good, so wonderful!" She died peacefully two weeks after the birth of our third daughter Xenia in March 1939.

Now the older generation of our family had reached their quiet haven after the many tempests they had gone through. They must have learned all they were expected to learn and were spared going through the difficult years of World War II. Clouds were gathering on the world political horizon and the international situation was getting more and more threatening, but our small family had a particularly happy and peaceful summer in 1939. Our responsibilities were lighter than they had been for years. The rent for the little cottage where Nikita's mother had lived and died ran for another three months. The wonderful old nurse, Anna Petrovna, who had taken care of my mother-in-law, wanted to stay there as long as the house was at our disposal. She invited us to come there for the week-ends, and she would cook for us. The new social laws effective in France, introducing the forty-hour week, were still fresh and new, and every long week-end felt like a small vacation. I remember well the wonderful relaxation of waking up on those Saturday mornings, in the sunny cottage attic. Elizabeth and Olga played endless games in the closets of the practically unfurnished house. Xenia was always a good baby, enjoying life. The good smells of freshly made coffee, still warm bread, and flowers, came up from the dining room downstairs. Anna

Petrovna was a pre-revolutionary type of nanny and at her touch everything acquired an old-time charm and dignity. Every time we came, her kindness to us and to the children found new ways to show itself. Nikita, the children, and I went on endless hikes. We pushed the well-worn pram with the baby; seven-year-old Elizabeth and five-year-old Olga proudly rode their little bikes which we had bought at a junk sale of scrap metal and which Nikita's magic touch put in good repair. The garden contributed cherries, raspberries, gooseberries, and Anna Petrovna made wonderful jams and tarts.

We took our two weeks' vacation in Biarritz with Nikita's sister and her husband, the young priest Father Alexander Rehbinder, who were living there with their three children.

Then suddenly our euphoria was destroyed. On September 1, 1939, Germany attacked Poland. On September 3 Great Britain and France declared war on Germany.

CHAPTER SEVEN

I suppose thousands and thousands of families felt the way we did: we were tiny drops in the huge waves of a catastrophic upheaval. We would be thrown about, smashed or saved, and would have little choice in the matter. In facing tragic world events we would be quite helpless, but there we were, a family with old people and small children, and we had faith in the strength of the ties that held us together. We had trust. An old Frenchman told me later that as long as the tiniest drop of water does not give up its vision of the ocean, its faith in the ocean as its goal, and keeps saying to itself "Ocean! Ocean!" it will never get lost.

Russians, French and Germans at War, 1939-1943

In September 1939 we thought it would be best to get the children away from Paris and send them with Aunt Mary to my sister-in-law who lived in Biarritz. Unfortunately hundreds of thousands of Parisians had the same bright idea. We had no trouble taking our little electric train from Chaville to the Gare des Invalides. There we found that the whole city section around the Gare d'Austerlitz (southwestern direction) was crammed full with crowds trying to reach the station. All the streets leading to it were blocked, and neither pedestrians nor cars could get through. In the pitch dark of the first "black-out" babies yelled, mothers cried for lost children, people stumbled on bags and suitcases. For several hours we waited in the crowd hoping to get closer to the station.

We were a rather unwieldy group: seventy-year-old Aunt Mary with a bad knee, two small children and a six-month-old baby for me to carry. Nikita carried the bags. I remember that during that night, sitting on the suitcase, I gave Xenia her last breast feeding.

At last we decided to give up the attempt to get a train that night. We settled Aunt Mary and the children in a small hotel nearby and went out to investigate how things were shaping up. We learned that very early in the morning, trains would be formed at the large suburban station of Quai d'Orsay and would move from there to the Gare d'Austerlitz.

At five A.M. we woke up Aunt Mary and the children and took them on foot to the Quai d'Orsay. The huge crowds had dispersed, the station was practically empty and the railroad personnel really wonderful — orderly, disciplined and good-spirited. By ten A.M. we got the children on a train. There was some pushing and crowding there and four-year-old Olga was frightened and cried a little, but Elizabeth, at six, realized she was the eldest and tried to be as helpful as she could. Little Xenia on Aunt Mary's lap looked like a flower in the hot and dusty crowd.

Of course, we know now that this spontaneous evacuation from Paris was a false alarm. The "phony war" lasted for eight months. I went to Biarritz and brought the children back. My sister-in-law had taken the invasion of her home by us and several other families quite in her stride. She loved all the children, enjoyed their presence and was completely indifferent to the chaos it created.

Nikita's youngest brother Yaroslav and his cousin Nicholas Koulomzin were drafted into the French army. None of us had ever applied for French citizenship and we were so-called "stateless foreigners." The military status of our men was now being determined and it was decided that all those born after January 1, 1904, were subject to military draft. Luckily for us, Nikita was born on December 18, 1903, and was thirteen days too old. I think we were quite loyal to France and willing to accept our responsibilities, yet I must say that there was a certain unfairness in the attitude of the French Government and French administration towards foreigners. Nicholas came to France when he was eight years old, the only child of a widowed father. All his schooling was done in France; he completed his university studies at the Sorbonne, got an engineering degree, but when he began looking for work, he was refused his "working papers" because he was a foreigner. It was a hopeless legal vicious circle: in order to get a working permit he had to prove that he had a job; in order to get a job he had to have a permit. Nicholas was a very intelligent, gentle and unaggressive man. He solved the problem by giving private lessons and coaching students for exams, earning the barest minimum for his own needs, and those of his father. There was no hesitation nor loss of time, however, in having him drafted into the French army. He took it in good spirit, but poor Uncle Tolia, his father, felt pretty bitter. With Nicholas's departure Uncle Tolia came to live with us.

I was rather amused at another instance of discrimination against foreigners which very much upset a nice young French soldier. A distribution of gas masks for all children was announced for a certain day at the Chaville city hall. When we presented ourselves we were told that children of foreign residents were excluded. I pointed out that two members of our immediate family were in the French armed forces, but, it appeared, this had nothing to do with the distribution of gas masks. When we left one of the young soldiers who were assigned to handle the masks ran out after us and stopped us in the street: "Please, please, do not take this to heart. There will be other shipments coming and all children will receive masks!" I comforted him as best I could, for I did not take the matter very seriously. In fact the only use I ever found for the gas masks was putting one on while peeling and chopping onions. It was extremely effective, but Nikita got quite a shock when he came into the kitchen and saw my "snout."

The winter of 1939/40 went by peacefully and quite comfortably for us. Events were happening elsewhere — Poland, Finland, Norway. There was no need to worry about Nicholas and Yaroslav who came to see us on their monthly leaves.

The winter was an unusually snowy one, but we had no trouble keeping our house warm and the children loved sleighing and building a snow house.

Then our whole world collapsed. Belgium was attacked and surrendered on May 28. French radio broadcasts denounced the Belgian surrender as an "infamous treason." The Allied Forces retreated to the sea coast. The evacuation of Dunkirk took place on June 6. Next day the Germans attacked France. The famous, supposedly indestructible, "Maginot" line was passed by and attacked from the back, or simply ignored. In four days one third of France was occupied by the Germans. Italy declared war too. A chaotic, irrepressible mass movement of refugees was fleeing the German advance. All the roads were crowded. People went mostly on foot, loading their belongings on carts and baby carriages. The lucky ones rode bicycles. Cars drove slowly, delayed by the pedestrians. To protect themselves from low-flying planes they loaded mattresses on the car roofs. Trains, insofar as they still ran, were crowded beyond belief. Air raids were constant. The French armed forces seemed to be completely demoralized and offered no resistance. The roads were so blocked by the movement of refugees that troops were paralyzed. On June 10, 1940, the French Government declared Paris an open city that would not be defended. The Government left for Bordeaux. Germans were within two days' march from the capital.

In such times every separate family unit has to make its own decision, and carry out its plans. Both Nikita and I felt that at such a tragic time he should take part in the defense of the country we lived in. He discovered the location in Paris of an engineering unit, applied there as a volunteer, and was told to report next day. The American firm Universal Pictures, Inc., in which I was employed, decided to leave Paris for Bordeaux, and since my salary was now our only source of income I had no choice but to go with them. Olga and Elizabeth were already registered for a summer camp run by the Russian Student Christian Movement in the southwest of France, not far from Pau. The camp's departure was now advanced and they were to leave on June 11 or 12. We were able to get Aunt Mary and Xenia, now almost sixteen months old, included in their group ticket. Fortunately for us, the same railroad line served Bordeaux, Pau and Biarritz (the latter with a change of trains in Bordeaux). Thus our route was easy to plan: Olga and Elizabeth would continue with their group to Pau; Aunt Mary, Xenia and I would get off in Bordeaux, where I would put them on the train to Biarritz. Uncle Tolia refused to budge. He would stay in our house in Chaville and see what would happen. We left him all our food supplies to see him through.

This time we avoided the chaotic rush of our first exodus. For organized groups of children places were reserved on the trains, and at five A.M. under the guidance of a uniformed social worker, we were shepherded to a train on a sidetrack outside the station. Nikita saw us off and at that time we did not know when we would see him again.

The train journey was longer than usual and somewhat nervewracking, since trains were being shelled. Our compartment was getting more and more crowded so that finally there were eighteen of us, including a helpless old woman and a drooling imbecile boy of eighteen. They had all followed the roads on foot for days until they could board a train and squeeze themselves in.

Elizabeth and Olga were asleep when I kissed them goodby and left the train in Bordeaux. Leaving Aunt Mary and Xenia in the crowded waiting room I went to look for the office of Universal Pictures.

With all the government institutions evacuated to Bordeaux, the city was a sight: streets crowded with people, not a room to be had for love or money, everybody excited and nervous. People rang bells of private apartments asking for permission to use the toilet, to wash their face and hands, to comb their hair.

Our Universal Pictures group was fortunate in that we had an agency in Bordeaux and its employees offered to put up their colleagues from Paris in their homes. I was assigned to the one-room apartment of Madame Fort, a simple, barely literate woman who worked in the film repair workshop. Her common-law husband was in the army and she lived alone with her baby.

Aunt Mary and Xenia left, and the very same day, I believe, on the last train leaving Paris Nikita arrived! His effort to "do his bit" had fallen flat. When he reported at the indicated time to the barracks of the Military Engineering Corps, there was no trace of anyone. The entire unit, lock, stock and barrel, had dissolved and disappeared no one knew where. There was no work for him in Paris and he decided to join us. My address was given to him at the Universal Pictures office in Bordeaux. We thought the best thing for him would be to go to Biarritz and take Xenia as much as possible off Aunt Mary's hands. Aunt Mary had been ill most of the winter and we were worrying about her getting too tired. It was wonderful to know that we were not separated for good and it made all the difference in the world to know that we were closer together to face whatever difficulties would come. Nikita left for Biarritz the same day.

That night Bordeaux experienced its first heavy bombing. No one had ever thought that military action would reach so far south and the city, crowded as it was, was not prepared for an air raid. There were only a very few public shelters, and the air raid wardens were not trained. At the sound of the alarm all the people in the big building where Madame Fort had her flat were herded into a long corridor on the ground floor. There we stood, in pitch dark, packed like sardines in a tin. The warden swore and slapped the hands of anyone who used a flashlight. At first all you could hear were babies crying, older children whimpering, people anxiously asking questions. Then the bombs began to fall, with the characteristic whistling sound followed by an explosion. Someone would look out into the street and announce: "That one hit No. 12, five houses away!" Then we listened with bated breath for the next whistle and the next explosion.

During the few air raids we experienced before we left Paris I thought that my fear was all for the children. If only they were safe, I thought, I would not be frightened. Now I realized how wrong I was! Then I had to remain calm for the children's sake. I had to make believe that everything was quite normal and even funny. In Chaville, which was not far from a military airport, we had only the shallow and damp basement of our small house to serve as a shelter.

Now I had to stand there, with nothing to do, alone in a crowd, in complete darkness, just listening to the sound of the bombs, trying to guess whether the next one was for us. Poor Madame Fort was in a terrible state. I began to comfort her as best I could and a woman standing nearby began to praise me for my courage. This one small compliment was enough for me to regain my spirits and overcome my fear. Next day crowds continued to roam around Bordeaux. A number of houses were destroyed. The dead and wounded were still being dug out from the piles of bricks and mortar. In comparison to later air raids in many cities, the damage was small, but it was a first and frightening experience. On the radio German broadcasts announced that next night the inhabitants of Bordeaux would learn what a really heavy air raid was like.

On Friday afternoon I was resting in one of the big Bordeaux churches. I did not want to impose my presence on Madame Fort during the day and there was nothing to do at the Universal office. As I left the church I suddenly heard someone calling me in Russian. Out of the window of a passing taxi three elderly faces were looking at me and gesturing frantically to catch my attention. It was Mr. Chilowsky, my husband's employer, his wife, and his sister.

Chilowsky was an old pre-World War I émigré from Russia. Though his milieu in France was mainly that of socialist exiles from Imperial Russia, his political interests had given way a long time ago to scientific work and inventions. Chilowsky was a strange man, very kind to people in need, yet quite impersonal and utterly absorbed in his own inventions, in his own trend of thought, to the complete exclusion of everything else. Working for Chilowsky suited Nikita perfectly; he had the same "inventor's mind," and the very process of solving technical problems absorbed him completely. I think it was not the practical result of their work that interested them most, but the process of solving difficulties.

At this time Chilowsky was working on an invention dealing with guided airplane bombs, somewhat similar to the guided missiles that were developed later. He was convinced that his invention was of great military importance, but he was never able to convince any authorities of this. Nikita thought that the practical value of his invention was far from certain.

The Chilowskys told me that in Paris they had hired a taxi with a Russian driver to take them to Bordeaux. They had arrived this morning and Chilowsky hoped to obtain from the French War Ministry a permit to leave France for North Africa on one of the boats that were being evacuated from Bayonne. Chilowsky realized that he might be unable to complete his work without Nikita's assistance. Finding me so unexpectedly in Bordeaux seemed a stroke of luck. He asked me to keep his sister company while he and his wife went to the ministry. I took his sister to the same big church where we could sit quietly and rest. Miss Chilowsky was a huge woman, old and pathetic. She always reminded me of an old elephant with her myopic small eyes, and her old skin hanging in little bags on her big frame. Now she was crushed by the events that had upset so completely the life and work of her beloved brother. "What will he do now?" she moaned gently. "How can he manage without Nikita? Who will carry our luggage if Nikita does not come? But how can your husband leave you and your children?" Dear Miss Chilowsky was the only one of the three who seemed to remember our existence.

Later that afternoon Mr. and Mrs. Chilowsky were back. He had obtained a permit to board a French Navy boat for himself, his wife, his sister and for Nikita alone, as his assistant, but not for Nikita's family.

"You were willing to let your husband enlist in the French army," Chilowsky said to me. "That would have meant your remaining alone with the children. Is it not the same now? My work is part of the war effort. You must let him go."

My thoughts were in a turmoil. If Chilowsky's work was really that important it might be Nikita's duty to leave us. But *was* it really important? Or was it one of his countless inventions that never worked out? Would Nikita be involved in an authentic war effort, or would it mean "carrying Chilowsky's luggage"?

"Nikita has to decide for himself," I answered. "I promise you that I will not try to influence him."

There is a small harbor in Bayonne a coastal town some 10 kilometers from Biarritz. The faithful Russian taxi driver from Paris agreed to drive the Chilowskys to Bayonne.

"Please come with us," Chilowsky asked me. "I am sure your husband will not consent to come with us unless he can see you first and take leave of you." Nothing held me back in Bordeaux for the week-end and I must admit that the German promise of a much heavier air raid for that night was not attractive either.

Off we went in the taxi to Bayonne. At first we threaded our way along endless lines of French military convoys loaded with ammunition and troops that were being evacuated. It was a somewhat uncomfortable proximity for they were certainly a very legitimate target for air attacks. Gradually our ways parted, however, and by the time it was getting dark we were rolling along country roads.

"I'll stop now," said the driver. "I've been driving for twenty-four hours and I must get some sleep." We all waited patiently while the poor man took a nap, his head resting on his hands folded on the steering wheel.

Dawn was breaking by the time we reached Bayonne. The Chilowskys remained there to look for the boat they were to board. I took a taxi to get to the Russian church in Biarritz. As we drove along the shady road we saw a detachment of Polish volunteers marching smartly, obviously making for the Spanish border. It was the only image of discipline, order, courage and decision that I saw during those days of chaos and fear. They were marching at full speed, in perfect formation, trying to reach their goal — not running away.

In Biarritz I managed to find Nikita. He was sleeping on the floor in the hall of the church building. I told him about Chilowsky's plans and that Chilowsky was waiting for him him in Bayonne. He was to leave next day.

By that time Nikita's sister Elizabeth joined us. Crouching down by Nikita's pad she spoke energetically: "Sonia may have promised not to try and influence you, but I have promised nothing. Nikita, you must not, you cannot abandon her and the children!" All day long the pros and the cons of the decision were discussed. Nikita went to see the Chilowsky's in Bayonne. The boat was to leave early next morning. He decided to go next morning again and make his final decision there.

Next morning was Sunday. Nikita left early and I did not know whether he would come back or not, so that our farewell was tentative. At ten A.M. I went upstairs to the church to attend the Divine Liturgy. What was keeping Nikita? The boat was supposed to leave early in the morning. Did he really leave? The service was drawing to its end. The Lord's Prayer was sung. Suddenly I saw Nikita entering the church. He went straight into the sanctuary, behind the icon screen. Normally Nikita is very shy and hates doing anything that attracts attention, but this time he asked Father Alexander, his brother-in-law, to hear his confession at this unusual time and then went up to receive Holy Communion. When he came back to me he whispered: "I have decided to stay." And in all the years to come he never expressed any hesitation or doubt about the rightness of his decision.

Some ten years later, we saw Chilowsky again, this time in the United States. Chilowsky told me then — very generously I thought — "I am glad Nikita stayed with you. Nothing worked out the way I thought and nothing came of my plans."

I believe that it was on the same day that Marshal Petain broadcasted his appeal to the French nation, announcing the armistice "in all honor." At that time Petain was still a figure of prestige for us, a hero of World War I. If he spoke thus, what could we, foreign residents in France, do but accept his decision?

By a lucky chance I was able to get back to Bordeaux by train, although railroads were closed to civilians. Everything was so disorganized that people were really not sure of any rules or regulations. It was very important for me to keep in touch with the Universal Pictures office. My salary there was our only source of income and I could not risk being cut away from my job. Now that I was sure that Nikita would not be separated from us, we could begin trying to reestablish our home. The first step was to get in touch with the children in the summer colony near Pau.

The armistice divided France into two zones, that "occupied" by the Germans and "free". Bordeaux and Biarritz were in the occupied zone and Pau in the free zone. There were no communications between the zones, so we were cut off from Eliabeth and Olga. The last letter I received from Elizabeth said:

"Dear Mummy, we are all right. Do not worry. We are both sick. When will you come? We are fine. Olga cries and asks for you. When will you come? We love you. Please come. Do not worry.

Your Elizabeth

P. S. Olga says, please come."

I did not know whether they were seriously sick or not. And with things as they were now, I did not know how long the Children's Summer Colony would remain open. I just knew that somehow we had to find the children and bring our family together again.

On Sunday morning I went to the little Russian Orthodox Church in Bordeaux. It was a modest, makeshift church in a large rented room, organized by a group of Russians settled in Bordeaux. It had paper ikons and all the decorations were made by the people themselves.

As I stood in this plain little church, I did not feel alone and lost. Aunt Mary, baby Xenia and Nikita must be attending Divine Liturgy in the Russian church in Biarritz, Elizabeth and Olga in the Children's Home chapel. I knew that something kept us all together, made us all one.

During the service I noticed a young man who certainly was not a member of this parish — a German soldier, in an airforce uniform. He must have been one of those who dropped bombs on us the other day, but there he was, praying, making the sign of the cross and when the priest came out with the chalice, he went up and received Holy Communion. When the service was over people surrounded him, asking questions. Yes, he was Orthodox; yes, his parents were Russians who had settled in Austria after the revolution. He was drafted into the German army. He found the address of the Russian church in the directory. This was his first chance to receive Holy Communion in a long time. So this "enemy" was part of that which kept us all together, made us all one.

Talking to people after church I learned that the Germans had set up a "Kommandatur" and this was the place where you could apply for any kind of permits — doctors to go out at night to visit the sick, bakers to deliver bread very early in the morning, permits to use cars, etc. Well, that was the place to begin my search for my children.

Early the next morning, I stood in a long line with some two hundred people in front of the "Kommandatur." A German soldier was walking up and down the line asking people what they wanted and giving them information. When he approached me, my knowledge of German came in handy. I told him that two of my children were in unoccupied France, that I wanted to find them and bring them home and that I needed a permit to take a train to Pau.

It is strange how much kindness you find when you can talk to people, get in touch with them. The German soldier told me he was father of a family, too. He took me out of the line, brought me into the building, spoke to an officer and in fifteen minutes I left with a signed and stamped permit that allowed me to take a train from Bordeaux to Pau and return. That very evening I took the train — the first one that went through.

We arrived in Pau at three o'clock in the morning and discovered that rules were even stricter in free France than in Bordeaux. No one was allowed in the streets before six o'clock in the morning and after nine o'clock at night. The station hall was crowded with people waiting for six o'clock so that they could leave the building. Most of them were French soldiers, returning home. But there were also quite a few families. One young mother held her hungry baby. She had no milk to give it. The baby's wailing went on and on, changing from screaming to whimpering and then back to screaming again. Everyone was tired and exhausted and at last one of the soldiers swore angrily about the "dirty brat." There was a chorus of indignation from the other soldiers: "You dirty brat yourself!" "Weren't you ever a kid?" "Shut up, you bastard!" I asked the young mother for the empty bottle. When I explained the situation, the guard at the station doors allowed me to cross the street and ask for warm milk in a coffee shop where someone was cleaning up. As peace and quiet reigned in the station hall, the baby hungrily sucked the bottle.

When we were allowed to leave the station I discovered several things of importance. There were no trains running from Pau to Bordeaux and the station was closed to passengers, only allowing those who arrived to get off the trains. No one was allowed to leave the city limits without a special permit and, of course, my German permit was of no use here. I discovered, too, that the children's home was some 20 miles beyond the city limits.

"All right, let's take one thing at a time," I thought. In talking to people, asking and listening, I finally discovered that there was still one bus that ran from Pau to occupied France. It had not yet been stopped because the Germans did not know about it. No one knew how long it would continue to run but I was able to get a ticket. Now I had 48 hours to find the children.

The problem of getting out of the city solved itself quite easily. A truck driver whom I asked to give me a lift told me he was delivering sand to a military airport outside the city gates. He crossed the checking post several times a day, so the soldiers did not stop him any more. "Let's hide your bag under the seat," he said. "We'll pretend you are my girl friend and that you are coming for the ride. I'm sure they'll let us pass."

In fifteen minutes we were over the hurdle. The truck driver was sorry he could not take me any further, but the airport was to the left and I had to take the road straight on.

Lots of people were on the move on the roads of France — people escaping Germans, returning home, looking for their

families — and in difficult times people are kind to each other.
I got several short lifts and did not have to walk all of the
twenty miles.

Around noon I saw the big building of the Children's
Home standing on a little hill and surrounded by fields. This
was it. Slowly I went up the steep path and drew near the
door. Suddenly I heard a piercing scream. "Mummy! Mummy!" and then the clatter of two pairs of feet racing,
tumbling down the stairs. I barely had time to drop my bag,
kneel down and stretch out my arms to catch the little girls.
"Mummy, Mummy! You are here . . . Mummy!" they sobbed.
I hugged and hugged them and could not help crying, too.
We were all so happy, so terribly happy.

Elizabeth and Olga had both been sick but they were both
well now. Yet the Home was crowded, the food very poor and
the children homesick. I told them that there were no trains
running just now but that I would get in touch with Daddy
as soon as I got back to Bordeaux. He would find a way to
fetch them and take them to Biarritz. I spent the whole day
with the children. At night I lay on the floor next to Elizabeth
and Olga, and very early in the morning, while they were still
sleeping, I started on my way back to Pau.

I was not worried about walking the twenty miles — I'd
probably get a lift. But how would I get into the city again?
I saw how soldiers were checking everyone and I had no
pass of any kind. Very soon I was offered a lift by two distin-
guished-looking elderly gentlemen. I mentioned that I had
visited my children and they did not ask any questions. On
and on we rolled towards Pau. In a half hour I could see the
striped wooden barrier across the road with soldiers standing
guard. My heart thumped, I clutched my hands, and said
nothing. A soldier stepped out. The car slowed down and
stopped. A soldier stretched out his hand. The older of the
two gentlemen drew out his wallet, and showed a pass. The
soldier stood at attention. "Oui, mon general!" he said and
saluted smartly. The car rolled on. I breathed deeply. Who
says there are no guardian angels? And why should not an
old French general play the part of a guardian angel?

That afternoon I called at the office of the woman who was

in charge of the Children's Home. Her advice to me was quite definite. "Do not leave the children at the Home," she said. "We have food enough for two days only, and I don't know what will happen then. We are trying to get all the parents to take the children back."

"But I have a ticket for just one person on the only bus that still runs between here and occupied France," I said. "And no one knows how many days it will be before this line is closed down."

"Coax the driver to accept the children. This bus goes down a road a mile away from the Children's Home. I'll send one of our senior boys on a bicycle there tonight and they will bring the children to the crossroads. Make sure the bus driver stops and picks them up."

I walked back across the city to the bus depot. I talked to the driver and he promised to stop at the agreed place. The bus was to leave at seven o'clock in the morning; the woman in charge of the Home told me it would pass at the crossroads near the Children's Home at eight. The children would be there.

I walked back to the Children's Home office, carefully measuring the time it took me: 45 minutes. That night I slept on a cot in the office. I willed myself to wake up at 5:30 to make sure to be in good time for the bus. But it was the third night that I had had very little sleep and when I woke up and looked at my wrist watch I saw that it was twenty minutes to seven . . . And the bus was leaving at seven!

It took me three minutes to dress and then I ran all the way that it had taken me 45 minutes to walk. I made it in twenty minutes. I was five minutes late, but the bus left ten minutes late anyway, so I made it.

I was still trying to catch my breath and being grateful for the small miracle of not missing the bus when I began to worry again. They told me that the bus would be at the crossroads where the children were to meet it at eight o'clock. It was seven twenty now and we had left the city already. It would not take us forty minutes to reach a place twenty miles away. This was the same road I had walked and driven along the day before and I began to recognize the landmarks. If only they would bring the children ahead of time! Perhaps they would realize that eight o'clock would be too late.

We were at the crossroads. The driver stopped and I got out. The side road stretched up-hill between vineyards. It was empty. The children were not there. Two French soldiers were hanging around, looking somewhat lost, as if they did not know what to do.

"My children are late! Can you wait for just a minute?" I asked the driver.

"Are you joking? And what about the other passengers? Of course, I cannot wait."

The man was right. What was I to do? Lose my job in Bordeaux if I did not return? Leave the children here? What would they feel when they finally came to the crossroads and I wasn't there?

I called to the two soldiers. I begged them to go up to the Children's Home at the top of the hill and find two little girls called Elizabeth and Olga and tell them that their father would come to fetch them. With a heavy heart I climbed into the bus. Grumbling, the driver shifted gears, the bus rolled.

And then, at the very top of the hill, I saw ... no, not the children, but the top of a plaid canvas bag, carried on the shoulders of a very tall man. The children's bag! They were coming, they were coming!

"Stop! Please stop! My children are there!" I shouted to the driver. But the other passengers were at the end of their patience. "What if we had to stop like that for every passenger?" "If you have children, then why do you leave them?" "Go ahead, driver!" At that moment I broke down and wept and begged: "Please, please stop! It will just take a minute!"

The driver stopped. I jumped out and ran up the road, shouting to the two soldiers, "Please, help me!" The French are never slow to understand and they did not stop to ask questions. They raced up the hill towards the tall young man and the two little girls. Each soldier snatched up one of them and they raced back. The young man with the canvas bag ran too. In a minute, breathless and somewhat tumbled about, we were all in the bus and it was rolling on, the passengers giving me dirty looks. I could not blame them, poor souls, each one of them nervous and worried on that uncertain, not quite lawful drive.

The trip lasted many hours and there was standing room only. Elizabeth, who always got carsick, found a place at the back, near an open window. I found space in front where I could stand on one knee and keep Olga seated. She was miserable with a bad toothache. From time to time I saw Elizabeth bend out of the window. Then she would give me a nod, her little jaw firmly set, as if to say: "It's all right. Don't worry."

We arrived safely in Bordeaux. I took Olga to a dentist. I took them both to a restaurant and it was a joy to see them attack the good food. Madame Fort put us all up for the night, and the three of us stretched out in her bed.

Next morning we took the train to Biarritz. The train journey was not very comforting. People told me frightening stories about new air raids by the English; Biarritz was in ruins. I felt depressed. With all these efforts have I brought the children into greater danger than before?

The stories were untrue. Biarritz was intact. There had been no air raids. My brother-in-law, the priest, and his wife and their children received us as warmly and as lovingly as ever into their home, over-crowded with all the strays and refugees they had already welcomed. I barely had time to wonder how they would manage to squeeze us in.

Now I heard familiar footsteps and the children shouted. "Daddy!" "Daddy!" I heard my husband's laugh, his voice saying, "Hold on! Hold on! We are not staying in the church house. Just wait and see!"

This was the last miracle that completed our adventure. A wealthy old lady, who owned a beautiful villa in Biarritz and lived there all alone with a staff of servants, was afraid the Germans would requisition her house for soldiers. She wanted to fill it and she invited us all to stay with her.

Half an hour later we were being shown to our rooms. Elizabeth and Olga had a beautiful room with a bathroom. My husband and I had an even more luxurious bedroom with a bathroom of its own. A maid with a flimsy white cap and apron was asking me whether the children preferred cocoa or milk, eggs or porridge for breakfast! It sounded like a fairy story.

The next two weeks turned out to be an unexpected vacation for all of us. The Universal Pictures office received instructions to return to Paris and since they did not want to get involved in paying employees for unused vacation time, we were all told to take two weeks vacation then and there. At the same time the French government announced that free railroad transportation home would be granted to all refugees displaced by current events. We stayed for two weeks in Biarritz and then returned to Chaville where we found Uncle Tolia unharmed and in good health. Quite soon his son Nicholas was discharged from the French army and joined our household too. Before the month of October was over, Universal Pictures decided to close down its offices in France and all the employees were dismissed.

The problem facing us now was to find some means of existence for our enlarged family of eight under one roof: Aunt Mary and Uncle Tolia both well over seventy, the three children and Nikita, Nicholas, and I, all jobless. In those early months of German occupation there seemed to be no way of finding jobs for our two men; all industry was at a complete standstill. When I asked my friend Sophie Zernov, who ran an employment agency and usually had no trouble providing me with secretarial jobs, she told me that there was only one kind of job available: working as an interpreter for German occupation forces. At the very moment she had a request for a German-speaking secretary from the German Kriegsmarine.

Frankly I had no choice. Eight mouths to feed, and no savings or resources of any kind, but I was rather unhappy at the prospect. Many White Russian émigrés tended at that time to be pro-German. I think they were influenced by years of a rather humiliating existence in France as "undesirable foreigners," as well as their sincere and strong anti-Communist feelings. During this first period of occupation, German military authorities were friendly to Russian émigrés. Nikita and I felt differently. We recognized National Socialism as an anti-Christian and evil power, especially its racial philosophy — the German "Uebermensch" wanting to rule the world and destroy the Jewish race. Also, the fact that my sister and brother lived in England and that so many of our close personal friends were on the other side made it impossible for us to accept the German cause. I took the job with a heavy heart. Nicholas resumed tutoring pupils in math, and Nikita used his imaginative talents to invent ways of earning money that unfortunately fell through, one after another. The most successful one was making soap. Local butchers gave him scraps of fat in exchange for half of the soap he made. Lye could still be had and from the old days of deprivation in Soviet Russia he remembered the recipe. Unfortunately shortage of fats brought this venture to a close.

The Kriegsmarine, where I got a job, occupied the ancient building of the French Ministère de la Marine on the Place de la Concorde, and the Department to which I was assigned was that of the "Werftbeauftragte" — the authority in charge of the work assigned to the French ship-building industry. My immediate boss was Korvettenkapitän Loenhold, who was to implement the construction of barges by small French firms destined for the transportation of troops and landing on beaches. All this was part of the famous project to invade England which bore the code name "Seelöwe" and was very soon scrapped because of some unsuccessful experiments which I believe cost the life of many German sailors.

There were two of us in the small cubicle assigned to interpreters, who were not supposed to have access to any other offices. My colleague Keller was a native of Alsace-Lorraine, and spoke French and German equally well. He was a well-educated, intelligent man, an architect by profession, married to a young German émigrée. The young Keller couple always remained something of a mystery to me. Keller was extremely kind and became a real friend, with a curious, almost nostalgic empathy for the kind of happy family life, family relations and family values which I took so much for granted. He was very generous with gifts of books for me and whatever food supplies he could find for the children. His wife, though a refugee, was not Jewish and identified herself quite easily with the German milieu of the occupation. I had at first the

impression that they really identified themselves with the
German cause. As time went on, however, and the German
victory turned to defeat, Keller became more and more frank
in his Communist sympathies. Whether he was a "collaborator," or a member of the resistance, or simply a climber or a
career man, I could never figure out. He left his job before
I did, brought wonderful farewell presents for the children
and me, and disappeared completely. By that time his wife
had had a baby. After the end of the war I tried to find the
Kellers, but they had left Paris. The "concierge" of the house
they had lived in told me they had had some trouble at the
time of liberation, but were now all right. Whatever his opinions, he was a thoughtful, kind man, open-minded to values
that were not familiar to him, and I keep him in grateful
memory.

The interpreters were quite carefully isolated from regular
administrative or office work. We had a small office of our
own and the German military or civilian staff members came
there when they needed help. We translated letters, documents
and reports from French into German and also acted as interpreters at meetings and interviews.

My first supervisor, Capt. Loenholdt, was a typical business-
man: super-active, aggressive, tense. There was no question
of stopping work because office hours were over. He was quite
frank and direct in his dealings with French shipyard owners:
"It is in your interest to work for us," he'd say. "If we win
the war, and I sincerely believe that we will, you will have
earned good money and established good contacts. If we lose
the war, which I hope we will not, you will have maintained
your boatyard in good working order and will have lost nothing." He was not inconsiderate of the people working
for him and when he learned that I had to take a train to get
home, he sent his personal driver to take me to the station
if he kept me working late. Like all the other Germans he was
anxious to buy for himself and his family all the good things
that were still so easily available in France (if one could afford
black-market prices). This got me into difficulties once, when
Loenholdt asked me to pick up boots he had ordered for his
wife and which would be ready during his absence. He gave

me quite a large amount of money to pay for them. On the day the boots were to be ready, I put the money in my handbag as I left home for the office. Rush-hour trains are always crowded and with the reduced war-time schedules it was a real fight to get on. In the struggle my handbag was snatched out of my grasp and, to my horror, disappeared as the train left.

Now I had a real problem on my hands. How on earth would I find the money to pay for the boots? We certainly had no such amounts available at home. Then, like so many other times, I thought of our old friend Paul Anderson, who was still in Paris, though his wife Margaret and the children had gone back to the United States. Paul willingly lent me the amount and I undertook to pay it back in monthly instalments. The story had an even better ending. Some three weeks later, as I was getting off the train in Chaville, our station master stopped me: "Have you lost anything recently?" he asked me. "Have I lost anything? Good heavens, yes, I should say so . . ." and I explained to him how my handbag had been wrenched off my hand. "Well, it was not stolen. It just fell out of the car door. We picked it up, but could not find your address in your bag. There was this card with your picture and your face seemed familiar, so I kept watching out for you." Nervously I pulled open the zipper of the inner compartment, and the money was all there. I was ready to embrace the station master, but I merely tipped him the amount of the first installment I had already paid Paul Anderson and he seemed quite satisfied. The whole incident seemed like a small miracle and I am mentioning it here because so many small miracles carried us through the difficult times we were facing.

And times were getting harder and harder. Our two major difficulties were lack of fuel and food shortages. It was a constant see-saw of either one or the other becoming unmanageable. The winter of 1940/41 was not as bad as that of next year, but we had not yet worked out ways and means of dealing with our troubles. Our little house had a central heating system, with the coal range in the kitchen serving as the source of heat. Coal was strictly rationed, barely enough to heat the stove a few days during the entire winter. Our attempt to keep the heating system going without coal, with the chips my husband gathered in the forest where trees were being felled, was a losing game. Radiators were barely warm and the chips disappeared faster than he could bring them in. Our rooms were getting colder and colder.

Poor Uncle Tolia was the one who suffered worst. Shivering, muffled in his overcoat, he spent days sitting close to the lukewarm stove. He just did not have the energy to go on. There seemed to be no future for Nicholas, no point to anything. Uncle Tolia was not really ill, but one night at dawn I heard Nicholas' frightened voice calling me: Uncle Tolia had died in his sleep.

Food was rationed and all staples like sugar, milk, meat, bread, fat, eggs, flour, macaroni, etc. were given in very small quantities. What we did not foresee that first year was that there would be a shortage of vegetables too — carrots, onions, potatoes.

It is against the background of these difficulties that I remember the many personal kindnesses that were shown to us by some of the Germans at the Kriegsmarine. I have already mentioned that I was not at all pro-German, but was very anti-Nazi and really unhappy about having to work there. But I always felt that it is impossible to come into contact with people, with individual human beings, and not to see them as such. For me, a person is a person, and not a little piece of a cause. A person is always interesting, always capable of goodness. I feel that it is part of the essence of Christian faith to see a breath of divinity in every human being. As I worked in this German military institution, that I basically considered an "enemy," little relationships of friendship, of sympathy, understanding, kindness and gratitude, compassion and appreciation began to weave into a kind of fabric that became part of life. I remember the strange feeling I experienced when a high ranking officer came into our interpreters' office to have me translate a letter. He began asking me personal questions: of whom did my family consist, was my husband working, how many children we had, what was our background in Russia. However matter-of-fact and noncommittal I tried to be, I felt that he was getting a picture in his mind of a human situation that somehow deeply touched him. This was very different from the kind of attitude I was used to on the part of one's employers. In a way I was touched by his being touched.

The secretaries, the girls, took me to their hearts. Most of them were considerably younger than I, and I suppose I was a kind of mother image to them, a symbol of something homey away from home. I could not help but have a sympathetic concern in their love affairs, their griefs and hopes, since news came quite frequently of brothers, lovers, and friends being lost in action.

The German military, and especially the German navy, was much less party-minded than civilian German institutions. My nonconformity did not irritate them; quite frequently they even sympathized with it. I remember a rather amusing dialogue I had with Herr Dure, an elderly Austrian engineer, uniformed but with silver braiding instead of the gold braiding worn by regular navy officers. The words "Heil Hitler!" were constantly used by everyone to say "good morning," or "good evening" or "goodbye." I made a point of never using the words, but this time, after chatting for a few minutes with old Herr Dure, of whom I was fond, quite unintentionally the words slipped out as I left the room. Instantly horrified, I clapped my hands to my mouth: "Oh, I did not want to say this!" Herr Dure gasped and almost fell back into his chair: "Frau Koulomzin, how can you? How can you say such a thing? It does not matter with me, you know . . . As a matter of fact, I rather like it . . ." Then suddenly the horror of what he had just said overwhelmed him. "Oh, I did not mean this! . . ." I laughed and left the room feeling it was wiser to drop the conversation. Poor Herr Dure was killed in action towards the end of the war.

Another typical incident happened in the spring of 1941. Part of the National Socialist program was encouraging comradely relationships between executives and the rank and file. With this purpose in mind, outdoor picnics were organized from time to time and attendance was compulsory. Even the interpreters had to attend. At the end of the day dinner was served in a hall with two long tables joined on one side by a short one. Our head, Admiral Kinzel, was sitting at the center of the short table and it happened that I was assigned the place just across the table from him. Admiral Kinzel was telling a joke to the few people within hearing distance, when the officer in charge, almost in the manner in which grace would be said at a church conference, proposed a toast in honor "of the glorious German army which, at this very moment, is victoriously overrunning Yugoslavia." Everyone stood up, lifted the right arm and shouted "Heil Hitler!" My arms remained glued to my sides, my mouth remained shut, and I remained seated. "Yugoslavia, Yugoslavia, my sister country! May God help you!" I mentally prayed. Chairs scraped everyone sat down, and Admiral Kinzel finished telling the joke without batting his eye.

Admiral Kinzel had a good sense of humor. At a later date, when all the German members of his staff were dining together as usual, word went round the table not to eat the éclairs (rather exceptionally served for dessert), but to send them to Mrs. Koulomzin's children. Admiral Kinzel announced firmly that he would not contribute his éclair, because "next thing, they will be sick, eating them all at once."

When operation "Seelöwe" was cancelled, Captain Loenholdt left for Germany. I did not know whether I would lose my job or be transferred to some other department, but at the request of Admiral Kinzel's chief of staff, Captain von Tirpitz, I remained assigned as translator and interpreter in their department.

Korvettenkapitän v. Tirpitz (Dr. v. Tirpitz in civilian life) was the son of Admiral Wolfgang v. Tirpitz, famous during World War I as the initiator of submarine warfare. In World War I he was a junior officer. The boat he sailed on was torpedoed and he was among the few survivors who was rescued from the sea and taken prisoner of war by the British. Winston Churchill, First Lord of the British Admiralty at that time, sent a telegram through the International Red Cross to Admiral v. Tirpitz that his son was safe, which is quite characteristic of the navy traditions of those days. Between the two world wars v. Tirpitz held a position in the German I. G. Farben Industry, travelled widely, spoke excellent French and English, and made friends in different countries. He was one of the most cultured men I had ever met. It is characteristic of his thoughts and feelings that his sons were prepared for confirmation by Pastor Niemöller, a former navy officer who was later imprisoned by Hitler. Tirpitz's brother-in-law, General v. Hassel, was involved in the so-called "generals' plot" against Hitler at the end of the war and was hanged as a traitor by the Nazis. To a certain degree v. Tirpitz had participated in the plot too. All of this I learned much later.

Tirpitz was a German patriot. The idea of Germany creating a kind of world "pax Romana" appealed to him, but for this very reason he felt grief and bitter resentment about everything that was being done and everything that was being destroyed by the Nazis. He possessed a somewhat old-world and knightly class-consciousness, but was certainly no snob in the vulgar sense of the word. His greatest quality was his interest and sensitivity to trends of thought, to spiritual values of other people, to anything that deepened one's understanding of life. I think this was how he became interested in an unknown and struggling Russian émigré interpreter in his office and why gradually we formed a strong personal friendship that lasted for more than twenty years and ended with his death. Tirpitz invited my husband and me to have dinner with him and Gerda Hüttner, his private secretary, also a member of an old naval family who became our good friend. We met at a French restaurant and spent a remarkable evening. All the conversation was in French since my husband spoke no German. We both were greatly impressed by Tirpitz's knowledge of Russian history, Russian culture and Russian political problems and charmed by his interest and courtesy.

After becoming officially assigned as interpreter to Admiral Kinzel's staff I became in a sense Tirpitz's subordinate, and my translation work was connected with the orders placed by the German Kriegsmarine to French shipyards. This included two specific tasks which allowed me to help people: granting permits to cross the boundary line between occupied France and the so-called Free France, and freeing from the work draft in Germany workmen of firms in which the Kriegsmarine was interested. From the point of view of German authorities these were very minor matters, but because of Tirpitz's attitude it allowed us to help many individuals, including Jews trying to escape. As a matter of fact in the case of a Jewish director of one of the French shipyards, Tirpitz, who had at one time obtained his release from prison, asked me to let the family know privately that he would be unable to protect the man in the future, but could still give him and his family a permit to cross over to free France. They all escaped safely.

In April 1941 our neighbor in Chaville, Monsieur Clement, a French reserve officer who, like my husband, had lost his job when France was occupied, found a small job with a provincial French road-building enterprise located in Bourges. Very generously, as soon as he became settled there, he persuaded his firm to hire Nikita, of all things as a German interpreter! Upon receipt of the telegram Nikita left immediately, with a German textbook under the arm, hoping to learn sufficient German during the train trip. Probably it would not have worked out on this basis, but fortunately his technical know-how and his good nature became so immediately useful that he was kept for good. This started a long period of separation for Nikita and me and I still have three thick folders of letters we exchanged from 1941-1943. These letters give a faithful impression of our life during the war years.

April 20, 1941

I am enclosing the children's Easter letter for you. It is too bad that you are missing all the services. We had a very unusual Easter night celebration, really funny. A few days ago Fräulein Gadow asked me whether she and her newest friend, the Admiral, Chief of Staff of the Kriegsmarine, could come to our Church and our home for Easter Night. The point was that at all Orthodox churches in Paris night services had been forbidden because of the curfew. One of our parishioners had the bright idea of bringing the German girl typist at the Chaville Kommandatur a dozen eggs and the dear girl (she

must have read some Russian novel about Easter night services) typed up "night passes" for every single member of
our parish. Our Chaville church was thus the only one with a
service during the night, the only one where an Admiral
could observe the "authentic thing!" I told Fräulein Gadow
that I had nothing against her friend's coming, but I could
not let a Russian chauffeur be drafted for Easter night to sit in
the car while the Admiral was breaking fast with us. All right,
she said, the chauffeur could share our meal. Aunt Mary and
I decided to take the three children for the Easter matins
service (from 12 at night until 1:30 A.M.). I could bring
them back, let them have their Easter breakfast and presents,
put them to bed and return myself to church for the Liturgy
and Holy Communion.

No sign of the Admiral as we started off to church, but
at the very beginning of the service, with our poor little church
crowded as it always is on Easter night, we heard a car drive
up and into the church walked Fräulein Gadow and the
Admiral in full uniform and regalia, his entire chest covered
with decorations. (When I came to the office on Monday
Fräulein Gadow told me that he was very much impressed
because his entrance caused no stir, no one turned round to
look at him. Good old Chaville Russians!) When I took the
children home, the admiral and Fräulein Gadow followed us,
and I invited the chauffeur to come in and they all joined in
our Easter spread, which was perhaps not as opulent as usual,
but quite good. The Admiral contributed a big box of choco-
lates. The children were so absorbed in their presents that they
were not at all impressed by his presence. Then it was
time for me to go back to church and I asked Elizabeth
(eight years old) to act as hostess. I don't know how long
the admiral stayed. All was quiet when I came home and
Aunt Mary and I broke fast. On Monday the office girls at
the Ministry were quite excited about the Admiral's visit.

April 25

I was a little depressed by the fact that both Elizabeth

and Olga have lost weight. I am making a tremendous effort to increase their rations. I have made an arrangement at the Catholic Foyer where I take my lunch to occasionally get two lunches to take home with me, and there is often a little meat in them. If you can possibly find any eggs or meat, do send them to us.

May 16

Last night Leshka (Olga, six years old) became upset about something, some little thing, and for a whole hour she cried and cried and could not calm down. I tried T.L.C., I tried speaking firmly, I tried to distract her — nothing helped. At last she seemed to be over it and ready to fall asleep, so I left her in her bed and went downstairs. Suddenly I heard Zishka calling me — she wanted to tell me something that Leshka should not hear. Leshka was sobbing again. On the landing, Elizabeth explained that Leshka is crying for two things and that she cannot tell me about the second thing, the sad thing, because "mama will be sad." I took Leshka out of bed, wrapped her up in her blanket and carried her into the bathroom where I tried again to calm her down. Gradually between sobs, I elucidated that, first, she does not want to go to school tomorrow, that she wants to stay the whole day in bed and I should *not* give her Xenia (two years old) to take care of. The second thing is that she heard that we were listening to the British news service and that she is so frightened, so frightened for Aunt Manichka (my sister and Leshka's godmother). She also added that she is hungry all the time, but she does not know "for what"; she wants something "juicy," but it's no use giving her anything because there is nothing at home of the kind she wants.

I decided to keep Leshka home for a week and I will try hard to get some fruit or berries for her . . .

May 19

I had a good weekend and everything went well. Saturday

afternoon at the village hall I got a "mother-of-three-children" priority card, so I brought home one hundred kg. of fire wood (the cart almost broke down at the doorstep), was able to order more at the woodcutter's and he promised to deliver it on Wednesday; went to church Saturday evening; bathed and washed the hair of all three girls. On Sunday morning, thanks to my priority card I was able to get some butter, six eggs, sardines and raisin-sugar. Went to church. Had old Parmanin for lunch with us (an old, sick and lonely man whom all the parishioners tried to feed in turn). Then I worked in the garden — planted beets and onions, built a cage for the rabbit where he spent the day (for the night we took him back because it began to rain and the children felt he was too young and might catch cold). My luck continued today; during lunch time because of my priority card I was able to get two half-pound packages of oatmeal.

The children have put on a little weight. I am glad.

I am so excited: Keller may, just may, get me a ticket for the one and only performance here of *Tristan und Isolde* of the Berlin Opera.

Aunt Mary went to see Dr. Lemmet. Her heart condition is not good and she has very high blood pressure; she is overworking, poor soul ...

The good weekend really boosted my morale. It is so easy to get depressed when everything is so unclear, so difficult to understand, even our immediate future.

May 30

I miss you so badly these days ... I really feel like "a goose in a fog" and it is so difficult for just "one half" of us to live alone, to make decisions, just as if you were breathing with only half of your lungs, and had only half a heart ... I get even more depressed when I think of all the endless millions of people who are now experiencing separation much worse than ours, so many broken homes, destroyed families, so much suffering, and all this huge ball of human suffering rushing on to some unknown future. One of the reasons my

bad mood is that I have not slept enough: many air-raid
alarms, Xenia unwell and sleepless, and I also had a small
translation that Tirpitz asked me to do at home — a quotation
from Goethe, so "compromising" that he did not want Keller
to see me doing it. I tried to do my best, polishing up my
French and going over it again and again.

We had a postcard from Yaroslav and he thinks that he
will be demobilized soon. We must think seriously of his future. If he gets no college education now, it means that he
will have no profession. What will he do? Think it all over.
We must write to Yaroslav and help him make the right
choice.

June 15

Thank you for your wonderful food parcel. Yesterday, on
Sunday, we had a real feast for our noonday meal — vegetables with bacon, strawberries with sour cream — all of which
you sent us. The day before I was able to get ten pounds of
oats that I can grind into flour on our coffee mill.

Though the Sunday was such a happy one I can't get rid
of my depression. I can't understand why I feel like that, why
I have a guilty feeling all the time. Is it because everything is
not all right with the way the children are growing up; is it
because we are separated from you, or is it just the horror of
everything that is happening in the world? Our faith is indeed weak and there is so little oil in our lamps . . .

At the end of June world events took another turn. On
June 22, 1941, Germany began war against Soviet Russia.
Many of the more pro-German White Russians welcomed
this event and saw in it the possible end of the Soviet regime.
Personally I never shared these feelings and felt that it was
a national war, that the aim of Germany was to conquer Russia and use it as a kind of stockpile of material riches to
build up Germany's strength. Under these circumstances
working in a German war institution seemed quite impossible
and I told Tirpitz that I wanted to resign. He persuaded me
not to do this right away, because such an action would com-

promise me to the point that I might be arrested. He argued
that none of the Germans at the Kriegsmarine would expect
me to share German feelings about this war, and that everything would be over in a few weeks anyway.

June 25, 1941

I guess the human capacity to digest events and settle
down is unlimited. Some things have become clearer. My
Germans are tactful. Those who know me less well talk about
the weather; those with whom I am closer bend over back-
wards to distinguish between "Russian" and "Communist."
In a sense it would probably be more difficult to talk to French
people in a French institution. Many Russian friends have
been arrested — Dourov, the headmaster of the Russian high
school, Th. Pianoff, Cyril Shevitch, and many, many others.
Probably, for the family's sake, I should not do anything
rash, especially when it is dictated by just acting the way I
feel. What do you think about it all? Perhaps, all by yourself, things seem clearer to you.

I must say I am rather comforted by the fact, that although
all our Russian people here vary in their opinions, you still
feel that their basic feeling is love for Russia, whether they
are willing to join the Germans as volunteers, or whether they
feel that this is impossible for them. I guess Tirpitz is right;
we are just drops in an ocean. We are all delivered into the
hands of the Living God, and we can only try and keep our
compass straight.

June 26

Mother's Day, and the children did all the little things
they were taught to do at school — brought little presents,
recited poetry, etc. After lunch I took them to a special program at the Maison des Enfants and when we came back,
and they started to play at home, I worked for two hours in
the garden and dug up two beds for potatoes. It rained at

first and when the sun came out, the earth steamed. It was so good — for my body and for my soul; the latter feels rather like a raw egg these days.

June 27

I am enclosing a "poem" Leshka wrote for me. Elizabeth had been taught a poem at school to recite to me on Mother's Day and Leshka, after going to bed, began going over it all in her mind and decided that she too would recite a poem. So she made one up — it took her an hour to do it — and then called me. With her shining, big "prune-eyes" she recited the following:

Sous mon village il y a l'eau qui coule
Dans tous les sens. Ça me fait rire —
Et quand je le dis à ma maman,
Ça la fait rire autant que moi.

Sur mon village il y a le soleil qui brille
Dans tous les sens et c'est le Bon Dieu
                              qui l'a fait briller.
Quand je fais ma priere je le dis a ma maman
Et elle la fait avec moi.

Under my village there is water running.
It runs everywhere and this makes me laugh.
When I say my prayers I tell this to Mother,
She laughs with me.

Over my village the sun is shining.
It shines everywhere and it's God who makes it shine.
When I say my prayers I tell this to Mother,
And she prays together with me.

June 30

The are passing around questionnaires for all Russians employed by Germans to sign. So the only topic of the day is "to sign or not to sign ..." On the first page you must indicate your name, address, profession, and to which part of Russia you would like to go back. On the reverse side there are two commitments: "I shall take part with all my strength in the fight of the German empire with Jewish Bolshevism" and "I shall carry out without questions in this struggle all the orders of the German National Socialist Party." And there are many who want to sign this!

I think we can consider that this will determine the question of my working here: I need not budge until they will require me to sign something like this.

The atmosphere is still rather tense. There are many more arrests among Russians. Bank accounts have been "frozen" so that Nicholas could not get his salary at the Russian high school.

And just now at the office, poor old Pfesdorff broke down completely and wept, his head on my desk. He received a letter from his son from the Russian front, written as the first shells of the battle began to explode. The boy wrote to say goodbye to him in case he never sees him again And the old man came to me, a Russian, to cry his heart out and I cried with him.

September 2

Poor Fräulein Huttner received the news that her young brother, 21 years old, is lost with his submarine in the Baltic Sea. Somehow death on a submarine seems worse than any other.

September 11

Quite urgent: I have to repair the children's shoes. I found a rubber strip in your drawer, but how do I glue it? Have you any rubber glue anywhere?

Elizabeth's namesday is on the 18th. Try and find something good to eat to send her. It will give her much pleasure.

September 15

Xenia is quite ill and unfortunately Dr. Lemmet is away on vacation. Though her temperature is not very high, she is very weak and indifferent to everything.

September 16

This morning Xenia is better. She asked for her doll, played with a flashlight, and swallowed a few spoonfuls at lunch.

September 18

Xenia's temperature went up again. Dr. Lemmet says she is in a generally run-down condition and does not fight the strep-throat infection she has. As soon as we get rid of the infection, we must build up her general condition.

She is so miserable . . . She won't eat, whimpers when we touch her, but every time we can get a spoonful of something down her throat, she perks up.

At the office, without my saying anything, Tirpitz told me to take a day off and I did it gladly.

Next day, at the office, there was a flood of kindly attention: old professor Noe arrived in the morning carrying a little package of biscuits for my children because he had heard they were sick. A sailor stopped me in the dark hall and slipped me a paper package with pieces of bread — leftovers from the mess table. "I remember how it was with us during World War I . . ." he whispered. Tirpitz brought ham from his last night's supper. The office girls discussed the situation

and decided to pick up leftovers from their table d'hote.
It is really terrible! But what can I do? And I have never
spoken to any of them of our difficulties.

September 25

Xenia is not getting any better. Little beads of sweat run
down her forehead even when she does not move and I have
to change her nighties frequently because they get soaking
wet. She does not sit up in bed. Dr. Lemmet says that if she
is not better tomorrow he would like to have another opinion.

Xenia did get better next day and from then on her recovery was steady. Dr. Lemmet was concerned about her lungs
and wanted X-rays to be taken at a good children's hospital
in Paris. Since her first bad relapse was caused by a very
fatiguing trip to see a specialist in Paris — by train, on foot,
in the subway — at the time when she was sick, I was wondering what to do. I think it is quite typical of the change in
human relationships and friendships that takes place in war-
time, that the director of a French firm solved the difficulty.
Mr. Gaston Bruneton drove all the way out to Chaville in
his car, picked up Xenia and me, spent the whole afternoon
with us at the children's hospital and brought us back in
the evening. Monsieur and Madame Bruneton became our
close friends and I often think with gratitude of them.

In January 1942 Nikita found a job in Paris and we re-
joiced at our reunion. But very shortly he was transferred by
his firm, "Société Française Radioelectrique," to their factory
in Cholet, Maine & Loire, some two hundred miles to the
west of Paris.

I was very much depressed by our new separation. Life
was getting more and more difficult. It was not only a matter
of food, but of fuel. How to keep our family, a rather vulnerable one with seventy-two-year-old Aunt Mary, constantly in
bad health, and three children under eight reasonably warm

and fed was almost more than I knew how to handle. Yaroslav was home from the army and enrolled at the École des Beaux Arts (School of Architecture) in Paris, but gentle, unpractical Yaroslav, fond as we were of him, was only another mouth to feed and never had Nikita's know-how in keeping a home running under difficult circumstances. Our tenth wedding anniversary was coming up in January and the fact that it had again to mark a separation discouraged me.

It was dark, cold and windy when I saw Nikita off to the station. A cold spell was starting and the biggest problem was not to let the house freeze. My letters to Nikita reflected my depression.

January 15

The first forty-eight hours after you left were frightening because the temperature in the house was falling rapidly and I just could not guess how far it would drop, and how bearable it would be. Now it has settled: on the first floor it is less than 30°F., and the water in the toilet is frozen solid. Upstairs, on the landing and in the bathroom, on the coldest days it is 44° in the children's room, and 49—50° in Aunt Mary's room. On less cold days it is about 5° warmer everywhere — in other words the temperature is quite O.K. in the rooms where we spend most of our time. I sleep quite comfortably downstairs putting hot water bottles in the bed. We have received our January coal ration and are all right for two weeks. I'll do my best to get some wood before the two weeks are over. We put Yaroslav's drafting table in the nursery so that he could work at night without disturbing Aunt Mary. We transferred the kitchen to the upstairs bathroom, so it all looks rather like an East End slum but it saves time and work.

January 17

. . . Coming home from the office found them all in pitch dark and smoke filled rooms. Replaced plugs and cleaned out the stove pipe and all was fine, but darling Aunt Mary was convinced I had performed a miracle . . .

January 19

Yesterday it thawed and the house became damp and even more cold and it dripped everywhere. The stove, like a bad-tempered wife, would not be coaxed to draw properly, then suddenly at ten P.M. it began to roar and radiate heat as if it had never caused any trouble and all the family sat exhausted around it.

All food except carrots has disappeared from the market, but we have a little stock of rutabaga turnips.

January 20

Have not quite mastered our stove yet. Last night I made a kind of paste of our garden soil (since they say it has a lot of clay) and filled all the cracks.

January 21

The cold wave continues. I learned to clean the stove pipe with one of Xenia's old nursing bottle brushes and my clay patches hold well: the stove roars and burns anything — green wood, old shoe soles, etc. Hans says he will give us coal if we can take care of the transportation ourselves. In a week's time there will be nothing at all to heat our stove and then the whole house will freeze and how will Aunt Mary and Xenia stand it?

But we have also received "comfort." Father John brought me a bag of four kilos of flour as his thanks for the evening passes I was able to obtain for all our parishioners to attend Christmas night service. Our bin was almost empty and now it is full again!

January 23

The cold wave has made things more difficult and water is frozen solid even in the upstairs bathroom. When I turn on the gas ring we can bring the temperature in the children's room up to 43°, but on the first floor it is several degrees below freezing point. I have enough coal until tomorrow.

January 31 (our tenth wedding anniversary)
Saturday

Came home for lunch and the table was laid with a white cloth and flower decorations. I spent the afternoon with the children and organized a big bath and hair washing for them.

They did *not* bring the coal. The truck went to fetch it, but the coal that was made available was coal dust, and without bags, so the truck could not transport it.

But that same day I received a special letter from Nikita that cheered me up a lot:

"I almost laughed when I received your letter written for our anniversary — we wrote exactly the same thing. We are really more together than we have ever been. You write about our wedding day and the sermon Father Sergius preached. To tell the truth I don't remember a word of it; probably if you had asked me on the very same day I would not have noticed anything, I was so scared. But I do remember another detail. When I put on the morning coat I had borrowed for the day, I discovered the pants had no buttons for my suspenders and I had no belt. So I came to the wedding with my pants tied up with a piece of rope! And I guess this was a prophetic symbol! I guess the way of life is a way of labor and need. As if to comfort you, when I opened the Gospel today, I fell on the account of the five thousand people fed by five loaves, so I guess that even if our budget doesn't work out it doesn't matter too much, for even worse budgets have been completed by the grace of God.

These days I have been thinking a lot about our life together — beginning with the lessons when we were children,
the balloons, our meeting in Moscow and then in Saint Juan
les-Pins, the Gare d'Orsay with all the camp luggage, and
all our life with all its difficulties. If you knew how grateful
I am to you and how I love you . . . And when we are separated I feel it all even more than when we are together . . ."

February
Sunday

In the day time I had to attend a tea party given by the
new Admiral Lietzman for all the staff, including the interpreters. It was funny to experience the contrast between our
unheated house, with our anxieties about getting or not getting some rutabaga, and the elegant tea in a Paris hotel, with
uniformed waiters serving "petits fours" and cups of real
tea with cream and sugar. You know, the question came to
my mind, "What is the real thing? What is reality? Our slum
home or this hotel? And where and what is the "new Europe"
they speak about? My own feeling is that "reality" is that
which does not depend on this external environment, is that
which can change from one set of circumstances into another
without being possessed by them. It was really funny to go
through this experience. And in addition to it, there was the
most beautiful musical program — Mozart's clavecin concerto
and Beethoven's Ninth in a beautiful Japanese recording. I
really have never heard such a good recording; it was as if
you were listening to the original orchestra. Let's go to a
concert when you come home next.
The coal has to be delivered tomorrow or Monday.

It was not. But finally, after several postponements
we received it on February 2. I wrote:
Tuesday, February 3. I simply cannot tell you what a
relief it is. It is beautiful coal; it burns slowly and smoothly,
is heavy and greasy. Unfortunately one ton looks an awfully

small pile and though I used up two pails to heat up our central heating system, and the air in the house did become less cellar-like, we still could not bring the temperature to more than 39°. We are all agreed not to attempt to heat the downstairs.

We are sharing the coal (not very generously) with Madame Leprêtre, and the little old Frenchwoman next door, whom the children call "Aia."

We are looking forward so much to your next visit. There are so many things to be repaired and arranged for a better and more efficient use of our precious coal.

February 17

You cannot imagine how we enjoy all the improvements you made during your visit: The kitchen is dry and warm and although the cold wave continues the upper floor is warm and comfortable, and, best of all, requires much less effort and work.

With the battle won in the "war against cold," the food situation worsened. Quite unexpectedly all vegetables disappeared from markets and stores. It was no more a matter of missing proteins and fats and sugar, but just absence of plain "stuffing" food. I spent hours shopping after work and came home with a jar of olives and a tin of sardines. How does one cook dinner for six with that? We had not expected that things like carrots and turnips and potatoes would disappear and had not made stocks. Again and again, just as it seemed to me that a dead end was reached, help always came — a friend would bring a few pounds of carrots; my sailor friend slipped me some pieces of bread wrapped up in a newspaper.

It was really "charity," "alms" in the true sense of the word (from the Greek "eleos" — compassion), the kind that enriches both the giver and the receiver.

Though Xenia was too young to attend the little private school where Zishka and Leshka went daily, the headmistress agreed to enroll her, so that she could get the daily school lunch. And then Nikita's job in Cholet proved to be a godsend. I wonder how we would have lived through this difficult time without his help. Almost every day after his working hours he got on his sturdy bicycle and visited farms in the vicinity of Cholet. Gradually he established friendly relations for there were often things out of order — especially radios that would not work — and Nikita was a wizard at repairing things. To show their appreciation farmers gave or sold him butter, eggs, home-made cheeses, sausages, potatoes, carrots, occasionally a rabbit or a chicken and even bread. Gradually he worked out a schedule of sending us food parcels by mail, and every time he came to visit us he was loaded with all the foodstuff he could carry. This too was tricky, for measures were taken against "black-marketing" and passengers were carefully checked and searched at the big stations in Paris. Nikita discovered that by getting off in Versailles, where there were no such controls, he could take a small suburban train to Chaville and reach home safely with all his relief supplies. In addition to his regular "food-hunt," Nikita had a plot assigned to him in the communal vegetable garden of his factory. Good as he is at everything mechanical or technical, he hates gardening, but, conscientiously, he spent hours and hours planting potatoes, carrots and beans, lugging water from quite a distance, hoeing, weeding and struggling with pests.

My letters to Nikita, besides reflecting the daily struggle for food and fuel and the growing discomfort of air raids, speak of many human contacts that deepen and expand in times of trouble:

February 19

Had a very interesting lunch at the Brunetons to meet their son-in-law who just returned from a German prisoner-of-war camp. He is more typically French than they. They are descendants of Huguenots, idealistic and optimistic French Protestants, while he is a real "Gaulois" with a sharp and caustic mind and an arrogance of manner. He does not idealize possible Franco-German relations, though he is not fanatically anti-German. I got carried away and invited them all to visit us, but now I am really at a loss on how to receive them. It will be interesting to talk to them some more — funny, how our friendships with the French have deepened — the Clements, the Pasquiers, and now the Brunetons and the Chevalliers.

February 28

Tania Ossorguin told me about a Russian engineer who went to Russia as an interpreter for the German authorities at one of the big power stations. His relationships with the Russian employees were good. The engineering staff impressed him as being better educated technically than he was himself, but culturally on a much lower level. The workmen on the other hand impressed him by the far higher cultural level than that of working men before the Revolution. They all treated him in a very friendly way and would bring him gifts of potatoes or lard. The Germans seemingly did not like his good relations with the local people, and after a month's time sent him back to France, paying him quite well. He asked the local Russians before leaving what message they would like him to give the other Russian émigrés. The answer was: "Let all those who are Russian come here as soon as they can . . ."

She also told me of the terrible conditions in the camps for the Russian prisoners of war — starvation and ill treatment. I think and think about it and nothing, neither thoughts, nor feeling, nor even prayer can help one to digest this. This morning, as I was crossing the Place de la Concorde, on my way to the office, just as the sun was rising — it is my best thinking time of the day — I was so full of bitterness for the Germans. But then I came to my desk, opened the drawer and there was the bread brought by my sailor. Somehow it is all so symbolic of the illogical confusion and tangle of our time. Where is hate and where is love?

April 17

Yesterday morning Tirpitz received the news that his middle son, whose eighteenth birthday they just celebrated, was killed. He was on his first submarine trip, just out of naval school, and it was actually an accident while the U-boat was in dock. Just the night before Tirpitz had invited me to dinner and talked to me about his family and especially about the two older sons and how impossible it was to open their eyes to truth when the boys are facing death, to make them realize that they are giving their lives for something that is all false. It is all so terrible and there is nothing, nothing one can do to help a man who has "fallen into the hand of the Living God." He can only go through the agony by himself, bear his own cross and we can only pray for him.

April 18

Bad news after bad news . . . Andrei Meyendorff is dead. A notice in the newspaper says he got lost in the desert and died poisoned by the too salty water. I do not even know whether his parents know of this. What is happening in this world of ours that so many of the best, of the young, have to lose their lives? We are desperately trying to get some details.

Why do we have to be separated, Nikitushka; when will we all be together again? It is so hard to go through all this by oneself.

At the beginning of the war my brother Iuri was in Estonia and his last letter was received by me in Bordeaux. He was a French citizen and the French Consul wanted him to leave Estonia because of the possibility that Soviet forces would occupy it. Like many other émigrés Iuri was too optimistic. He was hoping for changes in Russia and decided to stay. For more than a year we had no news from him. Then I heard of a Russian interpreter who was attached to the

German military forces and was going to Estonia. Through my cousin, who knew him well, I asked him to try and find out what happened. On his return he told my cousin (he said he hated giving such news to the families directly), that during the first night after Soviet troops occupied Tartu, where Iuri was at the time, all the Russian émigrés were arrested, placed on freight trains with the chalked inscription "volunteers for war work" and shipped into Soviet Russia.

As a matter of fact this was the very last we ever heard about Iuri, but at the time it did not seem quite so hopeless.

May 4

Imagine it, I have received some more news about Iuri. Some time ago I met a Mrs. Spechinsky and she writes me now that she met a woman who was being questioned by the GPU in Narva, Estonia. During the questioning a man entered and asked what answer he had to give to a woman inquiring about Shidlovsky. The investigator answered carelessly: "Just tell her he's been shot and she will leave you in peace." This may mean anything, of course . . . I know, I am absolutely sure, that even if Iuri did not always know how to live, he would know how to die. I am not so much afraid of death for him, but what if he was exiled, imprisoned, sent to a labor camp and is now suffering somewhere. We are all so scattered that we would not know how to gather our bones together . . . I feel almost guilty that you and I are so happy. My life is so filled with you, with the children, that my childhood friendship with Iuri has somehow been pushed aside. It is difficult for me to explain to you how much our friendship meant to us both, how we knew and understood each other. He was always such a complicated person; his whole life was complicated and now this . . . And we don't know whether his life is over or whether he is still suffering.

May 5

I keep thinking about Iuri and remembering all our life

together with him. I have little hope that he is still alive, that we might see him again. Last night I was looking at our three sleeping children and remembered Iuri's and my nursery and how little we thought of the possibility of living through the things we've lived through. I wonder what life will give our little ones.

June 10

A rather funny incident happened at the office. They were talking of introducing work on Sundays and you can imagine that my reaction was not enthusiastic. A German, and an SS-man at that, began arguing with me: "I'll explain to you why we have to accept this," he said. "You want us to win the war?" Dead silence on my part. "But you want us to win the war, don't you?" I take a deep breath and plunge: "I don't know." "How can you say this? You are working for us, aren't you?" "Well, do you think that every workman who works in a Ford automobile factory supports capitalism?" "But you want a new social world created, don't you?" "Well, I know what kind of world we lived in and we were pretty free and happy. How can I know what kind of a world will be created now, if Germany wins the war?" The poor man was deeply disgusted. Leaving the room he turned back, however, and said: "At least I cannot deny your frankness . . ."

May 3

There are more and more people in the streets wearing the yellow stars that the Germans require Jews to wear on armbands. Reactions are quite interesting. I was lining up before a store where some food was being sold. An old man with a star approached and *the whole line* stepped aside to let him pass.

During the summer of 1942 the persecution of Jews became much worse. As far as I know the French authorities tried to protect French Jews at the price of delivering to the Germans all foreign Jews living in France. This affected many Russian Jews. One day mass arrests were carried out and women and children were brought to the huge stadium called the Velodrome d'Hive. I was told that the sound of children crying and women calling was heard in all the adjoining streets Many French nurses volunteered to distribute food and look after the sick.

July 21

This morning I told Tirpitz about what was taking place in town. He reacted the way I would expect him to react and this did not surprise me. But two hours later I got a call from old Professor Noe, asking me to come to his office and help with a translation. When I came in he asked me to sit down and then said: "Will you please tell me what you told Kapitän v. Tirpitz this morning?" So the same sad story was told again. "It is terrible," said the old man, "to have lived and worked for Germany all my life, and then to learn to be ashamed of it. What has it become? . . ." He clutched his head and had tears in his eyes. He kept repeating, "If this can be done to Jews they will now think it can be done to any human being. But where is God? How can God bear such things being done?"

Tirpitz came to my office early this morning while I was still alone to get more details.

August 3

A rather funny incident took place today. It started when the owner of a small French building firm came complaining that almost half his workmen were being sent to work in Germany. Since he was working on some orders received from the German Kriegsmarine, his workmen should have been exempt from the draft. The papers relating to this matter were on the desk of one of the superior Navy officers, but unless something was done immediately the men would be shipped to Germany at the end of the week. Acting as interpreter, I was able to explain the situation to the Admiral. He showed a stack of correspondence a foot high lying on his desk. "If I look up your protegé now, someone else's request will remain unanswered that much longer..." he said rather reasonably, but still he did take note of the name and promised to call someone up. Then more of his precious time was used up as he began talking to me, trying to explain and defend what was being done. As usual, I could not help talking back. "I can understand your mistrust of capitalism, your concern for the welfare of the German people. But I cannot understand your attitude to the Jews. It seems to violate everything on which human culture and civilization is founded." He said something that sounded rather like an admission that many Germans were finding it difficult to accept what was being done.

The really funny consequence took place at lunch time. We have only one elevator, which can take up some twenty people, so that at rush hours you sometimes have to wait a while. I was standing in the crowd waiting for the next ride up, when the same admiral appeared. All the Germans, duly disciplined, stepped aside to let him through without waiting. Suddenly the Admiral saw me, a wretched civilian, standing behind the military staff, waved his hand to make me come forward, and with a most elaborately courteous gesture let me take the elevator first. I wonder what all the others thought; I wonder what a curious process went on in the Admiral's head, and what our conversation had to do with it.

October 1

You know, I've had a rather good thought: if we look at things *as a whole*, we really feel despair and everything looks quite hopeless, just a totality of horror. But if we look at every human life individually, at every individual suffering and grief, why then you can really see in it God's care and love. There *is* suffering, but this suffering does not deprive every

individual human being of God's love. I am not sure this
sounds very logical, but I really feel it.

Apart from efforts to supply food to his family Nikita was
facing another problem, another decision. During the first
months of the rapid German advance in the east, large areas
of Russia came out from underneath the Soviet rule and
were now administered by Germans. A number of White
Russian émigrés were employed there by Germans as interpreters. German firms began to hire Russian émigré technicians and engineers to work in the plants and factories in
Russia. Churches were reopened and priests allowed to serve.
All these Russians were sincerely motivated by their love for
Russia and an optimistic hope that they would be able to serve
her, Germans notwithstanding.

We began getting news from those of our friends who
went. Many of them established friendly relations with the
Soviet Russians — too friendly, in fact, from the German
point of view. Generally speaking their impressions could be
summarized quite simply: 1. To what a state the Soviets have
driven our people! 2. How terribly the Germans mishandle
the situation! 3. What a wonderful people today's Russians
are! 4. How hopelessly helpless we are to aid them in any
way! And still messages came back: come to us, help us.

Many of us wondered if the time had come for us to go
back, however difficult it might be, however hateful to do
it under German auspices. But would not a return to Russia
always be difficult? And was it not what we had been waiting
for for twenty years? Like others Nikita was asking himself
this question. We were living through a time when any moment you might have to make a difficult decision.

As time went on the measures taken by the German occu-
pying forces grew more and more harsh. Personally I
was particularly concerned with the case of Father Dimitri
Klepinin, who had sheltered escaping Jews. We had been
friends since the time when he was a student at the St. Sergius Russian Orthodox Seminary in Paris and came to our
summer camps as a church choir leader. Nikita knew him

since their childhood at the seashore in Odessa, when one day the Koulomzin dog chased the Klepinin cat right into the sea and the boys rescued it together. My friendship with Dimitri Klepinin went deep and influenced me strongly.

He was slight, short, very plain, not at all heroic-looking. He had a "potato-nose," uneven teeth, grey short-sighted eyes with a squint that peered through steel-rimmed spectacles. He had a wonderful sense of humor, he was simple, very humble and very kind, always interested in every person he met. And through this humble and humorous man, there shone a light of something that I cannot call anything but "holiness."

Dimitri graduated from the seminary in 1930, but seven years went by before he felt ready to become a priest. In 1939, on the eve of the war, he was appointed chaplain to the Home for the Unemployed, rue Lourmel, in Paris, organized by the very unusual nun Mother Mary.* He appeared in Lourmel in 1939, on the eve of war during a rainstorm, soaked but unconcerned. His green-blue eyes blinked short-sightedly at the formidable Mother Maria, a little uncertainly, too, for he was not an aggressive person. Neither Father Dimitri nor Mother Maria thought on that day that they would both die martyrs' deaths for a common cause.

Mother Maria became very active in the French Resistance Movement. It suited her love of danger, her energy. Father Dimitrii began his "mercy baptisms," at the same time. One day he entered Mother Maria's room in his usual self-effacing, sideways manner.

"What can I say to those people who come to me and say: "I must be baptized, Father, but I am not a believer," said Father Dimitri as if thinking aloud. "What shall I do?"

He hesitated a moment. Mother Maria did not speak. "I think Christ would give me that paper if I were in their place," he said quietly. "So I must do it."

Father Dimitri never baptized anyone who did not truly want to become a Christian. But he gave people baptismal certificates. Soon these ran into several dozen.

* The following information is taken from *The Rebel Nun* by Stratton Smith (Souvenir Press, London).

Father Dimitri's attitude to all that happened at this time was rather different from Mother Maria's. One day she read to him, with evident approval, a Resistance pamphlet, telling of how they would punish the people who helped the Germans. Father Dimitri said: "Dear God, what is all this talk of vengeance? Must we prolong this suffering forever?" Mother Maria flushed and said nothing. She felt it was a just reproof.

The overcrowding at Lourmel was terrible. An entire Jewish family was huddled in Father Dimitri's private room. On the days when there had been many arrests in the city the house at Lourmel was restless. Children sobbed fitfully, mothers wept for their lost husbands. Families were separated. Under the terrible physical strain, after many sleepless nights, Mother Maria's manner would become somewhat harsh. It was left to Father Dimitri to soothe the frightened people, to take their sorrow into his own heart. Many years later, the people who survived those dreadful days remembered Mother Maria with respect, but it was Father Dimitri whom they loved.

Father Dimitri and Mother Mary were arrested in February 1943. I immediately went to see Tamara, Father Dimitri's wife, to find out how I could help her. She was glad to let me take little Helen, their daughter, just slightly older than Xenia, to keep her out of the turmoil at rue Lourmel. Helen was a lovely child and we enjoyed having her for several weeks.

The German officer Hoffman, who examined Father Dimitri, was prepared to question the priest for a long time and was astonished when Father Dimitri told him frankly all he had done himself.

Hoffman said curtly: "And if we release you — will you promise never again to aid Jews?"

Dimitri's green-blue eyes looked fully at him. "I can say no such thing. I am a Christian, and must act as I must."

Hoffman stared at him in disbelief for a moment, then struck Dimitri across his face.

'Jew-lover!' screamed Hoffman. "How dare you talk of those pigs as being a Christian duty!"

The frail Dimitri recovered his balance. Still calm, he raised the Cross from his cassock and faced Hoffman with it. "Do you know this Jew?" he said quietly.

Two months later Father Dimitri, together with Mother Maria's son Iuri, was being transferred from their prison to a prison camp in Compiegne, France. His cassock torn and dirty, Father Dimitri was laughed at. To amuse a watching group of office girls, a German began pushing and hitting him, crying out "Jew! Jew!" Father Dimitri remained calm, but beside him, Iuri began to cry. Father Dimitri said gently: "Don't cry — remember that Jesus Christ had to bear much greater humiliations."

For almost a year Father Dimitri remained in the French camp. Then in January 1944 he and his friends were sent to the camp of Buchenwald in Germany. Two months later Father Dimitri was sent to the camp of Dora.

The frail Father Dimitri, who had been in normal health when he arrived at Dora, quickly grew weak. He could not carry out the work that was assigned to him. Some of his friends told the German foreman: "The priest is an old man; he cannot do this work." And indeed Father Dimitri looked old and unwell. But when the foreman asked him his age, he told the truth. "I am 39 years old," he said calmly and the man, angry because the prisoners had tried to deceive him, struck Father Dimitri.

Dimitri's forces continued to fail. He was dismissed from the work gang. He caught cold and ran a high fever. He was sent to the camp Death House. One of his friends was able to visit him there. He brought him the monthly letter-card on which he could write something to Tamara and his children. Father Dimitri stared at the card but wrote nothing. He was too weak. And he knew he was dying. That night he died. His friend survived to tell us the story of Father Dimitri's death.

With the beginning of 1943 Nikita and I began to think more and more of having our family leave Paris and join him in Cholet. Aunt Mary's health was failing, and willing as she was it was impossible for her to bear the burden of caring for the children and the household during my full-day absence at work, however much I tried to help her. Nikita's job seemed steady, and the possibility of his going to Russia disappeared with the failure of the German campaign. If we lived all together in Cholet my earnings would not be needed. The difficulty was that it seemed impossible to find any place to live there. However hard Nikita looked for a house, an apartment, or just a room or two, he was unable to find anything. Refugees from war areas crowded the small provincial town. At last a colleague of his agreed to let us use his apartment while he and his family went away on a three-week vacation in July. With this slender possibility in hand and very anxious about how everything would work out, I gave notice at the Kriegsmarine. Because I was a mother of three children I was not legally obliged to work and my resignation was accepted. I had no trouble finding a substitute.

We turned over our little house in Chaville to Tamara Klepinin and her two children. She accepted gladly, for the rue Lourmel home was closed. Aunt Mary was to remain with the Klepinins, who were very fond of her, until we could find something more stable in Cholet. Yaroslav would live with friends of his. I packed, cleaned house, tidied it up as best I could, and on July 1, 1943, the children and I took the train to Cholet.

CHAPTER EIGHT

Cholet is a small town in the Department of Maine et Loire, some two hundred miles to the southwest of Paris and fifty miles inland from the western coast. After the French Revolution Cholet was a center of the Vendée civil war, during which peasants and landowners fought in the name of their Catholic faith against the anti-church measures of the revolutionary government. They were called the "chouans" and the movement left a deep imprint on the people and the land. Old-fashioned patriotic songs were still popular at the time we lived there. The local Roman Catholic Church was vital and dynamic and the traditional piety of the people blended well with a strong social consciousness.

La Seguiniere, 1943-1945

It was a new experience for us to live in a small French provincial town, with its grey stone buildings, its narrow cobbled streets, its huge ancient cathedral and the quiet rhythm of its deep hourly chimes. I experienced a strange and rather peaceful feeling of loneliness; there was no Russian community, no daily job, no contacts with friends or foes, none of the intellectual stimulation of concerts, theatres, etc., which, poor as we were, we could afford in Paris. Nikita was away at work all day and the children and I took long walks discovering interesting places and mementoes of the Vendée war and, of course, looking for a place where we could live. Nikita's bicycle became our regular "means of public transportation." Elizabeth had her bike, and Nikita built a strong back seat with footrests for me. I would straddle it and hold

Xenia, while Olga perched in front on the handle bars. After two futile week-ends of driving around we at last rented a small one-room cottage in La Séguinière, a village four miles away from Cholet, which Nikita had originally rejected as unlivable. Nikita's factory was two miles outside Cholet on the other side of the town, so that it was within possible commutation distance by bike. It would do, we thought, for the summer, and if we did not find anything else by fall, we would have to return to Chaville.

There is no place in the world, I believe, where a Russian émigré can land without finding at least one other Russian. Thus we discovered in Cholet the Dimitrievs, father and daughter, who became our good friends. Vladimir Ivanovich Dimitriev, an officer of the Russian navy, was the last naval attaché to the Russian Imperial Embassy in France. His daughter's husband was prisoner of war in Germany. They were occasionally visited by his son George, who, as we found out much later, was very active in the French resistance movement. The Dimitrievs had deeper roots in France than we, and had made friends among the local landowners of the old French aristocracy, but we were very much of the same Russian background, so we discovered friends and relatives in common, spoke the same kind of language, and felt comfortable together.

Our last days in Cholet were spent under the sign of THE PIG! In his zeal to provide us with food Nikita bought a quarter of a pig, sharing it with a colleague. When one has to cut up the carcass, wash out the bowels, make endless "blood sausages," cook tripe, make "head cheese," render lard, all in addition to cooking all the meat thoroughly to put it up in glass jars, and when one has no experience of all this, it is a lot of work. And, of course, it is well-known that pork has to be cooked very, very thoroughly to be safe. It was difficult to get jars, it was almost impossible to get the rubber rings to seal them hermetically; this caused delays and some of the stuff had to be cooked all over again. We were having hot July weather, the apartment was small and unfamiliar and the whole undertaking became something of a nightmare. We were very happy to finally move to La Séguinière on July 22, with all our luggage, and all our cooked and still uncooked remainders of the pig.

La Séguinière was a small village stretched along one street that climbed up a steep hillside. At the bottom of the hill flowed a gurgling, shallow little river where the villagers did their laundry. Somewhat higher along the street stood the shoe factory, a stone building several centuries old. This factory was the mainstay of the village economy because the tops of the shoes were sewn by the village women at home. You could hear the whirring of the special sewing machines in almost every house. Some fifty people were employed at the factory itself.

Halfway up the hill one came to the village square where stood the big stone church, parts of which went back to the fifteenth century, the village hall with the mayor's office, and the village inn with the usual "bistro" on the ground floor. The street then climbed up and up until it finally ended in a fork where a big stone crucifix, in the shade of a huge parasol pine tree overlooked the whole village. All around stretched fields, meadows and vineyards, up and down hillocks and dales. It was a picturesque, peaceful landscape, not magnificent but somehow comforting in its changeless character.

Our cottage was the very last one. It stood behind the crucifix, along the road that flattened out there. Thick stone walls, a tiled roof, only one small window with a two-foot thick windowsill. The date above the door said 1795. The cottage had only one large, low room, with an uneven brick floor and a huge fireplace. An additional closet-like room with no door was tacked on in a corner. The large room had two small doors opening directly out to the street and to the vineyard behind the house. In summer they let in some sunshine. There was no electricity, no plumbing, no stove, no toilet. Water was drawn from a well in the vineyard right behind the cottage. There was some furniture — a heavy wooden table, two or three chairs with woven seats, three large wooden bed frames without springs or mattresses and a huge cupboard. A crawl-space of a cellar and an attic, where some old hay was still stored, completed our new residence. And we loved it, we loved our little fairy-story cottage that put our way of life several centuries back. We were young enough to feel confident that we would make it clean and comfortable. We were all together, we were happy.

Our rent began, as is usual in France, on July 15. We spent one weekend cleaning the house and making it as comfortable as we could. In a small pond nearby we washed and then dried out in the sun three huge canvas bags we found in the house and then stuffed them as tight as we could with fresh straw we bought at a nearby farm. We put them on heavy wooden bars placed across the bed frames and now had three double beds ready. The brick floor was easy to wash by throwing pails and pails of fresh water on it and sweeping the water out with a home made broom through a special hole near the door. The walls had been recently white-washed. We bought 20 bundles of faggot-wood — every year the trees along the road were heavily pruned and the branches, tied up in bundles called faggots, were sold for firewood. The following week we moved in.

Saturday, July 24th was Olga's namesday and we decided to celebrate by making a long bicycle hike to a picturesque region some 8 miles away from Cholet. We rented an additional bicycle for me, Elizabeth rode hers, Nikita had Olga on the back seat and our lunch in a basket on his handle bars. I took four-year-old Xenia on my back seat. Xenia asked me to stop and let her off. Trying to stop on a downgrade hill and jump off while the bike carried Xenia's additional weight proved beyond my skill and the front edge of the saddle hit me sharply in the pelvis. The pain was so strong that I realized I must been rather badly hurt, but it seemed a pity to spoil the children's outing when we were almost there. I insisted that we continue and Nikita took Xenia as a second passenger on his bike.

At the picnic site I just lay flat, hoping a couple of hours' rest would enable me to ride back. But the pains were getting worse and when it was time to go home I was completely unable to get on my bike.

Nikita went looking for help, and in about half an hour came back with a good-natured farmer driving a big horse-drawn wooden cart on two wheels. The peasant was willing to take us to La Séguinière for an appropriate fee. The sheer pain of the two-hour trip made me sick and feverish, but at last we were home. A doctor came to see me, and diagnosed a rather bad internal hemorrhage. He said I would have to stay flat on my back for two weeks.

The next ten days were hard on everybody. Our nice neighbor, Mère Jeannette, drew us a pail of water from the well twice a day, for I was afraid to let the children handle the heavy pail at the deep stone well, which they had never done before. According to La Séguinière standards two pails of water a day were more than plenty for a family of five. Ten-year-old Elizabeth would have managed simple cooking on a gas range, but we had to learn to cook at an open fireplace, to hang up the heavy iron pot on a hook above the flames, and adroitly to use for the more delicate cooking the red-hot charcoal left when the flames died down. We solved the problem by my dragging myself on my back from the bed to the fireplace where the children propped me up with the bags containing our laundry and brought me all the things I needed. And on top of all this there was THE PIG! Quantities of it still had to be cooked and put away in glass jars. This was Nikita's job in the evenings. The July heat, the smell of cooking, the flies, the discomfort and pain — all of this I remembered for a long time.

Everything has an end and things began to improve. I started to hobble around with a cane, doubled up like an old witch. Nikita built us a little outhouse against the wall of the cottage and it was a great boost to family morale. Actually it was only a semblance of a real outhouse, for a pail had to be emptied daily, for which a hole had to be dug every time somewhere beyond the vineyard. As I grew stronger this became one of my daily chores.

La Séguinière began to sprout little shoots of friendliness towards us. In my experience this small Catholic village was the most charitable, the most Christian community I had ever known. I appreciated it all the more because I realized that we were truly strangers for them and did not fit into any familiar social pattern — and social patterns were strongly crystallized in France. We spoke Russian to each other, we

236 MANY WORLDS: A RUSSIAN LIFE

were not Roman Catholic, Nikita was an engineer in a well known French firm, but we were obviously very poor and our tastes and requirements were very different from the village ones. When the villagers discovered that I spoke German, they often asked me to help them in their dealing with German authorities, but was not all of this rather suspicious? As time went on I realized that very probably we could not find better housing because we were suspect, for places where we were turned down as possible lodgers were later rented to French refugees.

Our first visitor was Monsieur le Curé, who brought us a present of a couple of fish freshly caught in the brook. He invited us heartily to attend Mass in his church and we said that we certainly intended to attend regularly, but could not partake of the Sacrament because we were Orthodox. He scratched his head and said he would have to take a look at his old seminary textbooks about the Orthodox church for he had not heard of it since seminary days.

Then came a nice young woman inviting the two older girls to join the local Catholic junior youth group for their summer activities. Unobtrusively she looked at the children's feet — they wore sandals with wooden soles — and said they would need leather shoes for the hikes. She could help us get them at the shoe factory.

There were two primary schools at the village. One was run by the nuns, and all the village children attended it. The other one was a state school with two teachers but the only children attending it were the postman's, who felt that since he was a civil servant, he had to support the state school.

Not far from La Sèguiniére was the manor of the Count de Terné. It was an ancient, square, low box of a stone building, surrounding a grass-grown yard, with remnants of a moat around it. At a little distance from the house was a grove of tall old trees that looked as if they had been part of a park. There were no woods around La Séguinière and, not realizing that this was private property, I went there once with the children for a walk. We were sitting in a shady place and I was reading aloud to the children, when we suddenly saw Count de Terné, a man in his forties, approaching us on his way to the manor. I realized then that we must be trespassing and got up excusing myself.

"You are welcome to walk anywhere you want and enjoy anything you like," he said. The children stood up too and Count de Terné lifted Elizabeth's chin with his finger. "Quels beaux yeux francs!" he said looking into her face.

The de Ternés had 12 children and were obviously hard up. No village girl would stay long as domestic help in their home, because the food was so poor, but every time a village woman gave birth to a baby, Countess de Terné would visit her bringing a traditional gift of bed sheets — good old hand-woven sheets from the family stock. Whenever money was being raised for an athletic field for the village young people or an improvement of some kind, the count's name stood first on the list of contributors. Later on, when Aunt Mary joined us, one of the de Terné girls or the mother would drop in to bring us fresh fruit from their garden or books from their library. In our fanatical determination to give our children the best education we could, we rented a small upright piano in Cholet, which was brought to our primitive cottage in an ox-cart, amidst dogs' barking and all the village children's excitement. The de Ternés had no piano in their manor and Countess de Terné asked our permission to have her daughter come to us to practice.

Another pillar of the La Séguinière society was Monsieur le Maire, the village mayor, a plump little fellow, whose round belly wrapped in a tricolor sash was to be seen at all official occasions. I particularly admired him at the occasion of the harvest feast towards the end of our two-years' stay at La Séguinière. All the threshing was done by one machine, moved from farm to farm, with all the farmers doing the work together and the farm family providing the food and the refreshments. When the turn came to the very last farm of the season, a celebration took place to mark the end of the harvest and the mayor always attended it. The girls from the participating farms were drafted to pass around the local red wine to the men while they carried on their dusty and thirsty work. One of them was supposed to offer the mayor a bouquet of flowers. Twelve-year-old Elizabeth was very proud that

she had been invited to help too, but could not quite understand why the older giggling girls pushed her forward to
offer the flowers to the mayor. The chubby mayor was in top
form: he accepted the flowers, kissed Elizabeth on both
cheeks (this was the reason the other girls did not want to
present the bouquet) and then made a wonderful French
political speech: he spoke of the joy of the first post-war
harvest in their village, of the traditional Franco-Russian
friendship, symbolized by a little Russian girl offering flowers
to him, the French mayor of a French village. He spoke of
their hopes for a peaceful future. Certainly Monsieur le Maire
always saw his village within the framework of world events.

Thus the little world of La Séguinière stood firmly on its
three pillars — Monsieur le Curé, Monsieur le Comte and
Monsieur le Maire, all three united in their devotion to it.
Gradually we learned to fit into the village way of life. One
of the first difficulties we had to overcome was our lack of
experience in living without some kind of garbage collection
or removal. I learned all food remnants went to the household
animals — chickens, a pig, rabbits, etc. Wood was burnt, any
kind of paper carefully saved to be used in the toilet. The real
trouble was shortage of paper. The only newspaper was published twice a week on a half-sheet of paper. The only other
steady source of paper was the children's school notebooks
written in deep violet ink. Use was found for most of the
broken things. We gradually learned to make sure that no
garbage accumulated near the cottage.

I also had to learn to do my laundry. In France the traditional way of washing clothes consisted of three steps: first
you scrubbed and hand-washed every piece of washing with
soap, then you boiled all the washing in a big galvanized con-
tainer with a double bottom and a tube going up to the top
with a mushroom-shaped shower head (somewhat like a coffee percolator). For an hour or so the boiling water went
again and again through the washing. Then you rinsed your
wash out, theoretically in clean, running water. And it was
this last step that stumped me at La Séguinière. Generally
speaking I preferred to wait for rainy weather and do the
rinsing in a tiny, even if somewhat muddy, pond close to our

cottage. In winter I had to break the ice on the pool first, but this was not too bad since the washing I rinsed was still hot from boiling. Hanging it up in freezing wind was much worse. I must admit that to my great envy all the village women got their wash snow white — much better than I ever did. Of course, there was also the trouble of having no soap, but in this we were better off than most people because Nikita knew how to make soap. I dumped all the cold ashes from our fireplace into an old kettle, poured water over it and let it stand for a few days. The water dissolved and absorbed the potash contained in the ashes. I poured it off, boiled it to make the solution stronger, added quicklime and then Nikita boiled it with the fat. The result was a jelly-like brown soap that he hardened by adding salt and then drying it out in bars.

Cooking on a fire in an open fireplace was not too difficult. From scouting days of my youth in Estonia I was pretty good at building and managing fires and, of course, you can bring a large kettle to boil much more quickly on an open fire than on a gas ring. The more demanding art was doing the delicate cooking on the charcoal one accumulated from the open fire place. Our best friend, Madame Champion, at whose farm we daily took our milk, was an excellent cook and made her wonderful "crême renversée" and "crêpes" on charcoal. She taught me how to use properly the local small round brazier and I even managed to bake my Easter cakes ("kulich") this way. In order to bake something you cover the red-hot charcoal in the brazier with a layer of ashes, put on your pan, cover it with a metal tray and heap red-hot charcoal on the tray. Your pan thus becomes a small oven, but the whole trick is to be able to maintain your charcoal at the right temperature, not too hot and not too cool, and keep it even.

The biggest and most important achievement was Nikita's, who provided our home with electric light. We would not have minded the lack of electricity so much if it had not been that it was impossible to get candles or oil for a lamp. The only light we had at first was that of our fireplace, and this is not much for six people to read, write, or work in the evenings. Nikita undertook to build us a wind generator. With no other tools than his pocket knife he whittled a five-foot long propeller from a $6' \times 1\frac{1}{2}'$ board. He fixed it on a ten-foot mast on the roof of our cottage, added a tail that made the propeller turn with the wind, and joined the propeller by means of old bicycle chains to a car generator. We had no trouble getting the latter in a garage, since so many people could not use their cars because of the gas rationing. The generator charged a car battery and this provided us with two small lamps of the type used inside a car, as well as with an old-fashioned radio-set with ear phones. Our wind generator served us faithfully for two years. As a matter of fact, towards the very end of the war, when there was no electricity in the village, neighbors came to us to get the news broadcast by the BBC about the landing and advance of the allied troops. Our radio was the only one that worked.

The only trouble with the wind generator was that La Séguinière, only fifty miles inland from the ocean, was a very windy place and our generator was not a very solid one. The first time it broke down was when Nikita was away, on a stormy, blustery day, with the wind growing steadily stronger. Up on the roof the propeller roared, the roof quivered, our little lamps gave out light as brilliant as 100 watt bulbs, and all the wires crackled. It did not last long. A stronger gust tore off the propeller and scattered its splinters all over the vine-yard, but we were glad to have the frightening racket stop. Undaunted Nikita whittled a new propeller, built a strong brake, and we were all right for several months. But in late spring in 1944, again at a time when Nikita was away on an overnight trip, we had another windstorm. By that time I was some three months pregnant with our fourth child. Again the brake failed and the whole house was shaking, the lights flashing, the wires crackling. Something had to be done immediately and we were short of such elementary things in those days! There was not a piece of solid rope in our household. I collected and tied together all the children's belts and climbed up on the roof. Then I climbed up a few crossbars we had fixed on the mast for this very purpose. The propeller roared above my head and I knew it could kill me right then and there if I were careless and climbed too high. Terrified, the children ran indoors and, at Aunt Mary's suggestion, began to pray that nothing would happen to me and the coming baby. I made a loop of the belts, threw it over the propeller's tail and turned the whole terrifying contraption against the wind. As by a stroke of magic the roaring stopped and the propeller was motionless, but I was still helpless. With one hand I held on to the mast; with the other I was holding the belts that kept the propeller-tail out of the wind. How could I tie it up solidly without a third hand? At this moment a most undesirable helper made his appearance on the roof — our neighbor, Père Ferdinand, well and legitimately in his cups on the Sunday afternoon. Reeling and weaving an unsteady path on the roof, happy and relaxed, he began telling me what to do: "Let it go, Madame Koulomzin, let it go! There is no wind any more... I'll fix it... Don't you worry, I'll fix it... Let go of it, Madame Koulomzin, I tell you, let go..." I was really worried; "Père Ferdinand, get off the roof, please do! I cannot let go. The wind has not stopped. Get off, will you! What will Madame Allard say if she sees you here?"

The mention of his wife seemed to impress him and at last he safely climbed down. By that time Elizabeth had run to the village carpenter, much lower down along the street, and asked for his help. He came with his 17-year-old son and a strong rope. The boy climbed up the mast and tied up the motionless propeller in a safe position. Then we all got down to our room and had a good glass of wine to comfort us all, Père Ferdinand joining gladly. I admit I felt very shaky and ever since then have had a nervous dislike of strong winds, which I used to enjoy before.

In the fall of 1943 we had to make up our mind whether we could stay in La Séguinière for the winter or should return to Chaville. By that time the allied air raids were at their high point and our home in Chaville was close to a military airport. The food situation was getting worse. With the general deterioration of the German situation their policy in occupied territories became harsher and harsher. In comparison to all this our difficulties in La Séguinière did not seem to matter too much. Our housing was very primitive, but we had enough plain and wholesome food — bread, milk, eggs, butter, vegetables, occasionally meat. We decided to stay. Aunt Mary came to join us; and Nikita and I rented an attic for us to sleep in a few houses down the street. It was unheated, of course, and had no furniture except one double bed, but we did not need more. I made a trip to Chaville and brought back all the things that could make our life more comfortable: a deck chair for Aunt Mary, our portable iron wood-burning stove, warm clothes, all the blankets I could round up, pots and pans and, finally, a big round flat tin tub for our ablutions. I believe that this last object caused the biggest sensation in the village. I kept up the principle of daily baths for the children with the help of our laundry tub. It took me only a few minutes to heat the water and the three of them took their bath in it one after another. (It was a moral satisfaction for me when the visiting school nurse told me my children were the only one to have a clean skin below their collars.) I washed when and how I could, but Nikita and Aunt Mary both were fanatics of daily top-to-bottom washing, so every evening when we went to our attic Nikita carried the tin tub hooked on his shoulder, like a Roman shield. In the morning, in the icy cold of our attic, he took his spartan "bath" and then brought it back to the cottage, which we kept warm, where Aunt Mary's ablutions could be performed with hot water.

All three children began to attend the village school run by the nuns. They felt happy there and very soon adapted to all the local mannerisms and habits. On weekdays they would clatter down the village street in their "sabots" and the French black school aprons that looked like dresses, warm scarves tied round the neck, since overcoats were strictly for Sunday use. When it was very cold they would carry a "chaufferette" to school — a wooden box-like contraption with a handle, into which you put a clay pot with red-hot charcoal. It is used as a footstool, with the feet placed on the slatted top.

On Sundays, dolled up in our best, we attended High Mass in the village church. Maybe this helped us to feel accepted in the kindly community. Maybe good Christians are not narrow minded and they would have shown us as much friendliness if we never attended church, but I must say that during the twenty-four years of life in France I never felt as warmly at home as I did in La Séguinière.

There was no Orthodox church anywhere close. We discovered however that several Russian families lived in Angers, a fairly large city sixty miles to the north of Cholet and that they were visited once a month by a Russian priest, a former monk from Mount Athos, who celebrated Divine Liturgy for them in an old shed they had converted into a chapel. The round trip by train to Angers, including attending the Saturday night and Sunday morning services, was a thirty-six hour venture. We left Saturday morning, and spent the night at Angers in the home of a traditionally hospitable Russian family who welcomed all five of us whom they had never seen before as if we were long lost friends. After Divine Liturgy on Sunday morning we had dinner at their home, took the afternoon train to Cholet and, picking up our bicycles there, rode the remaining four miles home. We did this several times, but later when I carried our fourth child, Nikita did the whole trip on his bicycle taking one of the children with him.

Elizabeth's best friends were not at school but at La Billauderie, the farm where she went daily to fetch our milk. I too was very fond of the farmer and of his wife, Monsieur and Madame Champion. He had that excellent, thinking French mind that seems to be quite unique. I remember him coming back from the fields, slipping the heavy "sabots" off his earth-blackened feet and stretching comfortably in his tilted chair near the fire, his pipe well packed with home grown tobacco. What good conversations he kept up — about the war, about Germany, England, France, China, Japan, his hopes for the future, the lessons to be drawn from the past. His son was prisoner of war in Germany, working on a German farm and his letters were read over and over again. He was thinking too and getting new ideas for farming which he wanted to try upon his return. Madame Champion was his step-mother, for M. Champion's first wife had died early. She loved the boy with a real mother's love. All her prayers, all her devotions were centered on that one, desperate petition — "Let him come back safely! Keep him safe!" With her we

talked about religion, about our families, about prayer and
faith. I remember her saying once, "I like what you tell me
about your Orthodox faith. I think you have one thing that
is better than in our church — you do not haggle with the
Good Lord ("vous ne marchandez pas avec le Bon Dieu").
This gave me some food for thought.

Elizabeth spent all her free time at the Billauderie and
Madame Champion had a real affection for her.

Olga got quite absorbed in the Catholic junior youth movement and became popular there. I was rather amused when
she was assigned the role of the Virgin Mary in the tableaux
presented at Christmas time, probably because of her long
heavy hair and her large expressive eyes.

Xenia lived at La Séguinière through her fifth and sixth
birthdays. Her special friend was the rather snivelly little
grandson of Père Ferdinand called René. They played endlessly together. One day I overheard their conversation as they
played house together. "Wife, go fetch me a pail of water!"
ordered the little husband René. "I cannot," answered Xenia
primly, holding her hands on her stomach. "I am pregnant.
You go fetch the water yourself."

During our stay in La Séguinière a very unexpected encounter brought us suddenly face to face with Russians from
the new Russia, not the Russian émigrés among whom we
had been living for twenty years. Nikita heard that a group
of Russian prisoners of war was brought to Cholet by the
Germans for some kind of work. I was excited, of course,
and felt that I could not miss this occasion to meet young
people from my home country.

My knowledge of German served me well. I unearthed the
officer in charge of the prisoners, and obtained his permission
to visit the boys, for boys they were, most of them 19-20 years
old. I brought them little gifts — cigarettes, home-made
cookies. They received them with great dignity and good
manners, thanking me, but not opening the package in my
presence, never asking for anything and always trying to find
a small gift for me. They wore uniforms given them by the
Germans and at this stage of their imprisonment were satis-
factorily fed. The only thing they asked for was news, news,

NEWS... How was the war going on? Were the Germans retreating? We brought them Russian émigré newspapers and these they snatched eagerly.

For Easter Sunday 1944 I prepared a somewhat more elaborate gift — a basket of traditional Russian Easter food — a cake called "Kulich", a cheesecake "Paskha", dyed hard-boiled eggs. That day I had some difficulty getting in, because there had been trouble. The prisoners had refused to work on Easter Sunday. Finally I was allowed to get through. This time I had the children with me and as we entered the room we greeted our soldiers with the word "Christ is risen!" and they all answered unanimously "Indeed He is risen!" and all four of us went down the rows exchanging the traditional three-fold kiss. Later I asked if they would like the children to sing them an Easter hymn — personally I am completely tone-deaf and voiceless. They seemed eager to hear this and as the children sang, I saw one of the older ones nudging a boy who had remained seated: "Get up, this is a prayer!" I told them we would be going to a Russian church next week and would they like to have their names and the names of their relatives remembered at the Divine Liturgy. Only one of them, Sergei, knew what this meant and gave me his name. Later I learned that he was killed a few days later in an air-raid.

All these boys took their Soviet regime for granted, knew no other life, and were eager to have the Germans defeated and so be able to return home. One of them, Peter, did say that collectivization had been "too hard on the people," but he was sure that when the war would be over things would get better.

I am running a little ahead of events in order to complete the story of our friendship with the prisoners of war. Easter was in April, and D-Day, when the allied British and American forces landed in France, was on June 5 and 6. As the fighting moved inland, our particular part of the country, towards the western coast, remained outside the field of action. Our Russian prisoners felt time was ripe for their escape attempt. We learned all the details of their adventures from Peter, who became our special friend.

Peter and his friends dug a tunnel from their barracks to beyond the barbed wire surrounding the compound. The tunnel entrance was hidden under one of the beds, and the dirt was carefully scattered outside the building. When the tunnel was ready, they chose a dark night for their escape and cautiously, one by one, crawled out, having agreed on the place where they would wait for each other. When they all got out and gathered together, they realized that one was missing — the one who always kept a bit apart and said he did not want to go back to Russia. Then Peter did something that I always thought required a great deal of courage: he wen back, crawled all the way through the tunnel into their barracks to check that nothing had gone wrong with their comrade. But the missing one had already left some other way; he wanted to escape on his own. Peter crawled through the tunnel for the third time and joined the group.

From now on they separated into smaller groups of three or four and found their way on foot to the farms of the neighborhood. Peter's group was received kindly, fed and clothed as civilians. They were then sent on with a handwritten paper which Peter showed me: "These men are escaped Russian prisoners of war. We have done our duty as Frenchmen; we gave them food and clothes. You do yours." From farm to farm they were helped and protected and they did their best to show their gratitude by helping with the farmwork. When the Germans had left, Peter and another one came to see us. Answering my questions, Peter expained that they did not ask us for help when they escaped because they thought it might draw the Germans' attention to us.

Dear Peter... Our primitive poor cottage, our family life, for him stood for some kind of "beautiful life" he yearned for, a kind of romantic vision. He would stand leaning on the piano, while Elizabeth practiced her dull little exercises, watching her and listening and I felt that it all was making up a picture for him, and he loved being part of the picture. He told us about his grandfather "who had many, many very old books" and how he read aloud from them that a day would come "when man would be like a wolf to other men..." When he was hiding in the fields here, said Peter, he remembered these words. His grandmother was a "staritza," a highly respected old woman, and people came to ask for her advice and her blessing. The Soviet authorities arrested her. They did not ill-treat her, Peter said; they just did not let people come to her any more.

Months later representatives of Soviet authorities came to Cholet to round up Russian prisoners of war and repatriate them. Most of them went willingly because they had families at home. Some avoided repatriation and some returned with misgivings. Peter was optimistic: "Oh, they'll lock me up for a year or two, and then it will be all over." One of them, a junior officer, asked us to help him obtain a certificate from the French police that he had escaped from German imprisonment. Being made prisoner of war was considered by the Soviets military crime. After reading Solzhenitsyn's *Gulag Archipelago* I wondered what became of our friends.

We saw Peter just once more. He came to Cholet with a Soldiers' Choir organized at the Repatriation Camp, to raise money and get food supplies. A concert was announced and, of course, our whole family and the Dimitrievs turned up in full force, taking up almost a whole row of seats. We attracted some attention for we were the only ones to understand and laugh at the jokes and funny songs and, I guess, our reactions were more spontaneous. During the intermission, a lottery was drawn for some prize contributed to the cause and they asked for a volunteer to draw the lots. Without hesitation we proposed our five-year-old Xenia, who was then passed over the peoples' heads onto the stage and, beaming proudly, performed her task unabashed. It was only on the next day that we learned from the local newspaper that the concert was organized by the local Communist party!

The eventful year of 1944, which saw the liberation of France, was an important one for our small family too. We were waiting for the birth of our fourth child, and our only son Iuri, or George, was born on December 17, 1944. It was a peaceful period in our lives. Of course, our life was not easy, world events were terrible and even in our small world we felt its repercussions. Even in Cholet there were frequent air raids and from the Crucifix at the crossroads we watched the bombs falling and wondered whether Nikita's factory was hit. For some time we gave asylum to another friend in our small cottage, George Dimitriev, who had been arrested by the Germans, had escaped and was now trying to reach the allied-occupied territory. He spent a week with us since it was too dangerous for him to stay with his father and sister and we enjoyed his company a great deal. While Aunt Mary washed and dressed, he modestly turned his back to her; when he washed, always in the same tin tub, Aunt Mary turned her back on him.

My major concern was to round up the things I would need for the new baby. Almost six years had gone since Xenia was born and I had given away most of the baby things we had. With great effort, gradually, we got the essentials — a basket for a crib, a worn out sheet for diapers, unraveled wool from old sweaters to knit baby clothes. A mattress could be made out of husks, but there was not a blanket to spare in our household and we were short of warm clothes that might have been cut up. I learned that in La Séguinière they made quilted wool blankets for babies, so that it was only a matter of gathering the necessary material. During the summer, whenever I heard of sheep being shorn at a farm, I asked for a small quantity of wool. When I had enough, I washed and washed it over and over again in our pool, dried it in the sun, bleached it, combed and fluffed it. A kind old woman in the village agreed to make the blanket and she even contributed a piece of cloth to serve as lining. I still needed some pretty material to cover the blanket and this I got under rather unusual circumstances.

Battles never reached Cholet, but by the end of the summer we saw many German detachments retreating along country roads, trying to avoid being encircled. Means of transportation were lacking, and it was said that Germans requisitioned on their way any bicycles and handcarts they could find, even baby carriages. Men hid their bicycles in the vineyards, and one day I found Xenia carefully hiding her small tricycle.

One day a detachment of some twenty or thirty German soldiers, led by a young officer, went past our house, pushing their bikes up the steep road. Standing in the doorway of our cottage watching them, I heard the officer say: "If I could only get some bread . . . I'd give a month's pay for a piece of bread." He looked sick and exhausted and even younger than the other soldiers.

"I don't want your pay," I said in German, "but you are welcome to some bread." To the sick German officer my words seemed little short of a miracle.

"I am sick," he explained," and I cannot keep down any of our regular rations. I've had almost nothing to eat for days. If you could give me a little soup I'd be ever so grateful . . ."

Half an hour later the troop of German cyclists settled for the night at a farm on the outskirts of the village.

The sick German officer came into the house and quickly gulped down the soup I gave him. His eyes were feverish, he was frantic and seemed unable to stop talking. "I must get home, I must get home! My wife and babies were bombed out of their home in Berlin. They were sent to East Germany. Now the Russians are there . . . I must get to them, I must . . ."

He asked me whether the road to Saumur was still open or in the hands of allied troops. I hesitated because the only news we were getting at this time were the BBC broadcasts and listening to enemy broadcasts during the occupation meant serious trouble. He understood my hesitation.

"What does it matter now?" he said irritably. "I don't care what you listen to. I just want to know whether we have a chance to get through."

I told him what I knew and very sincerely wished him good luck in finding his family.

Then Eilzabeth and nine-year old Olga clattered in, in their wooden shoes, and said, "Mother, you know, there are two Russian soldiers with the Germans — Russian prisoners of war. They wear a different kind of uniform. They asked us to get them some wine. We'll run over to Madame Champion at La Billauderie. She'll let us have some for Russian prisoners of war."

An hour later we sat down to a very cheerful supper. The two Russians were Red Army soldiers, made prisoners by the Germans and brought to France to work for them. These two in particular had worked putting out fires caused by the allied bombings. They were both husky, cheerful fellows, who knew how "to land on their feet" and find their way in any difficult situation. Elizabeth and Olga came back laden with butter, bread and a bottle of wine. The two prisoners contributed eggs, and next morning Madame Baudry from the farm just a little above us on the road told us laughing that all the eggs had disappeared last night from the nests where the hens had laid them.

We sat down in front of the fireplace at our heavy well-scrubbed wooden table to a really good meal. Before beginning it we made the sign of the cross, as we always did. This impressed our two new friends. "Now, that's good," said the older one. "That's real good. You have not forgotten the old ways and your children have not forgotten them." And both men crossed themselves, looking pleased.

Next morning the Germans were leaving for good. Down the hill they rode on their bicycles, the two Russians at the rear. As they passed our house, one of the Russians jumped off his bicycle, ran up the steps and thrust a package into my aunt's hands. "Here, that's for the young mother," he said. "God bless you all!" and he was off.

We opened the package. There was a beautiful piece of white silk cloth in it, shinning white with a white design woven into the fabric. He must have picked it up in one of the bombed stores. I dyed it pale blue, and now the quilt for the baby was complete.

What happened to all of them? Did they reach their homes? Did the young officer find his family? God knows! But the old quilted blanket, well worn by now, is still with me and I often tell its story to my grandchildren.

Nikita's birthday is on December 18 and as a present for him I had asked the village carpenter to make a wooden box for his tools. He did not get this present on time, but a much better one instead. December 17 was a Sunday and we were busily getting our quarters ready for the baby who was to arrive in a week's time. It would not be possible any more for us to sleep in Cécile Payoux's attic, so we had to move the furniture in the cottage around and squeeze one of the big beds into the closetlike space in the corner, which from now on would be our bedroom and the baby's room.

By nighttime everything was ready. Nikita went off to the Billauderie to fetch our milk and I lay down for a rest. Suddenly the baby decided to come, and it was obviously in a hurry. Elizabeth was asleep in bed, down sick with flu, so Olga rushed off on her bike into the night to fetch her father. She made it in record time announcing breathlessly, "Come home quick, the baby is coming!" Luckily the owner of the small bus that made the trip to Cholet twice a week had just received his gas ration and in ten minutes we were careening down the village street, the people looking out of their doors, wondering why the bus was making its trip so late at night. We arrived at the hospital just in time and the midwife had not even time to take off her hat before she announced proudly: "Un petit gars!" — "A little boy!"

The days I spent at the hospital were simply heavenly! Clean sheets, electric lights, a comfortable bed, a bathroom, everything done for me by the kindly angel-like nuns, not a worry, not a responsibility on my mind! It was marvelous to stay there and rest for almost ten days, as was practiced in those times.

The day I returned home I realized at once that Aunt Mary was very ill. When I took her temperature it was 103°. It appeared that she had a kidney infection, which kept her in a critical condition for several weeks. Antibiotics were not widely used in those days, or maybe their use did not reach La Séguinière.

The big event in January was our son's baptism. And it was really an undertaking! Old Father Barnabas still traveled around visiting small groups of Russian Orthodox people, but there were very few trains running now. It took us several weeks to get the whole project organized. Father Barnabas would come to Angers. From there he would take a bus to a town a little closer to us and there my husband would meet him and bring him to us riding "piggy back" on his bike.

For a day our little cottage was to become a real church, with five sacraments celebrated. Everyone chipped in with the preparations. We scrubbed our cottage shining clean. Eleven-

year-old Elizabeth, who was to be the godmother, mumbled
and muttered the Creed all day long, for she was to recite it
during the ceremony. Our neighbor Madame Allard said she
would cook dinner for the great event, for how could a dinner
be cooked in a room at the same time that a baptism
was going on? Monsieur le Curé offered to put up Father
Barnabas for the night and asked whether he could attend the
service. A tub was loaned by a neighbor to serve as a font.
We even had guests. The Dimitrievs decided to walk the
four miles that separated us in order to attend the service and
receive Communion. We invited Mr. Dimitriev to be godfather
with Elizabeth. Two of our Russian prisoner-of-war friends
turned up too.

On the eve Father Barnabas sat with us and under his
direction I baked the prosphora (holy bread) for the sacrament. He had the carved wooden seal, and we had the flour
and the yeast and I had already learned how to bake on a
charcoal brazier. My prosphora came out as shapely and as
good as any I saw in a parish church. Wine was not difficult
to get for all the farmers made their own wine.

After a good night's rest (Monsieur le Curé had even
provided a hot water bottle) Father Barnabas came to our
house.

He heard our confessions. He gave the sacrament of Holy
Unction to Aunt Mary and she lay there, her mild thin face
shining with oil and a serene look of happiness. By the time
Father Barnabas started the Divine Liturgy our guests had
arrived: Monsieur le Curé, for whom our only comfortable
seat was reserved, the Dimitrievs, Peter and his friend. These
two were a little awkward not knowing how to greet a priest.
They had heard from their parents that you kiss a priest's
hand when he gives you his blessing but they did not know
how it should be done. Father Barnabas did not know
whether they'd want him to give them his blessing, so he
just shook hands with them. What they really got was a poke
in their teeth, but everyone felt they'd done their best and
was satisfied.

I am hopelessly tone-deaf and voiceless, but my husband and the children did their best to sing the responses and

my aunt's thin voice joined them occasionally. Our one and only table became an altar for the Sacrament.

Then came the Baptism and Chrismation. Elizabeth and the Mr. Dimitriev gave the responses. To Elizabeth's disappointment it was the godfather who recited the Creed, since the baptized baby was a boy. But together they blew and spat on the devil, acknowledged Christ and went around the bathtub font. The baby howled at the appropriate moments, while being dipped in water, slept peacefully through the rest. The silk quilt looked beautifully festive.

Monsieur le Curé woke up with a start from the snooze into which he dropped during the long service. The baptism was over, and the servant of God George was now an Orthodox Christian.

When the services were over, our neighbor, Madame Allard, brought in the steaming rabbit stew and a wonderful cake she had baked for us. Bottles of wine were opened and toasts were made in the best French tradition: for France, for Russia, for the safe return home of Peter and his friends, for the safe return of all the village boys still imprisoned in Germany, for the newly baptized George and for all his family.

One more event took place before war could be considered finished for La Séguinière. In the middle of the village square, in front of the church, there was a stone monument to the fifty-six villagers and farmers killed during World War I. Such monuments are to be found in every French village and town. Many of the names had become familiar to us — Champion, Baudry, Allard and many others. Curiously enough the number of men held prisoners of war in Germany or drafted for work in Germany was almost exactly the same — fifty-seven, if I remember correctly. For almost five years the whole village thought of these boys and prayed for their safe return. Every morning around six A.M. (and war-time six A.M. at that!) Nikita and I awoke to the sound of footsteps in the street — people going to early Mass before they began work, and all these Masses were offered for the same intention. During our long twilight chats with Madame Champion we talked again and again about the same burning question:

would her son return safely? At every gathering, on every public occasion, the boys in Germany would be remembered with concern and affection.

The first one to come back (though he was not really one of the villagers) was a young priest, who had developed some lung trouble in captivity and was released early because of this. He was assigned assistant pastor in La Séguinière, and everyone called him Monsieur l'Abbé. He was very different from Monsieur le Curé — young, dynamic, of the type of Roman Catholic priests who became "worker-priests" in Paris. He took over all the work with young people and even produced a ballet on the theme of the liberation of France.

One of the drafted boys had become ill and died at the very beginning of the war. Now the others began to come back, in twos and threes, then a dozen at a time. The villagers counted the returnees. Weeks went on, then months. Forty-nine, fifty, fifty-one. For two weeks there was no more news, then came back the fifty-second, the fifty-third. The summer of 1944 was drawing to its end when news came that the fifty-sixth man had safely reached Angers. Monsieur le Curé announced that when the truck bringing the last man to La Séguinière had passed Cholet, he would have the church bells rung. Everyone waited anxiously and then at last in the afternoon of that grey, blustery, windy day, we heard the church bell and hurried down. The village square in front of the church and the streets leading to it were crowded: old men and women, workers from the shoe factory, children, women with babies, all were milling there. At last we heard the truck, moving slowly up the steep road. People began waving and yelling. The truck stopped at the church entrance and before "the fifty-sixth man" had a change to get out, the crowd was at him — women kissed him, thrust their babies at him, men clapped him on the shoulders, everyone was laughing and crying at the same time.

High above, on the church porch stood Monsieur le Curé, smiling at his people, tears glistening in his eyes. He watched them for a while and then his voiced echoed across the square: "Eh bien, voila ... It has happened ... They are all home ... Now, children, let's go inside and thank the good

Lord!" The crowd poured into the church, women not worrying about their uncovered heads. Monsieur le Curé intoned and the old walls vibrated to the powerful sounds of "Magnificat anima mea Dominum . . ." sung by the hundreds of people crowding the church. I will never forget it.

Curiously enough, as a kind of footnote to the celebration, I remember that at this occasion, for the first time during our two years' stay at La Séguinière, I felt an inimical reaction to us as foreigners. A man, not one of the villagers, brusquely addressed us: "Don't speak a foreign language! You'll land in trouble." "But we are Russian," I said "We've been together in this war." "If you want to avoid trouble, just don't speak it!" he answered angrily. This was a first hint I saw of the rather shady side of the liberation in France. People suspected of having collaborated with Germans were arrested, women had their heads shaved and were paraded, almost naked, around the city streets.

We had no trouble, even though we were foreigners and I spoke German. La Séguinière was not the kind of place where such things happened. Nikita was once stopped in the street in Cholet by one of his colleagues. "Monsieur Koulomzin," he asked. "Have you had any trouble since the liberation?" "No," answered Nikita. "Frankly, I was even surprised, because some others did have trouble, and after all, I am a foreigner and was hired while the factory was under German management." "I'll tell you why you were not bothered. You remember our conversation in the screen room?"

Then Nikita remembered, how one day while he was working in the electromagnetic screen room with two other technicians, one of them began to abuse the American and English flyers, their air raids and their bombing of civilians. With his usual emphasis on objectivity, Nikita argued that it is practically impossible to pin-point bombings, that in war and during air-raids it is impossible to avoid destruction of civilian buildings and people. It appeared that the conversation had been set up on purpose to test his political opinions.

During this period Nikita once had to make a special effort to protect some Russian prisoners of war. One morning at six A.M. we heard knocking at our door. It was one of the villagers and he said that a group of men wearing German uniforms had been discovered near one of the farms. No one could understand their language; it was not German. Would Nikita come and help interpret. But even to Nikita their language was unintelligible, for the men belonged to some minority group of the Soviet Union, perhaps Georgian or Armenian. Fortunately one of them spoke Russian and could explain to Nikita that they had been made prisoners of war by the Germans, issued uniforms and used for war work.

I was getting bread at the village bakery when I saw the procession marching down the street, Nikita in front, grinning broadly, then the armed local "resistants" surrounding a bedraggled group of prisoners in some kind of grey uniform. Nikita wanted to make sure that the prisoners would be turned over to proper French military authorities for it was rather doubtful how the case would be handled by late-day "resistants" trying to show off their heroism.

During that summer of 1945 we had to decide whether we should now return to Paris. One important reason for returning was the matter of schooling. Elizabeth was twelve years old and the village school had no grades for her level. Even during the school year 1944/45 she had to attend the lycée in Cholet, which meant a daily round trip on her bike, up-hill and down-hill, eight miles in all. In winter weather, rain, sleet and occasional snow, this proved too much for her and she ended up with pneumonia. George, six months old now, was not doing well. We were lucky to find an excellent young doctor in Cholet, a pediatrician, who took real interest in his case. Quite early he insisted that I give up nursing the baby, because I was so run-down that my milk was too watery and not nutritious enough. There were no baby foods or condensed milk available to supplement unsatisfactory breast feeding. At two months George weighed less than at birth. Now the doctor said George had all the symptoms of rickets— thickened wrist joints, a chaplet of little bumps down his chest and bow legs. "You cannot stay in this house another winter," said the doctor. "There is no sunshine and it is damp. The child urgently needs treatment by ultraviolet rays and this is impossible here."

"But, doctor," I argued. "Here we have plenty of milk, butter, eggs, and vegetables, and you know what trouble we'll have getting all this in Paris."

"At this stage ultra-violet rays are more important," was his answer.

We decided to go back. Tamara Klepinin did not need our house any longer and was being helped as a victim of the Nazis. Nikita was told that it would be possible to have him eventually transferred to a factory of the same firm near Paris. Aunt Mary was overjoyed at the thought of being close to a church again. We were somewhat anxious whether my work as an interpreter at the German Kriegsmarine would cause us trouble, but after all it is always better to face possible trouble than to build your decision on the fear of it. We made up our minds to go back to Paris, or rather to Chaville.

We left early in August, 1945. It was not difficult to pack up our few belongings, but it was difficult to say goodbye to our friends. We all cried as we hugged Madame Champion and her family. We promised to come back to see them again. The same bus that took me to the hospital when George was born came very early in the morning to pick us up. For the last time I saw Madame Allard's face in the window, weeping unrestrainedly. A good chapter of our life was over, we had been greatly enriched and now a new chapter was about to begin.

It was strange to be home again. Our little house in Chaville looked somewhat sad and neglected after all the war-time makeshift adaptations and the months of standing empty since Tamara Klepinin and her children had left. But our children were wildly excited at meeting old friends and showing off the new baby. Before we even unpacked, I decided to check on our status with the local post-liberation authorities. Would I be considered a "collaborator" because I had been employed as an interpreter by Germans? Was I to face any kind of investigation?

Postwar Interim: Paris, 1945-1948

In France, as in many other European countries, every resident has to be duly registered with the local police. Now, after our two years' absence, I had to register at the Chaville police station and I was a little nervous about what the consequences would be. But my anxiety was shortlived and was resolved rather ridiculously. In truth, the mountain gave birth to a mouse.

I presented the certificate made out by the mayor of La Séguinière and George's birth certificate. The policeman examined them carefully. Then he hemmed and hawed. It was known, he said, that I had been employed by the German occupation authorities. Yes, I answered, but what could I do with seven mouths to feed, my husband unemployed and two members of our family in the French Army? The neighbors had confirmed our "good morality," the policeman admitted, but still ... Then I did something that made me feel very embarrassed: I took out a package of cigarettes (cigarettes were still rationed), negligently put them on the policeman's desk next to our papers, and continued talking. Just as negligently he placed his hand on the package and the cigarettes disappeared. "Well, I guess there isn't much to be said..." he remarked. In a minute all our identity cards were duly stamped and registered. We did not have to worry about being accused of war crimes.

The next ten days were a merry-go-round of friends' and relatives' visits, of cleaning and painting the house, of estimating the repairs that would gradually have to be made — burst pipes, broken windows, etc. Aunt Mary was settled in a sunny room downstairs, with windows opening into our small garden. The downstairs room facing the street became our living room, the three girls shared the nursery above Aunt Mary's room, and Nikita, George and I had the room next to it. Yaroslav was glad to return to his closet above the stairs; he had lodged with some friends during our absence.

In a few days our kindly doctor Lemmet took charge of George and arranged for him to have the ultraviolet ray treatment for his rickets at the local children's clinic. Elizabeth and Olga were entered at the excellent Lycée de Sèvres which involved a twenty-minute walk and a short train ride daily. Since the little private beginners' school they had attended was now closed, we were glad to avail ourselves of its headmistress' advice to have Xenia tutored by a retired elderly teacher living in a Home for the Aged in Chaville. Xenia had to get rid of the Séguinière "patois" accent and be prepared to enter the Lycée de Sèvres preparatory class next year.

I was hoping I would not have to work anywhere, but less than two weeks after our arrival a secretarial job at a good salary was offered me that I did not have the heart to refuse. The American YMCA was carrying on its War Prisoners' Aid work, staffed by secretaries of neutral nationalities — Swedes, Swiss, and Danes. They were willing to have me work part-time, allowing me to be home when the children returned from school. Our household was joined by a cheerful and loveable fifteen-year-old helper named Erica, and her mother, of Estonian background, who were part of the early wave of displaced persons reaching France. What Erica lacked in housekeeping experience, she made up in enthusiasm and good nature. We helped her to register for classes in the afternoon and everything worked out very well. Elizabeth and Erica became good friends and their friendship continued for many years, until Elizabeth became the mother of a family in the United States and Erica in Canada.

This early post war period was very much like any time following some disaster, a flood or a fire. Not everything could be repaired or rebuilt at once; not everything went smoothly. George's health was causing us concern. As I had feared, the milk supply was poor, with insufficient refrigeration, and often the milk we received turned sour. Baby foods were unobtainable, the bread in the bakeries was made with hard-to-digest additives George developed diarrhea and had to be kept for weeks at a time on a diet of strained mashed potatoes. Elizabeth looked delicate and suffered from headaches, but it was Olga, with her rosy cheeks and round face, who proved to be severely decalcified and developed a deviation of the spine. A comparatively slight fall resulted in a broken arm, both bones of her forearm snapping, so that when I picked her up her hand and wrist were at right angles to her forearm. She was in great pain after her arm had been set at the Versailles Hospital and she came home again. As I sat up with her, helpless to alleviate her suffering, I wondered bitterly whether this accident was necessary to draw more of my attention and concern to this child — so scrupulously conscientious, so unselfish, so loving, somewhat reserved, whose good nature and health tended to be taken for granted.

But conditions were improving — for us, specifically, because of the regular stream of most generous parcels and gifts coming from our friends in the United States: CARE food parcels, cocoa, tea, coffee, sugar, condensed milk, tinned food of all kinds. Clothes — beautiful warm, scarcely used clothes for the children and for us stockings, shoes, sweaters . . . Our most faithful friends were the Scotts, Celia Ann Van Waveren (formerly Mayer) and the Huntingtons. We were again in touch with my sister and my brother in

England. Although Mania had suffered a great personal loss during the war, her professional career grew by leaps and bounds and I believe she was the first woman to hold a position of such responsibility in the world of investment brokers.

My work with the YMCA War Prisoners' Aid proved to be very interesting. Now the roles were reversed and the German soldiers were at the mercy of their French guards. The food situation in the American camps was not too bad, but in the camps administered by the French authorities conditions were often terrible. The "Y" secretaries were in a rather awkward situation: they were not supposed to do any relief work (theoretically this was the province of the International Red Cross) but to distribute recreational and cultural supplies. "What can I do?" exclaimed a young Swede. "I enter a dark cellar and stumble against emaciated bodies, packed like sardines, lying on the damp earthen floor. With the help of my flashlight I can barely distinguish their faces. And I am supposed to ask them whether they need ping-pong balls, or musical instruments, or chess sets?"

At all times and in all countries, when helpless people find themselves under the uncontrolled power of other men, abuses will take place and when wartime resentments and feelings of revenge are mixed up with it, the situation can become terrible. There were cases of corruption and willful cruelty, sexual abuse, barracks were allowed to burn with locked-up prisoners helpless inside, prisoners of war were used, without sufficient equipment or protection, to defuse mines ... The "Y" men had no right to report any such cases. Again it was the exclusive responsibility of the International Red Cross.

I must say that, however terrible some of the incidents were, there was a very important difference between the French attitude to their German prisoners and the German treatment of Jews or Russian prisoners of war. The French general-in-charge of the POW camps was approached by the senior "Y" secretary, who described some of the things that secretaries saw and had no right to report. The general's reaction was immediate and perfectly clear-cut. He insisted that no reports be sent to the International Red Cross Headquarters, and none be given any publicity or sent abroad, but

that any cases of unjustified ill treatment or hardship be passed
on to him personally. The only thing he insisted on was *speed.*
He wanted to be informed as soon as anything happened. This,
of course, involved speed in our secretarial work, translating
and typing the "Y" men's reports.

I am glad to say that human kindness shows itself at least
as often as human cruelty. I remember how I once mentioned
to the saleswoman at the dairy where I was getting my milk
the case of a seventeen-year-old German prisoner of war,
made to defuse land mines, who lost both his arms and his
eyesight when a land mine exploded in his face. The woman
suddenly snatched a couple of cheeses from the shelf and gave
them to me: "Send the kid a food parcel . . ." she said.

Looking over lists of prisoners of war in England I came
across the name of Tirpitz's eldest son and was glad to know
he had come through alive. I was able to get in touch with
him and send him some packages and books he wanted.

In January 1946, Nikita was transferred from Cholet to
a factory of the same firm in a Parisian suburb. He could now
live at home and our family was reunited again. Our friendship with La Séguinière was not broken off. We exchanged
letters and both Elizabeth and Olga spent some of their Christmas and Easter vacations at Madame Champion's farm.

The girls' world expanded in a new direction. In the summer of 1946, thirteen-year-old Elizabeth went to England to
spend two weeks at an English summer camp, and to visit my
brother and his wife and my sister Mania. Next year Olga
joined her and both girls learned to speak English. Everyone
was very friendly to them, but a very special and deep relationship developed between the girls and my sister. It meant a
great deal to them and somewhat helped her in her great loneliness and allowed her to come back to life. In 1947 eight-year-
old Xenia had her first fling at independence, going to a Russian summer camp in the Haute Savoie.

About a year after our return to Paris, Paul B. Anderson
came there on a short visit. He was again instrumental in a
new development in my work which became very important
for me.

The World Council of Churches assigned considerable

funds for the reconstruction of churches that had suffered
during the war. This was understood not merely as a reconstruction of buildings, but as a strengthening of church life
and work, especially in relation to youth. The Orthodox
Church was included in the program, and a grant was made
providing a part-time salary for a person to serve the needs
of the Russian Orthodox Church in France. They were offering
me the position. After an interval of thirteen years I was
again given the opportunity to take up the work I loved so
much. The scope was quite limited: out of the time I could
give to a job outside my home, I could use one-half for the
development of this new project, and the other half would
have to be used for secretarial work for Donald A. Lowrie,
YMCA representative in France. This allowed me, however,
to give time to some preliminary research — talking to people
who were actually involved in work with Russian Orthodox
children — in orphanages, in summer camps, in church
schools, asking for the advice of priests, teachers and social
workers, learning their needs and sharing their experience.
There was no doubt that the desire to give children a Christian
outlook on life was there, and the sense that it had to be
rooted in the Orthodox tradition was also strong, but there
was also a recognition that the few religious educational materials available were quite unsatisfactory. How could books
written for children in pre-revolutionary Russia serve the
needs of children born and raised in West European countries,
educated in western schools, having just lived through World
War II? The Orthodox Christian tradition had to be translated into the concepts and language of the children of today.
Thus our project became the production of several books, published by the YMCA Press. Personally I was involved in the
production of the first two, for children of 8 to 10 and 10 to
12. Three more books were produced later for adolescents
and young adults. In many ways these books set a new stand-
ard for Russian religious educational books as regards language, objectivity, closeness to life. The illustrations were
done by an excellent artist, M. Dobujinsky. I did not know
at the time that this work would prepare me for my future
activity in the United States on a much larger scale.

I do not remember just when or why we began thinking of emigrating to the United States. To a certain extent we were influenced by the collapse of our hopes that World War II would change the situation in Russia and we would be able to return there. As a matter of fact a number of Russian émigrés, many of them very devoted church members, did go back to Russia at this time and faced courageously the hardships they met there. Even Metropolitan Evlogy, the venerable old bishop heading the Russian Church in Western Europe at the request of Patriarch Tikhon, succumbed to the wishful thinking that the time had come for him to lead his flock back to its Mother Church. He was losing strength and rapidly approaching his end. One day, when I called with the three older children, the nurse told me he was not allowed to receive visitors, but seeing the children would give him pleasure. She took them in and a few minutes later they came out looking pleased and sucking candy bars he gave them. "I always bless children with candy," he told them, smiling. Only on his deathbed did Metropolitan Evlogy begin to realize that his decision was premature. He appointed as his successor the very much beloved Archbishop Vladimir, who was quite firm in his conviction that the Russian émigré church had to continue its existence abroad and be independent of Moscow.

Nikita and I realized that we would not be able to bring up our children in Russia according to our beliefs. We also felt somewhat frustrated because after so many years of hard work, our joint earnings were barely sufficient to pay for not quite adequate food, housing and fuel. Our major concern, however, was not an economic one. I realized that our children could not and should not remain "émigrés" all their life, the way our generation had, "a nation within other nations," with no deep ties and no responsibilities. France had too crystallized, too old a culture to absorb new elements. I could not imagine our children becoming fully French, unless they completely abandoned their "Russianness". The same was true of most other European countries. Only in America could I see the possibility of striking root, of becoming truly part of an adopted country and yet preserving our own spiritual values, our spiritual heritage. There were also the strong ties of friendship that linked us with many people in America; there was warmth, understanding, and real affection reaching out to us — the Andersons, the Huntingtons, the Scotts, the Van Waverens and so many others. One particular letter that I received at this time touched me deeply. Old Dr. George A. Coe, a pioneer in new methods of religious education, retired from Teachers College, Columbia University, at the time I was studying there in 1926. During the war years, when our only contact with the free world was occasional broadcasts we managed to catch of the usual war-time, "sabre-rattling" patriotic kind, I often felt comforted by the thought that beyond this there are thoughtful, objective, truth-seeking men, like Dr. Coe. In 1947, quite by chance, I heard that Dr. Coe was still alive and I wrote him a letter. He answered immediately:

My dear Sophie Shidlovsky,

Permit me to call you by the name that has been bright in my memory for all these twenty years. Only a few days before the receipt of your much esteemed letter, I fell to wondering upon how the marvellous events of the two decades had affected you. Now comes your own answer, giving me happy assurance that you have not only survived and become the mother of four children — how I should like to see them! — but in addition have continued even until now your labors in religious education.

Your belief that I am still a dissenter from the passions and policies of most of the rulers and ruling classes in the world is correct. You are right also in your confidence that I still base my judgements upon public policies on my firm and ever firmer conviction of the inherent value of human personality . . .

. . . Now guess where I stand with respect to the international strains of the present hour! How do you suppose I interpret the duty and privilege to which reference is made in "I was hungry and ye fed me"? What do you suppose my attitude is to the "relief" projects of my own country? Or my attitude towards its insist-

ence upon monopolizing atom bombs for the good of
all the nations and peoples?

Enough of this! At this moment the great thing in
my feelings is the bond that has united you to your old
teacher, and your old teacher to you these many years.

I am nearly eighty-six years old, in good health
and active,

Affectionately yours,

George A. Coe

Of course, there were plenty of other considerations concerning our emigration that had to be taken into account. In
Paris our children could attend excellent schools and receive
the best of education. The very cream of European culture
was within our reach. In France we were secure and we were
happy. The risk of arriving in the United States, with five
people in our charge, with jobs to be found for Nikita and
for myself and no savings to serve as cushioning, could be
rather frightening. Two pieces of advice that we received at
this time helped us to make our decision.

Of our American friends, Mrs. Chapin Huntington was
the most practical-minded, businesslike and best qualified to
judge the practicability of our project. In comparison to our
other friends the Huntingtons were wealthy and their affidavit would carry most weight with the American Consulate.
I wrote Mrs. Huntington at some length, explaining the pros
and cons of our plan and asking for her advice. The answer
came by telegram, saying that if housing were available they
believed our plan reasonable and promising, that they were
sending an affidavit to the American Consul in Paris right
away and that they would be glad to send us money if we
needed it. This was very encouraging, offering us more than
we had asked and more than we actually needed.

The other advice we received was of a very different
nature, but it helped us to feel at peace and unworried about
the whole project.

Nikita and I were very fond of a Russian hierarch, Bishop
Sergius of Prague, who knew us both well. A man of great
spirituality and wisdom, he was in appearance a very cheerful,

friendly man, with a strong sense of humor, who could roar with laughter at something funny. We heard that Bishop Sergius was in Paris for a few days to discuss with Metropolitan Evlogy the new church situation in Eastern Europe, completely changed by the post-war expansion of the Soviets' dominion.

Both Nikita and I tried to live according to the teachings of our Church. Self-assertion, adventurousness, "taking one's life in one's own hands," "building one's own future," "shaping one's own fate," are not virtues in the light of the teachings of the Eastern Fathers of the Church. There was really no major reason forcing us to emigrate, nothing threatened us, we were in no danger. Was it right for us to change the course of our life so drastically? Was it "in obedience to God's will," or was it just "self-will"?

We came to Bishop Sergius with this question in mind. He received us as warmly as ever and laughed at us as merrily as usual. "Yes, you want me to give advice, so that afterwards you could say it was all my fault? Oh no, I will not let you catch me in *this* trap!" On and on he talked in cheerful good nature. A sentence here, a thought there, a suggestion that set off our own train of thinking. As we left, I looked with surprise at Nikita: "Do you realize that without giving us any advice, he made the way perfectly clear: do whatever you consider reasonable and right, but do not feel that your decision, your action, will determine your future. Everything will happen according to God's will." We made up our minds then and there that we would start planning to emigrate and would accept willingly and cheerfully whatever would be the results, going to America, or staying in France.

Much later I learned that Bishop Sergius had come to France to make a decision of his own. His diocese was occupied by the Soviets. Should he return to it or stay in Vienna, Austria, where he was at present with a number of Russian refugees who had fled the advance of the Red Army? Seemingly, his superior, Metropolitan Evlogy, told him to go back to Prague. Bishop Sergius obeyed cheerfully. He was then assigned to the diocese of Kazan in Russia, where he became as beloved by the people as he was in Prague. He died there a few years later.

We applied for a visa to the United States in 1946 and had to wait for our quota for two years. By the summer of 1948 we knew that we would be leaving some time in November.

A few events took place in our home life during these last few months. One more member joined our family, Nikita's Aunt Mary Meyendorff, who thirty-six years before, in 1922, had helped his mother and all her children escape from Russia. She had remained in Russia for all these years, supporting herself by giving mathematics lessons, and an excellent teacher she was. Unmarried and alone, she went through all the usual experiences of life in Soviet Russia: imprisonment, exile, poverty, hunger. By World War II she was back in Odessa, her family's home town. During the German occupation of Odessa she was able to set up a little fruit stand on a street corner and thus support herself at the age of seventy-seven. As the war drew to its end people in occupied territories had to make up their minds whether to stay or leave. Aunt Mary Meyendorff decided it was her last chance to see the members of her family who were still alive and living abroad. Her German name made it possible for her to be evacuated from Odessa at the time of the German retreat and she was duly plunged into all the turmoil of the last months of war in Europe — air raids, destroyed cities, arrests, disappearances, sudden deaths. For four years, completely unfazed, cheerful and matter-of-fact, she fitted into any family situation where help was needed, took care of her young grandnephew while his father was in prison, supported her sister-in-law when her husband (Aunt Mary's last living brother) disappeared, never to be seen again. Just as cheerfully she accepted being taken in by her sister's family, even though she was the fifth person sleeping on the floor in the same room. She finally settled in a camp for Displaced Persons. We wrote to her asking her to come and live with us and she gladly accepted our invitation.

The two Aunt Marys knew each other since the old days of their youth in Petersburg. The only way Aunt Mary M. could be sqeezed into our small house was by having my Aunt

Mary share her room with her. "This will be a big sacrifice for you, darling," I said. "We will not ask her unless you are really willing." Aunt Mary Sabouroff answered: "When I was released from prison in Moscow and sent into exile, I went to Nizhni Novgorod because I had a cousin living there. She took me in, though there were already three of them living in one room. Don't you think that I am happy at last to partially repay my debt now?"

Soon after Aunt Mary M.'s arrival, Yaroslav left our home for good. He had graduated from the Department of Architecture of the École des Beaux Arts in Paris and decided to emigrate to Canada, where Nikita's other brother Fedor was already settled with his wife and four daughters.

Our very last summer in France was a delightful one. We usually spent our vacations in Biarritz, at the home of Nikita's sister. By now Father Alexander Rehbinder and Elizabeth had seven children so that with our four and a few cousins on Father's side, the house would be really too crowded. We decided to camp out and bought a second-hand American Army tent for six. Some six kilometers away from Biarritz, on the way to Bayonne, we found a meadow on a hillside dotted with a few pine trees. At the foot of the hillside was a small lake. We asked the men mowing the grass whether they would allow us to camp there, and since it was long before private camping became popular and strict rules for camping were laid down, they just shrugged their shoulders and said "Why not?". There we settled with our tent, a small stove and a bottle of butane fuel for our cooking. We had the children camp out with us by turns, in "mixed couples"—one Koulomzin and one Rehbinder child—which seemed to be better fun. Occasionally, in the evening, the whole clan would walk over from Biarritz, settle around our small campfire and sing all those endless Russian songs we have sung for generations. The heat of the summer day cooled down gradually, a slight wind whispered in the tall pine trees, the sky grew darker and darker and the stars shone brightly. It remains a memory to cherish.

Upon our return to Paris our departure suddenly loomed quite close. Like pieces of a puzzle details began to fall into place. My sister generously undertook to pay our boat fares on the "Queen Elizabeth." We received a letter from Mrs. Schaufuss, director of the Tolstoy Foundation, inviting us to stay upon our arrival at their re-settlement home in Valley Cottage, N.Y., until we could find jobs and housing, with payment for board and room to be made later. Our second Aunt Mary would have to wait for her quota for two or three years. We arranged to continue the rental of our Chaville house, but since she was too old to live by herself another niece of hers, Nikita's cousin, Anna Tcherkoff, would come to live there with her husband and children. This, at least, was the official version for our landlord, though the real issue was the desperate need of the Tchertkoffs for better accommodations. With the recent birth of twin girls they were a family of seven crowded into two small rooms. They were fond of Aunt Mary and delighted at moving into a house and having her become a member of their family. The sale of our household things and furniture brought in enough money to pay for our passports, visas, railroad fare to Cherbourg and left us a small capital of one hundred dollars to start life in the new world.

One thing we were unable to sell: Nikita's bicycle, that faithful vehicle of family transportation that had served us so loyally through all the war years. Three days before our departure, as Nikita was riding it in Paris across the Place des Ternes, it collapsed and its frame broke in two. It would not serve another master.

The date of our departure was set for November 20. The last days were filled with a round of send-off parties, with heart-warming good wishes, prayers, and even tears. A last visit to the Russian cemetery at Ste. Geneviève des Bois, the last service in our little church in Chaville which we had helped to build, the group of friends waving good bye at the Gare St. Lazare . . .

And then came the hitch! As the boat-train arrived in Cherbourg, large posters announced that the departure of the "Queen Elizabeth" was being postponed because of a strike of dock workers in England. Announcements would be made as soon as a new date could be set. Travelers could be accommodated at the company's expense in Cherbourg hotels.

We knew that the Tchertkoffs had already moved into our house. We could not afford to spend our precious "capital" on extra railroad fares and meals. Anyway, perhaps the strike would be over next day! Obviously it was better to wait in Cherbourg at the company's expense.

I am sure this unexpected pause had a special meaning for us. It was something of a preparation for what we would need to have and to be when beginning our new life. But it was really a funny experience. We stayed in Cherbourg for twelve days, every day expecting we would sail tomorrow. We took rather skimpy meals at the hotel. We went on long walks. Our pillar of strength proved to be a one-volume Russian edition of Tolstoy's *War and Peace* which we had with us and which I read aloud to the family. The hotel was almost unheated, and the radiators became lukewarm during the small hours of the night only. We would huddle all together on one of the big double beds, cover ourselves with the warm eiderdowns, order hot water to make tea, and I'd read aloud until I got hoarse. Even three-year-old George was fond of this whole procedure. He came lugging the book and calling out: "Let's go and read *War and Peace.*

My major problem was laundering our clothes. I could not risk giving our things to a laundry, for we might be leaving tomorrow, and how do you keep four children clean for twelve days without washing their clothes? So I washed panties and shirts in the sink and spread them out on radiators hoping they would dry during the lukewarm period.

It was an unexpected pause at a moment when our sense of security was at a low ebb. It was like having to stop suddenly just as you are starting to make a jump over a wide and somewhat dangerous space. It was a little frightening and yet it gave a sense of perspective. Friends sent us encouraging letters and telegrams.

And then it was all over. On December 2, 1948, we were installed in our cabins on the "Queen Elizabeth" and saw the shores of Europe slowly disappear in the foggy afternoon.

December crossings tend to be rough and dramamine was not used in France in 1948. Being the worst sailor in the world, I booked a berth for myself in a different cabin from the rest of the family, so as not to inflict my misery on them. Fortunately they all did rather well. On one day only Nikita and Olga had practically the whole empty dining room to themselves.

Our Life in the United States, 1949-1970

After three days the weather grew pleasant and even I revived, encouraged to do so by little George who developed a sore throat and ran a high temperature. The nice ship doctor treated him and, as we drew near the coast and were told that the immigration authorities would be checking us on deck around 10 P.M., he suggested I leave George in the cabin and explain about his illness. I followed the doctor's advice, but this turned out to be a mistake. The immigration agent looked grave and said he could not let us off the boat unless he saw everyone. Nervously I suggested I could run down to our deck and bring George up. No, this would not do either. There was a doctor with the immigration team, checking for infectious diseases and he would go down with me and take a look at George. That poor doctor was the most sober, the most sad-looking man I had ever seen. My attempts to explain the situation to him while we were going down were met with dead silence. In our cabin George lay asleep, his cheeks flushed, his damp hair curling in tendrils, his long lashes like shadows under his eyes. In his mother's eyes he looked angelic, but the doctor remained quite unimpressed.

"Has he got laryngitis?" he asked.

With all my fluency in English, I had never had to deal with doctors or illness in that language and had no idea what laryngitis was. Perhaps it was a dangerous contagious disease and they will not allow us to disembark if George has it?

"I don't know . . ." I said. "His throat is very red and he has a temperature of 103°. The ship doctor saw him."

"I am asking you: has he got laryngitis?" the doctor repeated mournfully.

He wrote something on a pad and again we marched the long way up to the deck in complete silence. He stopped off on the way to make a phone call. Maybe he is late for a date, I thought, or maybe he has trouble at home? Perhaps the phone call will make him feel happier.

When we returned, the upper deck had emptied and only our family stood in a corner, looking worried and uncomfortable. The agent began checking our papers. When it came to presenting our vaccination certificates, oh horror of horrors, Nikita could not find the seventh one. A certificate was missing . . . "They will not let us in! What shall we do?" the thought flashed in my mind and my feet got cold. "Nikita," I said, "check the certificates, see which one is missing." It was Aunt Mary's, and with relief I turned to the official:

"We cannot find the vaccination certificate for Mary Sabouroff, but look at her arm." Aunt Mary was the only one whose vaccination "took"; her arm was still swollen and the scab of the vaccination was clearly visible. The official was satisfied and after a few more questions we were told we could disembark, or spend the night in our cabin and leave in the morning. We were in, we were admitted.

Nine-year-old Xenia hung on my arm as we went through the door.

"Mummy, Mummy, are we in America? Are we really in America?"

"Yes, darling, we are. We are really in America!"

Xenia jumped up and down, pulling my arm, chanting excitedly:

"Our America! Our France! Our Russia!"

Alexander the Great and Napoleon had not felt more triumphant than she did at this moment! The world was hers.

Then came the wonderful experience of seeing our friends patiently waiting for us on the pier: Dr. Ernest Scott, my teacher and friend from the Union Theological Seminary days, his daughter Nora, my godmother Countess Sophie Panin, Paul and Margaret Anderson, and a cousin of Nikita's.

If I remember right, Aunt Mary and Xenia left that night with the Andersons to spend a week or two with them. Because of George's "laryngitis" we decided to spend the night on the boat and Nikita's cousin picked us up in her car in the morning and drove us to Reed Farm, in Valley Cottage, N.Y., where the Tolstoy Foundation had its resettlement home.

The Tolstoy Foundation was created and directed by two outstanding women — Alexandra Tolstoy, the youngest daughter of Leo Tolstoy, and Tatiana Schaufuss, whom I knew since my childhood days in Voltchy when she was a war-time Red Cross nurse working in the same unit as my cousin. As well as giving her famous name to the Foundation, Alexandra Lvovna was its heart, warm and responsive; Tatiana Schaufuss was its brain, its authority and its rather ruthless driving power. The farm was at first a regular chicken and vegetable farm, to the joy of Alexandra Lvovna, who liked nothing better than hard, physical farm labor. Then it became a rest home for Russian authors, scientists and artists. A camp for Russian children was run in the summer. At the end of World War II a more urgent need called for the creation of a resettlement home for displaced persons of Russian origin arriving from Europe. In 1948, when we were there, this activity was just beginning, and it grew to its peak in the mid-fifties. By that time new dormitory buildings and a church were built and actual farm work and the children's home and camp were closed down. In the sixties the emphasis changed again and the Tolstoy Farm was turned into a home for the aged for some fifty elderly Russians. Later a nursing home for ninety-seven people was added.

At the time of our arrival the whole of Reed Farm was
still run like a large family. The matron was Martha Andreevna Knudsen, a friend of the Tolstoy family who took a
motherly interest in all of us. To the girls' disgust, she packed
them both off the very next day after our arrival to the Nyack
High School, thrusting them into the group of Russian adolescents who daily were driven to school by the farm car. Some
of the youngsters were American-born; others had come recently from Germany, Austria, France, or the U.S.S.R., and
their one language in common was Russian. During those
first weeks at Reed Farm, before they all switched to English,
the girls' spoken Russian improved greatly, and this was certainly an unexpected dividend of our coming to America. Our
two older girls already spoke English when we came and this
made their debut in school much easier, but the fact that right
away they felt part of a foreign group, that they were not
the only foreigners in an all-American environment, greatly
influenced the process of their acclimatization. It probably
slowed it down somewhat, and would not have been a good
thing if it had lasted too long, but it certainly made for a less
traumatic sudden change.

When Aunt Mary and Xenia joined us at the Farm, Xenia
began attending the little grade school in Valley Cottage,
alone with a group of other Russian children. I was concerned
that she was not learning any English. According to Xenia,
the teacher left their Russian group in peace, and did not
attempt to teach them. I told Xenia she should try and learn
some English words herself and to encourage her I promised
to give her a dime if, by my return from work in New York,
she could tell me three new words she had learned. In
the evening Xenia presented herself, cheerfully claiming her
dime: "But did you learn three new English words?" I asked.
"Yes, I did," twinkled Xenia, "I have learned three — boy
friend, girl friend and shut up."

I had no trouble getting a job. A few days after our arrival
Tatiana Schaufuss and Alexandra Lvovna offered me a job in
their New York office, where the activity of the Tolstoy Foundation was growing astronomically. The morning trip to New
York took me over two hours, so I had to leave at seven A.M.

but quite often in the evening I could return with Alexandra Lvovna, who drove her own car.

Nikita had a somewhat harder time, but in January, 1949, he landed an engineering job in Detroit, with a firm that planned to open an agency in New York. They said they would be willing to transfer him to New York when it became feasible.

We stayed at Reed Farm from December until March. Grateful as I was for having this temporary home, I have not kept a happy memory of it. We had no home of our own; Nikita and I were again separated; because of commuting my work kept me away from the children from seven A.M. to seven P.M. Every day of our stay was increasing our financial obligation to the Tolstoy Foundation. Sixteen-year-old Elizabeth was right in the throes of adolescence, enthusiastically making new friendships and getting very irritated with her own family. Olga found herself suddenly abandoned by her sister; she was lonely for her French friendships and not as quick as Elizabeth to make new ones. Xenia felt at home wherever she was, but George was always underfoot and getting into all the scrapes a four-year-old boy can find: eating rat-poison, tumbling into the ice-covered brook, climbing up the roof. Aunt Mary was exhausted, but fortunately dear Martha Andreevna took it all in her stride. On top of it all, unused to American electrical appliances, I got my hand caught in the wringer of an old-fashioned washing machine. The pain was so agonizing that I almost lost consciousness, but fortunately Olga, who was helping me with the laundry, was quick at turning off the current. Again this shows the kind of person Martha Andreevna was, for my only thought at the moment was to reach her. Horrified as she was, seeing my hand white and flat as a pancake, she calmly comforted me, took me to the doctor and did everything necessary efficiently and kindly. My wrist and hand were badly crushed, but no bones were broken and I recovered completely, though for quite a while it was very painful.

Everything comes to an end, and the time came for us to think of finding a home of our own.

While we were still in Paris, when I received a letter on

Tolstoy Foundation stationery, I noticed on the list of board
members the name of Crawford Wheeler and wondered
whether he was one of the young American YMCA secretaries
who used to visit us in Moscow in 1918. One Saturday morning
in January, 1949, while I was standing in the Farm driveway,
I saw a car drive up and a middle-aged man get out of it.
Thirty years had gone since I saw him last, but I thought I
recognized him: "Crawford..." I began hesitantly, and the
man called out: "Why, Sophie Shidlovsky, is this really you?!"
Thus was resumed an old friendship.

Crawford Wheeler lived in Nyack, a charming little town
some six miles away from Reed Farm. He was married and
had two grown-up sons and a married daughter. His eldest
son, Crawford Jr., was killed during the last months of World
War II.

It is really strange how all the members of that group of
Americans who were in Russia during the tragic days of revolution and civil war had never forgotten that experience.
Thirty and forty years later they continued to meet occasionally, to share their memories, collect pictures and letters and
to keep up their interest in Russian affairs. Paul Anderson
belonged to that group too, and I remember how at a testi-
monial dinner given him on his eightieth birthday, Harrison
Salisbury noted the strong impact their Russian experience
had had on the life of these young Americans. Crawford
Wheeler and his wife Margaret were helping very actively
in the resettlement of Russian displaced persons, helping them
to find jobs and homes.

Now Crawford and Margaret put all their hearts into
helping us find a home. Their generosity and the warmth of
their friendship always remains for me one of the greatest
miracles of American life — what we Orthodox would call
its "grace" or "charisma." We decided to settle in Nyack, a
charming town stretched out along the Hudson River against
the background of Bear Mountain. The children had made
good friends among the other Russian young people, there was
a beautiful little church at Reed Farm, and we had grown
very fond of Father Michael, its priest. More and more friends

and relatives from Europe were arriving and starting their new life around the Tolstoy Foundation farm.

Crawford and Margaret looked for a house or an apartment for rent. They were horrified at the prices and after a week or two came to us with a quite unbelievable proposal: we should *buy* a house. I simply laughed at the suggestion. Must one not have money to buy a house? The capital of eighty dollars we brought with us (our original hundred thawed a bit during the long enforced wait in Cherbourg) had already disappeared and we had run up a bill of five hundred dollars at the Tolstoy Resettlement Home. But Crawford persisted. He said he could get us a loan from the local bank for a third of the total amount. He was willing to deposit as a collateral his bonds for the other two thirds. I was so naive that I did not fully understand what "collateral" meant and how very generous the Wheelers were, what a trust they showed in us. Margaret began looking for a house for sale. Nikita and I were both scared.

"Are we not being dishonest?" I wrote to Nikita. "You are always so insistent on not cheating even in small things, like a bus fare, or the children's ages, etc., but here we accept a large loan, and how can we be sure that we will be able to repay it?" Nikita's hesitations were rather characteristic of him: "I am so anxious to hear from you," he wrote. "How do matters stand with the house? I am getting pretty scared about the whole thing. *We* getting to be *house owners?* Where will this lead us? I do hope we are not doing anything against God's will, becoming owners of such property! But, after all, there are lots of people who do live in houses of their own, so maybe there is nothing wrong with doing it . . ."

Finally our house was bought, our lovely, hundred-year-old, white frame house, with a beautiful view on the Hudson, its front all overgrown with wisteria and a large yard with several old elms, pine trees and maples. As I write this, thirty years later, still living in the house with our youngest daughter and her family, it seems unbelievable that we were able to buy it for $12,500, with an additional thousand dollars to rebuild the heating system. Our monthly payment, including taxes, was one hundred-twenty dollars. Nikita was making three hundred dollars a month, and I two hundred. We could make monthly payments on our debt to the Tolstoy Foundation, we could send money to Aunt Mary in France, and we could still swing it.

Crawford, Margaret and I were leaving their house on the way to the bank to sign the deed when Crawford called me back to their living room. On the grand piano stood a large photo in a silver frame of Crawford, Jr. who at twenty-two years of age was killed in the Battle of the Bulge, just a few weeks after he came to Europe as a freshly commissioned young lieutenant. He found himself, with his unit, facing unprotected an advancing heavy German tank. He ordered his men to retreat, while he, with a buddy, stood up and tried to stop the tank's progress with a bazooka.

"Sophie," said Crawford. "I want you to know that whatever we have done for you and your family, we've done in his memory." I could hardly hold back my tears. Curiously enough Crawford Wheeler Jr. was killer on the eve of the day when our son George was born in war-torn France.

Crawford Wheeler was very fond of my mother, and as we were leaving the bank he said: "I think she must be happy for you today."

Nikita was transferred from Detroit to New York, and we moved into the house while the new heating was still being installed. There was a lovely old coal range which kept the kitchen warm and even heated the room above it.

During the next two weeks we assisted at a kind of miracle. Crawford and Margaret must have spoken of us to all their friends in Nyack and we were literally flooded with gifts: tables, chairs, beds, chests, old rugs and curtains, sheets and towels, pots and pans, dishes and plates. Some things were offered for sale at unbelievable prices — a dining room set for seventy-five dollars, an old-fashioned washing machine for five dollars. Margaret spent days at our house, helping me wash the windows, hang up curtains, paint furniture. The Huntingtons sent us a generous check as their contribution to our setting up our own household. The whole Reed Farm family turned up for the house-warming party. Martha Andreevna brought us a big rug, freshly cleaned, as her present.

Father Michael celebrated a service of thanksgiving and many of our friends, so very recently arrived themselves, brought little presents too.

One of the most eloquent expressions of our appreciation of our new home was made by four-year-old George. For almost three months he had been losing one home after another: first our Chaville house, then the Cherbourg hotel, then the Queen Elizabeth cabin, then Reed Farm. At four years old a few days are enough for a place to become a home and its disappearance is hard to understand. During all these temporary stays he was being constantly admonished not to make a mess, to be very tidy, and careful, to make no disorder. As I opened the door to his new room, a small one next to Nikita's and my bedroom, he asked me: "Will this be my room, my very own room?" "Yes, George, your very own room." "And can I make disorder in it?" "Yes, you can," I said, unable to react differently. George sighed deeply, went into his room, locked the door behind him and during the next half-hour unloaded on its floor every box and every drawer in which I had stored his toys and his clothes. It was his room and he could "make disorder" in it!

All our family loved the house. To me it felt like a kindly old friend, giving me security and protection. Nikita's job in New York disintegrated very soon and for two months he could find no other work. His very qualifications were a handicap, for making complicated electronic equipment and instruments was usually connected with Government orders and thus demanded "clearance" of the engineers employed, which he did not yet have. But the good old house helped us to manage. A home was needed for the eighty-four-year-old mother of a friend of ours, Countess Elena Mikhailovna Tolstoy, and we were asked to take her in as a paying guest. She stayed with us until her death six years later and all our family, young and old, learned to love her and appreciate her keen mind, her sense of humor and her fine spirit. In moments of crisis, the house was large enough to accommodate more people and over the years we had a series of "lodgers." Even the nephew of the former owners of the house, Ed Mann, a young lawyer in Nyack, came to live with us for a year or two because he wanted to have a room where he could keep his dog with him and was pleased to find it in the home of his childhood.

I believe we were the first Russian family to settle in Nyack, certainly the first to buy a house, but very soon other people arriving from Europe, and with the assistance of Tolstoy Foundation began to find jobs and homes in and around Nyack. Finally over one hundred and fifty families settled there and a new ethnic community was born in Rockland county.

At the time when we moved to our new home, the Tappan Zee bridge across the Hudson and the New York Thruway had not yet been built. A wooded area began two houses away from us and, between the river and the wood, George and his neighborhood friends had a most wonderful, somewhat Tom Sawyer-like childhood, with mysterious hide-aways and forts in the woods, fishing adventures and even a little home-made rowboat. While the thruway was being built, some fifty houses had to be moved and the wooded area disappeared, but the boys had a lot of fun watching the work. I remember a hot day in July, as I was returning from work on the bus, we stopped because a large two-storey house was being towed on a platform across the road. We all got out to watch. It was very sunny and very hot and suddenly I saw, right underneath the very middle of the house, seven-year-old George, completely unconcerned, squatting down in the only shady and cool place.

The two older girls had a more difficult time adjusting in high school. The easy mixing of parent-organized birthday parties of the younger children in grade school is over by the time children reach high school. Teenagers have a hard enough time to establish their own identity, their own rapport, their own groups of friends. "Belonging" or "not belonging" is a painful problem under any circumstances. And here was an American suburban high school world suddenly forced to accept groups of foreigners, large enough to be noticeable, bearing the somewhat dubious tag of being "Russian," speaking either no English or very little, dressed differently, reflecting different customs, different standards — "D.P.'s."

The teachers, without exception, were outstandingly sympathetic and helpful, but it is the recognition by their peers that matters to teenagers, not the teachers' approval. Elizabeth, with her "British accent" and her sensitivity, had the most difficult time in adjusting. She had stayed for only a little over a year in high school at the time she graduated. In those days the senior prom, held in the high school gymnasium, was a big formal affair, with girls in long white dresses and boys in tuxedos. With something like despair she confided to me that she knew no American boy would invite her and she would *not* be taken to the prom by one of her two Russian classmates, who simply would not know how to behave. I realized that all of this was very superficial and did not really matter too much, but how can one remain indifferent to the desperate hurt of a youngster?

The senior prom took place after the commencement ceremony. After the formal dance, parties would be held in private homes. It would be quite acceptable to have a big party at our house immediately following the graduation ceremony. And our lovely old house, with its arched drawing room and beautiful parquet floors, was such a wonderful setting for a formal party! I spoke to one of the older boys within our Russian youth clan (as a matter of fact the older brother of the boy Elizabeth married four years later). He enthusiastically agreed to organize what one might call a "surprise graduation party" for Elizabeth and the other Russian girl who was graduating with her.

The party was a great success. There was nothing uncouth about our boys and girls, and certainly there was nothing wrong with their dancing and their singing ... I think this first party started off a tradition that greatly helped the creation of a friendly group of young Russians in Nyack, who called themselves "compania." The same type of graduation party was repeated two years later for Olga, with quite a few American boys and girls attending, and seven years later for Xenia with a half-and-half ethnic mixture. How many gatherings, parties, plays, and dances filled our house to capacity throughout these years! They even became known among

American boys and girls as the "Russian-style party," and they sometimes asked for it specifically.

Following the example of endless small Russian communities scattered all over the world, our Nyack group very soon organized a parish. A priest, who was also, by marriage, a member of our family clan, Father Seraphim Slobodskoy, was an inspired leader. A former Red Army soldier, son of a priest who had disappeared in the prisons of the Gulag Archipelago, a painter of some talent, and an ardent football player, he had been made prisoner during the war and chose not to return to Russia. He became priest in the Displaced Persons' camps in Germany and he brought to his priesthood the zeal, the self-sacrifice, the simplicity and the enthusiasm of a new post-revolutionary type of clergy. Even before his arrival a church school was started on Saturday afternoons (again in our hospitable old house) with some twenty-five children attending. (In later years attendance grew to one hundred fifty.) Father Seraphim helped blend in our Nyack community two generations, or rather two types of Russian émigrés: those who had left Russia soon after the Revolution, in the twenties, generally speaking of a somewhat higher cultural and social level, and those who left the U.S.S.R. after World War II and were molded by almost thirty years of life under the Soviet regime. Father Seraphim had a natural and excellent approach to children and young people, warmhearted, humorous, devoid of pomposity. Unfortunately, in later years, as he grew older and his health deteriorated, he somewhat lost touch with the more Americanized, college-age young people. He was unable to learn to speak English and this created a block. At first church services were held in the parish hall of the Nyack Presbyterian Church, then in an old garage, then in a large room on the third floor of a shabby business building, but very early it was decided to buy a piece of land and build a church of our own. It took four years to carry out the project. The rather remarkable aspect of it was that the entire work was done by the members of the parish, in their spare time, on a volunteer basis: architectural design, actual building of walls, all the plumbing, wiring, plastering, wood carving, mosaics, frescoes, icons, gilding of the dome, landscaping of the grounds, etc.— all was done by members of the parish among whom were professionals in all the fields involved.

Besides the Tolstoy Farm and the Russian parish in Nyack, a third Russian center came into existence in Spring Valley, New York, within some seven miles of Nyack. A group of Russian nuns, led by Father Adrian Rymarenko, a remarkable priest who had undergone great hardships in Soviet Russia, settled there, bought some land and had it turned into a Russian Orthodox Cemetery. This became a necropolis of Russians outside Russia with several thousand graves, a place of comfort for the bereaved and a haven for those who had lost their home country.

I think I can sum up this first period of our life in America by saying that we created a little Russian world of our own. This was not a new experience in émigré life, but there was a difference. This small world was not completely isolated from its environment, especially for the younger generation. Our American environment of this period was open-minded to us, friendly, even if not always understanding. Young roots and tendrils grew and penetrated into the soil of our environment; we did not remain protected by a dead shell.

One of my vivid memories of this process is connected with our naturalization as American citizens. We had never applied for French citizenship, and my own and my husband's decision to apply for citizenship in the United States was not just a matter of convenience. As our applications went through the regular routine, I received pamphlets and booklets containing the information about the American constitution, American history, etc., that I should know to pass the test. In the mail was also included a pamphlet by "The Daughters of the American Revolution" which I disliked very much. It said among other things: "Remember, when you become an American citizen, you are no longer an 'Irish-American' or an 'Italian-American', or a 'Polish-American'; you are just plain American." At that time I was working in an office of the National Council of Churches, as secretary to a charming and intelligent elderly lady, Miss Sue Weddel, of whom I was very fond. I brought the letter to her. "This makes me wonder whether I should become an American citizen," I said. "My main reason for emigrating to the United States was that I thought one could be American and yet preserve one's national cultural heritage." "Sophie," answered Miss Weddel, "my family has been American for generations, but if I thought that the Daughters of the American Revolution stood for what America is, I'l give up my citizenship right away."

The final touch to a true concept of American citizenship was given by the judge before whom we pledged our allegiance to the United States of America in a group of some two hundred people. I shall always remember his words: "What does it mean to be American? Does it mean to forget your old country, to forget its language and its culture? No, *this* means being a bad American. A good American is the person who is always open-minded, who will help his neighbor, who is glad to share what he has. Be proud of your ancestry, be proud of your culture and your old language. And when you go to visit your old country, make sure you are not a bad American — do not boast of your refrigerator, your TV set, your car . . . You are American if you can show your appreciation, your love, your understanding of your heritage."

* * *

When my husband's first job disintegrated in 1949 and he could find no other engineering one, he took the job of a drill-press operator in a small factory in Nyack, a branch of the firm Wilcox & Gibbs, builders of industrial sewing machines. Nikita was always very skillful mechanically, good-natured and unpretentious in his relationships with others. He adapted easily to his position as a skilled laborer, joined the union, and was popular among his fellow workers. In order to make more money he chose to work on a night shift, from four P.M. to twelve P.M. Since I had to leave at seven A.M. for my job in New York and came back at seven P.M. we did not see much of each other. Saturdays were taken up for me by running the church school and for Nikita by building the church. In 1951 Nikita was "discovered" by a government committee that was looking for foreign scientists and specialists working at jobs that did not make use of their knowledge and experience. He was offered an engineering job with Lavoie Laboratories in Morganville, N.J., which he gladly accepted, though the starting salary was a little less than he was earning as a skilled laborer. The really difficult part of the decision was that we would again have to be separated. Morganville is sixty miles away from Nyack, and driving a hundred and twenty miles a day would be too fatiguing and too expensive. Should we all move to southern New Jersey? Should we give up our house? Should we again uproot the children? Nikita's decision was firm: "No, Sonia, it is not right for us to destroy that which has come to life here. We've been separated often enough. We will manage it again."

And manage it we did for nineteen years, until Nikita retired. He came home for the weekends only at first, and then also on Wednesday nights, going back to work on Thursday morning. We spent our summer vacation with him since Morganville is close to all the New Jersey beaches. Later, two of our girls went to Douglass College at Rutgers University, in New Brunswick, N.J., which meant that he could often give them rides home, and I believe those long drives together resulted in a closer friendship between the girls and their father.

The house on 38 Glen Byron Avenue in Nyack adapted itself well to a full and varied life. It was somewhat like wheels turning within wheels, that run smoothly, without catch or snag. There was the world of George and his friends, active and exciting, centered mainly in the yard, the basement and the attic. There was the world of the girls, with their boy and girl friends, their parties, gatherings, and romantic involvements. There was the world of our own involvement with the larger family clan and the Russian community, people coming to stay with us because of some family emergency. In addition to all this, our house was a peaceful haven for much loved old persons who ended their life there.

I have already mentioned the old Countess Elena Mikhailovna Tolstoy who came to live with us and who died at the age of ninety-one in 1955. She was very hard of hearing, very firm in many of her old regime attitudes, but she managed to establish a close friendship with each member of our family. In her quiet room she would play card games for hours with George; she would willingly attend christening and wedding ceremonies staged by Xenia for her dolls; Elizabeth would have long heart-to-heart talks with her. She was extremely intelligent and highly cultured and I enjoyed talking to her about problems involved in bringing up children. She shared memories with Aunt Mary. At first the arrangement made with Elena Mikhailovna included having a woman to take care of her. She provided a small salary and we provided room and board (in exchange for dishwashing for the whole family), and at the time of the massive arrival of displaced persons it was not difficult to find a lonely elderly woman who was glad to take such a job. For most of these women a time of adjustment in a Russian environment, before they settled in the new world, was really useful.

I remember especially an incident which took place with one of our "helpers," Matrena Alexeevna, a heavy-built, elderly woman from a Cossack family. She came to us just before Easter, and on Holy Friday she helped me bake the Easter cakes. It was quite a revelation for me to see how meaningful she made the whole procedure: she made the sign of the cross on each cake as we put them into the oven and as she sat watching them bake, in the agelong Russian womanly posture of sorrow — the left hand supported at the elbow by the right one and the left palm supporting the face — she would sigh and say sadly: "And to think what took place at this very time! There He was, nailed to the Cross, suffering for us!" On Easter Sunday afternoon we were all relaxing and resting after the nightlong Easter service. Matrena Alexeevna met me in the kitchen and suddenly blew up: "I know you sent him on purpose! You sent George to see what I was eating . . . And I was eating an orange and I bought it myself, and it was nothing of yours!" I almost blew up too: "Matrena Alexeevna, how can you say such things? I've told you again and again that you are welcome to eat anything you want, at any time, that all the cupboards and the refrigerator are at your disposal . . .

How can you speak like this today, on Easter Sunday, after the time we've had with you on Holy Friday?"

I went back to the living room and told Nikita about our spat. I felt badly about having such a quarrel on Easter Sunday. "Do go and make it up with her. You'll do it much better than I."

He certainly did. As he knocked and entered Matrena Alexeevna's room, where she was resting on her bed, Nikita said that we did not want to hurt her feelings, or check on her in any way. "And if we've done anything wrong, then forgive us, for the sake of the great feast." And, quite naturally, he bowed in the traditional old Russian way, touching the floor with his fingers. Matrena Alexeevna jumped up from her bed. "Forgive me, a sinner, forgive me!" she cried out, and threw herself on her knees bowing down with her head to the floor. Not to be outdone, Nikita knelt down and bowed too and I stood there watching the two of them, wanting to laugh and to cry at the same time.

Soon after Elena Mikhailovna Tolstoy's death, our household was joined by Aunt Mary Meyendorff, Nikita's aunt, whom we had left in France. She had moved to Nikita's brother in Canada and now finally got her visa for the United States and came to live with us. Since by this time both older girls were in college, the two old aunts could have separate rooms, but later, when Elizabeth, her husband and their children (the number growing from one to three) came to share our house, they again lived in one room. This time the sacrifice was on Aunt Mary Meyendorff's part, for my Aunt Mary had a stroke in 1956 and for the last seven years of her life she was completely helpless, immobile and gradually more and more childlike in her mind. She also lost her eyesight, while Aunt Mary Meyendorff could read and thread a needle without glasses, and every day, for hours, she read aloud to her sightless companion.

I wish I could find words tender and loving enough to speak of those two nonagenarian spinsters, who never had a family of their own, but whose capacity to love others was so great that they both ended their lives without knowing loneliness or bitterness, surrounded by the affection and care of their nephews and nieces and their children.

Aunt Mary Meyendorff was brisk, energetic, rationalistic in her thinking, an excellent teacher of mathematics, whose teaching methods were very close to the new math taught in American schools today. She had decided opinions about everything and liked to give advice, which could sometimes be very exasperating, but she had an excellent sense of humor and took criticism well. Aunt Mary S.'s favourite reading was the prayer book, the Bible, and books on spiritual life, and though this was not the kind of literature Aunt Mary M. enjoyed, devout Orthodox Christian though she was, she read aloud faithfully for many hours a day.

Aunt Mary S. lived seven more years with us, like a small vigil light that burns before an icon, barely noticeable, yet giving a different atmosphere to the whole family. After her stroke I thought she would not live more than a few months, but she lived on and on, outliving Aunt Mary Meyendorff by two years. She could not move at all and I had to turn her in her bed every two hours, day and night, to avoid pressure sores. During the day I lifted her with the help of a special harness, cranking it up in a steady iron frame on wheels. This allowed me to settle her in an armchair and even to bathe her. Her mind was getting dim, but her love for us all was so great that it always made itself felt. All her life she had cared for others — for her parents, for my mother, for me, and it seemed that sacrificing herself was a kind of joy to her. Now she had to accept others taking care of her. "You know," she said one day to me, in her strange new expressionless voice, "I was all my life afraid of the very thing that happened to me, and you know, it is not so bad . . . Not bad at all."

I must bear witness to the fact that having a member of the family who needs constant care and understanding, without an actual exchange in communication, contributes something very valuable to the life of the family. Even George, our youngest and thus somewhat spoiled only boy, was affected by it. One evening when Nikita and I went out and unexpectedly were unable to return on time, twelve-year-old George was alone at home to "baby-sit" Aunt Mary. It was time for her to get her bed-pan and I knew we would not be home for another two hours. I called George and explained to him he would have to cope with the situation. George heaved a sigh and said: "Don't worry. We've already done it. We had a hard time, but we made it!"

Aunt Mary Meyendorff died first, from cancer of the breast that erupted suddenly and violently. She died while all the members of her family clan, some twelve or fifteen of them, stood around her with lighted candles, singing the responses as Father Seraphim read the prayers "for the departure of the soul."

Aunt Mary S. died two years later, in my daughter Elizabeth's arms, without any suffering, gently falling asleep. Nikita and I had just left for our vacation and the message that Aunt Mary had taken a turn for the worse reached us by phone. We left immediately and drove for three or four hours to reach home. During this ride I suddenly felt my tension and nervousness leave me and a feeling of peace take their place. Elizabeth was waiting for us in the driveway. "It is all over, Mother," she said through her tears. "She died peacefully," and she named the precise time when I stopped worrying.

* * *

So far I have spoken of the Russian community in Nyack and the peaceful haven it was for our old ones. This, of course, is not a complete picture of our experience. Russian Nyack was a good start, a good place to emerge *from*, but each one of us had to find a new life of his own. In school, in summer camps, on summer jobs, and especially in college the children learned to live on their own, to make friends, to find a place and establish themselves in the American way of life without losing their own personality.

I sometimes wonder what qualities or values rooted in their own earlier experiences they brought to this new life. As I look through their letters of that period there seems to be at least one trait that is common to them all: they knew happiness; feeling happy was part of their experience of family life. They could evaluate life from this experience, from this "taste of happiness" they had had. Writing from a summer camp, twelve-year-old Xenia called herself "the happiest girl in the world" (if we would come to fetch her) and "the second happiest girl in the world" (if she had to come home by train).

I think none of our children attached too much importance to material values, to economic status or security. They knew well enough the meaning of financial difficulties, of "making do" and "doing without." Early in life they learned to work and to earn money for their needs. But I think they also knew, and it was part of their nature to know, that these values were secondary. Of course we had no savings and they knew that it never entered our heads to worry about this. We took it for granted that they would all go to college, that it would somehow become possible, that a way would open up. Elizabeth was accepted at Connecticut College for Women with a big scholarship and lived in a house where the girls did their own housekeeping. Olga and Xenia went to Douglass College, Rutgers University, with a student loan. By the time George graduated from Junior High School we were somewhat concerned about his poor working habits and the quality of education and social life in the public high school. We were able to send him to Wooster School in Danbury, Connecticut, and I cannot speak highly enough of the school, of its headmaster Rev. John Verdery, and of what the school did for George. And who cared that we never could afford to buy anything but cheap second-hand cars, which Nikita tinkered with endlessly?

All the children were strongly conscious of the need to discover themselves, to find their own identity. Quite definitely the Russian community in Nyack was a small world to emerge *from*, not to remain *in*. They loved their home and their family and yet they knew, and we, their parents, knew, that they had to become independent of it. I think Olga put it quite well in one of her letters from college:

"Is it not silly? When I am here, I want to be home and when I am home, I seem to run away all the time. It's rather like a yo-yo which is thrown out and then pulled in. My whole life consists of constantly leaving home and then being drawn back. Even when I am away from home, I am back there in thoughts. But when I *am* home I cannot remain there, or the whole game is up."

All our children took a trip back to Europe at some time and it was important for their discovery of their own identity. Olga's visit in 1958 included a trip to Russia. "I wanted to find out once and for all," she wrote, "who am I? Am I Russian? Am I American? Am I French? And you know what I found out? I am I. I am just Olga, myself, and no other definition adequately describes who I am."

All our children, except Elizabeth, who became engaged while she was still in college and married soon after graduation, lived independently for some time, sharing an apartment with a roommate. They had their own jobs, their own friends, they discovered their own way of life. And yet for all four of them the Orthodox Church (not necessarily the *Russian* Orthodox Church) remained a vital part of their life. Their experience of church life remained the heart of their life experience. Curiously enough all four of them married Russians, or rather persons of Russian origin.

* * *

Quite unexpectedly our settling in the United States brought me personally a call to a work, a vocation, as meaningful for me as my family life. It was tied in with the little known life of Orthodoxy in the United States.

There are several million Orthodox people in the United States, most of them affliated with the Orthodox Church because of their ethnic origin: Greek, Russian, Ukrainian, Syrian, Bulgarian, Serbian, etc. The first settlers from these countries came in mid-nineteenth and early twentieth centuries, because of economic pressure in their home countries. They were a source of cheap labor in America, in the coal mines, in the steel mills in Pennsylvania, the sponge fleets in Florida, as farm hands and factory laborers in many other states. Their isolation, their difficulties, their helplessness were far greater than those of the immigrants in our time, when the world has grown so much smaller and life in any of its parts is not unfamiliar to people living elsewhere. Most of these early immigrants were simple people who had little opportunity for education. Their strength lay in their faith, in their indomitable spirit, in their patience and devotion. They supported each other by creating communities, building their own little dome-capped churches, having their own priests, speaking their own language. For them their parish church was their home away from home. They created Russian, or Greek, or Serbian schools that tried to teach the old language to their children, so that they would preserve their old faith. But this was the one thing in which most of them failed: passing on an understanding of their faith to the next American-born, American-educated generation, eager to conform to the American way of life. Within the third generation a certain interest awoke among young adults concerning the faith of their forefathers. In the case of the Russian Orthodox people their church life was influenced by the breakdown of the official church administration in Russia after the revolution of 1917. The parishes in America were deprived of any support they had been receiving and forced to become much more independent. On the other hand the renaissance of Russian Orthodox theology, thought, and piety within the Russian emigration in Europe brought to America a number of highly educated, active and challenging Orthodox leaders. St. Vladimir's Orthodox Theological Seminary became the focus where Russian theologians, formed at St. Sergius in Paris, came in touch with the reawakening of the Orthodox Church in America. The seminary was founded in 1938 and after a few rather tottering first years began to grow and gain strength. In 1962 it moved to a beautiful campus in Crestwood, New York, and became fully accredited as a graduate school of theology, with all the teaching done in English and an enrollment of around one hundred students of different ethnic backgrounds.

My own special interest has always been work with children, and I gradually became involved in the process of re-awakening that was taking place in the young American churches in this field. American-born Orthodox parents wanted to set up something that would be more effective than the "Russian schools" they had attended in their own childhood. They wanted this Orthodox religious education to fit in with the total American way of life, to be relevant to the problems children have to face today. Rather naturally they took for their model the Protestant Sunday School system and set up a system of classes on Sunday morning, taught in English by volunteer lay teachers. Most priests eagerly supported this movement, but there were many difficulties. The need was there, untrained volunteers were available, but there were no books, no guidelines, no textbooks for teachers or students, no programs, no teaching aids, and practically no one, even among the priests, qualified to train teachers. Methods of teaching were not taught in the seminaries and the best of priests could only contribute to the work their own inspiration and untrained educational talent. Old Russian catechisms and textbooks were hopelessly out of date, uninspiring and dull, and, of course, written in Russian. The very essence of Orthodoxy — the wholeness of life under God, the fullness of the children's participation in the life of church worship, the involvement of the children's own creative spirit in their religious experience — was left out. Protestant customs were introduced that many Protestant churches had already rejected, such as replacing family attendance of church worship by children attending Sunday School while parents are in church.

Groups like our Nyack parish were unfortunately not sympathetic or understanding to such "Americanized Orthodoxy." "What kind of Orthodox are they?" thought the new Russian émigré. They have pews in their churches, they do not speak Russian, they do not bake "kulichi," their services are too short and they skip half the holy days. The new arrivals ignored the American Orthodox parishes and founded their own, which were administered by their own church administration of the Russian Church in Exile.

I was eager to become acquainted with the American Or-

thodox Church and participate in its growth, but as a matter
of fact it proved to be not that easy to get in touch with its
"growing edge." Finally, quite by accident, I met Father
Nicholas Kiryluk, an Orthodox U.S. Army Chaplain, at the
office of the Tolstoy Foundation. He told me that there existed
a Sunday School Committee of the Russian Orthodox Church
in America. He arranged for me to become a member and
this activity proved to be very rewarding. We undertook to
translate into English and publish the books I had helped to
produce in Paris, which was certainly a step forward.

I was asked to prepare new texts for younger children and
a church history for teenagers. By that time I had left the
Tolstoy Foundation office and found a new secretarial job in
the National Council of Churches, which was much less demanding. The woman for whom I worked, an former missionary in India, Miss Sue Weddell, was very sympathetic to my
involvement with the educational work of the Orthodox
Church and allowed me to switch to a four-day week, which
left me one full day a week for writing. The writing of a
church history for young people was a real challenge and I
was very grateful for the attention and assistance that was
given me by Father Georges Florovsky, the dean of the
St. Vladimir's Seminary. At about the same time Father
Georges introduced a course in religious education into the
Seminary curriculum and asked me to teach it. For seventeen
years, from 1956 until 1973, I taught it with great interest
and enthusiasm and thus came to know well a whole generation of young priests who did so much to reform the life
of the parishes.

My first and unforgettable contact with the young American church was at a gathering of clergy where Father Florovsky asked me to speak on Orthodox Christian education.
There were nearly a hundred priests present, most of them
young, or at least they seemed young to me, unused as I was
to beardless, clean-shaven priests, wearing civilian clothes,
with only a clerical collar to distinguish them. To address an
audience of priests, speaking as if I were an authority on a
subject in which they were interested, was a completely new
and practically unimaginable situation for me that would

have been impossible in Europe. Whatever I said in my lecture that day must have been very ordinary and contained no particular innovations or discoveries. I tried to share with them my concept of what is involved in the growth of the child within the Church.

When I finished there was a second of silence and then they all stood up and applauded, and the applause went on and on. I was really shattered. This reversed my life's experience of relationships with priests: my "fathers" were treating me as if I were their mother. I am sure that it was no talent of mine that impressed them, but through me they caught a glimpse of a kind of life in the church which was new to them and which they recognized as something true and desirable.

The work of St. Vladimir's Seminary acquired a new impetus when its staff was joined by new men from St. Sergius Academy in France, especially Father Alexander Schmemann and Father John Meyendorff. Father Alexander became dean of St. Vladimir's in 1955. He was a much younger man than Father Florovsky and I remembered him as an eight-year-old boy, a pupil in a class I taught in our Thursday-and-Sunday School in Paris. He was gifted and brilliant, and an outstanding liturgist, but I would say that his real genius lies in his ability to see and recognize new needs, new situations and to react to them in a truly prophetic way. He was a champion of new causes, but for him no cause was ever bigger than the individual human person involved. Personal, pastoral care was never driven out by the important role he played in establishing new church policies. I think there was never an "uninteresting" person for him. Also he was quite incapable of stylizing himself into the traditional image of the classic, pious, Orthodox priest. His sense of humor ran away with him and occasionally gave offense to Russian traditionalists, but it was the very quality that allowed him to reach the younger generation and make Christian faith alive and meaningful to them. He was a remarkable speaker, omitting all the usual religious oratory, and the unexpected, unusual, plain turns of his speaking reached the core of attention and understanding in his listeners.

The impact of Father Schmemann, Father Meyendorff, and the other young theologians caused many people to recognize Orthodoxy in America not as a surviving national tradition — Russian, Greek, Serbian, or other — but as a vision of the Christian way of life, based on Christian faith and witnessing its faith in a world of eroded Christian values. They were truly representative of the best of Russian culture and tradition, the best of West European education, and St. Vladimir's Seminary became a center of Orthodox Christian revival, a powerhouse for the Orthodox Church in America, and it provided education to students of many different ethnic backgrounds, as well as to converts of non-Orthodox background.

My close contact with St. Vladimir's helped me to realize that any efforts at improving the religious education of our children and young people must be made along the lines of our common faith and not our different national backgrounds. I also felt that, first of all, we had to make an effort to think deeply concerning our philosophy of the child's place in the life of the Church. We had to understand our problems thoroughly, before we tried to do anything immediately practical. The first difficulty was to find a good starting point. I knew that if the initiative of reform in Orthodox religious education were to be taken by any one national jurisdiction, the others would brand it as "Russian" or "Greek" or something else and would feel it was none of their business.

At this point the friendships I made during my secreterial work in the National Council of Churches helped me to find a solution. Through mutual friends I met Dr. Gerald Knoff, head of the Division of Christian Education of the NCC, and asked him whether he would be willing to convene a consultation on Christian education, with representatives of Orthodox churches in America. Most of these churches were nominally members of the National Council of Churches and though they took very little part in its work, they always punctiliously responded to formal invitations. Gerald Knoff willingly agreed, Father Schmemann threw himself enthusiastically into the project, and helped me make out a list of key priests to be invited from every jurisdiction — men who were interested in church educational work. About twelve of us met for the first time in 1954 and from then on continued to meet for some two years in the conference room of the Division of Christian Education. The topics we discussed helped us to understand the basic principles on which we wanted to build our work. Papers were given on the meaning of doctrine, of liturgical worship, of ethics, of Bible study in the life of children. We studied aspects of children's religious growth, principles of teaching, and we reviewed and compared different approaches.

In October, 1956, we held a two-day conference at Reed Farm, with some twenty-five people attending. It was decided to found an Orthodox Christian Education Commission, with Orthodox churches of all ethnic backgrounds taking part, and to publish twice a year a Bulletin which would contain articles on Christian education. For all of us taking part in the work it was a period of enthusiasm and inspiration. We believed in the importance of our work and were supported by the real hunger for any kind of religious educational material in the parishes all over the United States. We had no money, no budget, no staff, no address but this did not worry us.

By that time, between Nikita's increased earnings and the nursing care needed at home for my aunt, I felt it possible to give up doing any paid work. My last job, as assistant librarian in the Nyack High School, demanded much less time but in 1957 I gave that up to. Now I had all the time I need to promote my new venture in church work.

We published a Bulletin regularly, and in 1959 one of its issues took the form of a 135-page teacher-training manual. In 1962 we again used a Bulletin issue to produce a 100-page illustrated book giving guidelines for two years' work with pre-school children. In a review of our materials, Father Paul Schneirla of the Antiochian Orthodox Church called them "a mediation of our church tradition through the techniques of modern educational methods."

During this period we attained the best inter-Orthodox cooperation I had ever experienced. Church groups that did not even recognize each other's canonical status worked together. All the typing and reproduction was contributed by the Religious Education Department of the Greek Archdiocese; Federated Russian Orthodox Clubs contributed the small amounts of money we needed. A Ukrainian priest, acting as our secretary, contributed his boundless enthusiasm and faith in the future of our work. I will always remember how we were helped at a moment of our lowest ebb by Father Hategan and his wife of the Romanian diocese: a meeting of our Committee was called at the Antiochian parish in Brooklyn and nobody turned up. I was sitting alone in the empty room, discouraged and wondering whether it was wise to continue our efforts. Suddenly the door opened and in bustled the cheerful, exuberant and portly Father Hategan and his wife, who came all the way from Cleveland, Ohio, to attend the meeting.

We printed two thousand copies of the pre-school manual and these were sold within six weeks. With the proceeds we printed another two thousand copies and these sold within the year. Inexorably, without experience or funds, we were being pushed into publishing books.

By that time a talented young teacher, Constance Tarasar, joined our work. She enrolled at St. Vladimir's and became the first woman to complete a full course of graduate Orthodox theological studies. Connie and I worked together on producing new texts. At all stages of the work key priests and theologians of different national jurisdictions read and revised the manuscripts. Our financial policy was optimistic, to say the least, but the books sold rapidly. Our income and expenses grew equally fast. In my old records I find that our yearly turnover was four hundred sixty-six dollars in 1957 and it had grown to more than one hundred thousand dollars by 1969. We had published pupils' workbooks and teachers' manuals for all elementary and high school grades. In 1965 we started on a project that became my favorite piece of work: a monthly magazine for children called *Young Life*, with a circulation of over five thousand. Tom Kazich, a member of the Serbian Church, became my inspired co-worker. Of all the people I worked with during these years, Tom was the one who shared most closely my understanding of our work with children and I had great hopes for his future. A little later we began publishing *Upbeat*, a monthly magazine for adolescents, and then a college-level quarterly *Concern*, which later became independent.

Nurturing and stimulating this activity were our contacts with people in parishes of all ethnic backgrounds, all over the United States. Many times a year I had to fly out to conduct teacher training seminars in New England, in the Midwest, in Pennsylvania, on the West coast. In 1966 I spent an unforgettable month in Alaska, visiting the Indian and Aleutian Orthodox parishes there.

What was so wonderful about this work? What inspired us? I think for all of us, it was a time of discovery. The people who gathered at the seminars and conferences discovered the meaning of Christianity, not simply as a set of old ethnic traditions and homey rituals inherited from their immigrant forefathers. They began to see suddenly the depth and breadth of life in the Church. For me it was the inspiring experience of coming in touch with growth in a church body, discerning "the growing edge" of the church. People's ears and eyes were open to hear and see as they had not done before. Of course, their appreciation of my personal work was often exaggerated. As a matter of fact I was an elderly woman, a housewife, a mother and grandmother, with no theological education, but bearing within me the heritage of a great Christian culture and of a great Orthodox revival, shaped by catastrophic historic events. I could speak to teachers and parents in our common, family-life kind of language, making our daily life experience part of our experience of life with God. My particular capacities happened to meet at the right moment the strong need of the people. The greatness of their need and of their receptivity conferred on me a dimension I did not really have.

By 1969 I felt that it was time for me to turn over my work to a younger generation which was ready to try out new ideas and new approaches. Our Commission had become sufficiently solid to pay small salaries and it was really opening the way to a new vocation in our church. I was sixty-six years old and I wanted to sum up my educational experience and thinking in a book that St. Vladimir's Press was willing to publish, *Our Church and Our Children*, (1976).

On October 16, 1969, I was given a fantastic farewell banquet. Letters from all the different church jurisdictions in America, letters from Japan, from Canada, from Alaska, from all the corners of the United States, letters from bishops, priests, teachers, parents and children were bound into an impressive volume and presented to me. St. Vladimir's Seminary conferred on me the degree of Doctor of Divinity "honoris causa." A service of thanksgiving was celebrated by Metropolitan Ireney, primate of the former Russian Orthodox Church in America, now called the Orthodox Church in America. A dinner for close to two hundred people was served, which was also attended by all my family, including my two oldest granddaughters and Father Seraphim of our Nyack parish. At the end of the dinner, Connie Tarasar, who had been the organizer of all this splendor, presented me with a check for fifteen hundred dollars, "to take a trip to Russia," which had been my unexpressed dream for many years.

CHAPTER ELEVEN

On July 28, 1970, I was on a plane approaching the Sheremetievo airport, near Moscow, exactly fifty years — a whole lifetime — after my mother and I walked away from our home and Gania came to see us off and we both wept so bitterly as I kept saying: "Gania, I'll come back, Gania, I promise you, I'll come back!" Now I was coming back for a short visit, as a stranger: a mother and a grandmother of a family in America, and Gania had died from tuberculosis in the early forties during the war.

Russia, Revisited, 1970

The TWA plane captain announced that we were beginning our descent to Sheremetievo, "the most beautiful and modern airport in the world, the Russians call it ..." he added sarcastically and I caught myself at this point resenting his making fun of "my" people. But there was no doubt about it; the airport was extremely shabby and drab, more so than any American or European airport I had ever seen, with the typical shabbiness and poor taste of most of the new buildings I was to see in the Soviet Union.

We lined up to pass inspection at customs and a tourist family right in front of me was in trouble. They looked like Armenians from the United States and they had a huge amount of luggage. As I watched the scene the customs official pulled out twenty colored mohair shawls, one after another, eight fur coats and endless other pieces of clothing. His argument with the owners of the luggage seemed to have been going on for a long time. They insisted they were bringing gifts for family and friends; he was sure it was for the black market. The official was frantic and exasperated and most of the luggage was finally held back. I waited rather anxiously for my turn.

"Have you anything newly purchased that you are bringing in?" the official asked. "Yes . . . why, yes . . ." I almost stuttered. "I have a plastic dinner-ware set I am bringing as a wedding present for my niece . . ." "For goodness' sake, let's not lose any time on such nonsense! Have you any shawls?" I nervously pulled out three small nylon head scarfs I had brought to be able to give them as presents to friends. "Nonsense, nonsense . . ." he repeated. Curiously enough, the only thing that attracted his attention was a little paper icon in an imitation leather case which I always take with me on trips, a postcard reproduction of an ancient Russian icon. "You know, when you will be leaving, you will not be allowed to take out any Russian art objects," he said. "This is not an art object, it's a cheap reproduction of an old icon," I answered. "Well, I've warned you anyway and you'll argue about it when you leave. Next, please!" I must add that I had no trouble whatsoever with my icon when I was leaving.

I travelled "luxury class" because I wanted to be on my own, not part of a group, shown around by a guide. "Luxury class" included a taxi ride from Sheremetievo to the Metropole Hotel in Moscow, where I was assigned. It was a trip about an hour long. I looked hungrily at the landscape — the familiar woods with birch trees, some log houses in the traditional "izba" style, the grass meadows, and the unfamiliar new suburban communities with high-rise buildings and electric trains. The taxi-driver was interested and sympathetic. "Where did you live in Moscow?" he asked. I knew that many street names had been changed, but I could give him some landmarks, such as the Central Post Office building and the main thoroughfares. He insisted it was not much out of our way and drove me along familiar streets. It was amazing to recognize buildings, even a familiar store, that used to be the famous Kuznetzov porcelain store on Miasnitskaya Street, and was now still selling dishes, tea-sets, etc., as a State store.

I registered at the Hotel Metropole and was given a large room on the third floor. It was a curious detail of Soviet tourism that tourists are not given advance information about the name or address of their hotel. I knew the Hotel Metropole well by sight, though surroundings had changed. A busy city square with heavy traffic replaced the old open-air food market and there was an underground passage for pedestrians. At the hotel the typical early twentieth-century Russian grandeur made itself felt in the size of the rooms, the width of the corridors, the marble fixtures in the bathroom, the large windows, the occasional chandeliers, the beautiful dining room. Along with this went shabby, cheap rugs, curtains, and upholstery, poor quality towels and bedlinen, the ugly wall paper. Yet the friendly and pleasant woman at the floor desk told me that the particular room I was assigned had recently won a prize for "the best hotel room."

I quickly unpacked and went out to roam in the Moscow streets. It was a pleasant late afternoon, sunny yet cool, the kind of weather I had almost forgotten in New York. My first impression was of crowds. The car traffic was less dense than in New York, but the wide sidewalks were crowded with millions of people hurrying on their way somewhere, working people, wholesome, sunburnt, neatly and plainly dressed, all of them with parcels, shopping bags, or briefcases stuffed with things. I did not see any woman that would be called elegant in Paris or New York, nor did I see anyone tattered, or barefoot, or long-haired. Plenty of shady trees, but no trimmed lawns. The streets were kept very clean, not a shred of paper anywhere. In the side streets were old Moscow private houses, the charming old eighteenth-century houses in rather bad repair and shabby. I was glad to realize that I neither looked nor felt like a foreigner. During the very first half-hour of my walk someone asked me for directions and I never felt that I attracted anyone's attention. During my whole stay in Moscow and Leningrad I easily got involved in conversations with strangers, and it always came to them as a shock that I was "from America," a United States citizen, and they found it hard to believe. I really had no difficulty in establishing rapport with people. Throughout my stay I would leave my

hotel early in the morning and return at night, roaming around
completely on my own, mixing with people in street cars,
subways, restaurants, churches, visiting old friends and making
new ones. I noticed that during my first night in Moscow, the
telephone bell rang in my room at two A.M., but when I
lifted the receiver no one answered. Maybe this was a formal
way of checking on me.

My first day in Moscow was spent visiting the part of the
town where I had lived in the years 1917-1920, the "Doctor
Zhivago" years of famine, disruption and fear, when all the
life I had known as a child went to pieces and was destroyed.
Names of streets had been changed, but I had no trouble finding our old "pereulok" (lane) and our house was all the more
recognizable because the author Maxim Gorky used to live
there at the same time we did and now a bronze plaque com-
memorated this event. The house must have been fairly modern in the early decades of the twentieth century and I was
again impressed by its basic architectural good quality, similar
to houses of that time and type in Paris or London. Now the
elevators worked again, although the staircase was carpetless
and the walls chipped. On the door of our former apartment
(which we had considered very small in those early post-
revolutionary days when we came to live there) were seven
names. Seven families lived in the apartment. I rang the bell
again and again but no one answered. It was a weekday and
everyone must have been at work.

Disappointed, I was leaving the building when I saw a
very old woman entering. I thought, perhaps, since Gania and
Peter had lived here for twenty-five years, she might have
known them and tried to ask her a question. She looked scared,
mumbled something about not knowing anyone and scurried
away. This was the only time I met with the kind of fear which
must have been general in Stalin's time, a constant fear it must
be difficult for the older generation to outgrow.

I went around the corner to look for the church we had
attended, the church where my mother and I stopped on the
day of our flight and Father Vassili blessed my mother. There
was no trace of it ... A young woman passing by willingly
informed me that she remembered the old church: it had been

torn down in the thirties to make room for an apartment
building. Only a few old trees and the heavy wrought iron
fence around the site helped me to recognize the place.

Worse than this was the sight of an old church, probably
seventeenth century, in another side street. Plaster had fallen
off, the dark brick framework was crumbling away, empty
window spaces stared like blind eyes. The nave and sanctuary
were used for storage and dumping. Trucks rolled up and unloaded some kind of rubbish. The old church stood like a
skeleton among living people. I stood and stared until people
began to turn round and look at me.

Next day I found my first "functioning" church, as they
are called. Suddenly I saw a glimpse of a well-kept gilded
dome in a small side street. As I approached I saw an icon
on the sidewall, quite high up. On the narrow ledge in front
of it lay a small bunch of field flowers placed by someone.
The flowers were still fresh. It was a week-day and a few old
women were waiting for the service to begin. As we talked
they spoke of their three parish priests. All three were good,
they said, but the third, the young one, was really wonderful!
One of the women spoke of her pilgrimage to the St. Sergius
Monastery near Moscow, of the great crowds there, the services, people spending the night sitting on the grass around
the church, singing hymns and religious folk songs.

When the service of Matins began I watched this congregation curiously. There were some forty or fifty women,
aged from forty to seventy, but I also counted up to fourteen
young people in their twenties who came in singly and in
couples. They watched, listened, looked respectfully and
quietly, and left after ten minutes or so. They were not wor-
shipers in the real sense of the word, but they seemed typical
of the young Russian generation, tired of the shoddy drabness
of official bureaucracy, industrialization and materialism. I
saw them in old churches, in art galleries, at concerts of classical music, collecting objects of old Russian art, as if they were
searching for some beauty or spiritual dimension of life that
they missed in their day-to-day Soviet reality. The two vested
readers in the church, in their late teens or early twenties,

looked like students. A young woman dressed in black acted as an altar boy. I learned that this is quite usual now.

Next day I took the train to St. Sergius. This was one of the few "illegal" things I did, for tourists are not allowed to leave the city unless accompanied by an interpreter. There were many women on the train and our conversation was easy and friendly. They were all greatly interested in the snapshots I had of my grandchildren dyeing Easter eggs, our home, the church we built in Nyack, the children's Easter procession. The two things that impressed them most were the un-crowdedness of our home and the fact that there were Ortho-dox people in such a distant land, living and praying in the Orthodox way.

I became particularly friendly with one woman in her late forties. She had come all the way from Kazakhstan (in Asia) for this personal pilgrimage and it was not the first time she was doing it. She spoke enthusiastically of how she would abstain from food all this day, go to the evening service, spend the night in church and receive Holy Communion in the morn-ing. As we talked on, she looked at me searchingly and asked: "Tell me, what do you love more, your motherland, or where you are now?" It was a difficult question to answer, and one that had to be answered with complete sincerity. I said: "It is very difficult to say what you love more, your motherland or freedom." She did not answer.

When we left the train and went down the road a bit, our ways parted. I was going straight to the monastery and she was going to the peasants' home where she would stay for a few days. "Goodbye," she said, "goodbye! You will re-member my name — Anna." "Goodbye!" I answered. "My name is Sophie." We embraced each other and we were both crying. We did not have to explain that we would remember each other's name in prayer.

The monastery, which dates back to the fourteenth century, has been carefully restored and is kept up as a national historic monument. Church services are held in two of the churches, one building is used for the Theological Seminary, and the rest remains a museum. As I went through the gate in the ancient thick walls, the sheer beauty of it all stopped my breath: pink, blue, white and yellow buildings, golden domes, original ancient architectural shapes, frescoes ... The first and most ancient building I entered was the church where the relics of Saint Sergius are venerated. It was dark and crowded. Services are chanted all day long and the crowd of pilgrims flows steadily through, singing, blessing themselves, putting up little candles, praying with sighs and tears. Standing in that crowd I really felt lifted on a wave of prayer.

I knew how strongly children are discouraged from attending church in Russia. I knew that the law forbidding religious education can be interpreted so as to prohibit their presence in church, yet at St. Sergius I saw a number of school-age children coming in with their families and praying in church. As I left the church I spoke to a little girl about eleven years old. "I am so happy to see you here," I said. "I come from America and there are many Orthodox children in America who pray as you do. They will be glad to know that there are children praying in church here. "At this moment the little girl's mother and grandmother caught up with us. For a moment they looked worried, seeing a stranger speak to their child, but when they heard my words, they beamed at me smilingly.

In the same church I saw three teenage girls listening attentively to explanations given them by one of the old women. I was glad to see this for I heard that some of the old women who bore on their shoulders the brunt of the years of persecution, during which young Communists entered church buildings to light their cigarettes from vigil lights, resent the presence of young people, even when they enter with respectful curiosity.

The church in Moscow that impressed me most was a focus for the new "intelligentsia." I attended it on the day of the Prophet Elijah and I still remember the priest's sermon. "Who is a prophet?" he said. "A prophet is a man who moves around. He is not a priest, he is not tied down to a church building. Every human grief, every human trouble, every human sin concerns him. He enters into everything that happens in life. And at the same time he is enveloped in a flame, the pure spiritual flame that lifts him up to God. Each one

of us, the least one of us, has to have something of this prophetic spirit . . ."

I was introduced to this priest by an old friend of mine
who had returned to Russia after the end of World War II.
As was typical of the reverent attitude of the faithful crowding the churches in Russia, we did not approach each other
in church, nor exchange greetings until the service was over,
though our eyes showed us that we recognized each other
after twenty-five years of separation. The priest invited us to
have a cup of tea with him in a small room adjoining the
church. Smilingly he unplugged the phone before we began
talking — he had reason to believe that there was a monitoring
device in the phone. We discussed such matters as the new
independence of the Russian Orthodox Church in America,
of which he thoroughly approved. I asked him whether there
really is an "underground" church in Russia, as opposed to
the official church collaborating with the Soviet government.
"Underground church . . ." he said. "What do you call an
underground church? The underground church has many
floors to it. The higher up they go, the smaller they are. And
on the very last floor, that is above ground, visible to all, there
stands just one man (he meant the Patriarch). Everyone sees
him, everyone sees all he does, but no one can see his feet, for
they are still hidden." This kind of talk I found very typical
of the Russians today. They expect you to understand meta-
phors; they speak in images.

Father spoke of the young people he sees more and more
frequently in his church. "I noticed a young girl coming quite
frequently to the services. I invited her for a talk. 'Are you
familiar with church services?' — 'No.' 'Do you understand
anything you hear in church?' 'No, not a word.' 'But *why*
do you come then?' 'Because it is all so wonderful, because
I feel a different person when I am in church.' Oh," continued
Father, "she will learn to understand, we will take care of it,
but this shows how and why young people come to church."

After leaving the church, my friend and I spent the day
roaming around Moscow, eating our lunch on a bench in a
small square, visiting the famous Tretiakovsky Art Gallery,
talking endlessly about the different experiences she and her

children, now grown up, went through, about the life and work
and faith of the Russian people. Speaking of the church she
said: "The hardest to bear was not the persecutions, not the
arrests and exiles. The hardest of all was that period of com-
parative prosperity after the end of the war, when for a while
the priesthood became a profitable profession. Priests earned
a lot of money, went about well dressed, owned cars, and a
lot of unworthy men became priests. This was the hardest
of all, but even this we had to bear, we had to be patient and
silent. What mattered most was preserving the Church, bringing the sacraments to the people."

On my last day in Moscow that same friend was talking
to me in my hotel room. "Tell me," I asked. "What is the
greatest difficulty in your life here? What is the hardest to
bear?" She looked suspiciously at the desk phone and turned
her back to it. On a slip of paper she wrote one word in
French and then carefully tore the paper up. The word was
"mensonge" — lie, falsehood.

I had hoped to find in Moscow my old friend Igor Alexeev, son of Stanislavsky. I called at his parents' old home,
which had been turned into the Stanislavsky Museum and
preserved exactly as it used to be. The secretary told me that
Igor was away on vacation. Too bad, I thought, but the very
next day, at the home of Nikita's cousin who lived in Moscow
with her married daughter, I saw Igor. He had heard from
her of my forthcoming visit and sacrificed a whole week of
his vacation in order to see me. Yes, mistrustful as Russians
are today of casual acquaintances, their capacity for friendship and their need of friends is very great.

There is really quite a difference in human relations involved in daily city encounters between the United States and
the Soviet Union. Russian society does not function around
the principle of "serving the customer"; there is none of the
professional amiability we are used to in Western Europe,
and many foreign tourists are upset by the poor service in
restaurants, the lack of courtesy in stores. Yet the man in the
street is amazingly friendly and willing to go to a lot of trouble
to help you. Another contrast is that while Americans who
happen to share the same table in a restaurant will inevitably

start sharing information about themselves and exchanging opinions, Russians are extremely reserved when talking to strangers. You have to be very careful not to let people feel that you are "fishing for information," prodding them. I think my contacts were helped by the fact that I belonged to a recognizable type — an "old émigré," a grandmother, an elderly Orthodox church woman. On the other hand real friendships are quite unaffected by our modern American acute consciousness of lack of time. The friends I met spent hours and hours with me, and could not tear themselves away. Our conversations could have gone on for days.

I was strongly impressed by my cousin's son-in-law, a young man called Iura. He was an artist, particularly interested in old Russian art. Officially he held some minor position which safeguarded him from being prosecuted as a "parasite," but his real vocation was creating beautiful "objets d'art" of leather, gold, silver and semi-precious stones. "Does your art work pay?" I asked, admiring a bracelet he had made. "I could earn well," he answered, "if I worked in series, repeating the same model twenty times over, but this . . . this would be like spitting into my own soul . . ." A strange feeling for a man born and raised in a completely industrialized society, yet I believe it is quite typical of many Russians today. Before I left Iura sent me the bracelet I had admired, as a present.

Of a different type was another couple I met. The husband, of Russian origin, had been educated in America. While in college he was carried away by Communist teachings and decided to go back to Soviet Russia, breaking all ties with his family and the White Russian émigré clan. After quite a few years of efforts spent in satellite countries, he was granted Soviet citizenship and given a good job in Moscow, on the staff of a magazine dealing with agriculture and economics. Sasha's former enthusiasm and convictions had considerably faded. He thought with nostalgia of his family in the United States, but he believed that he was serving a useful purpose, supporting ideas expressed by some Soviet economists about a new and realistic approach to the price levels established by the Government, i.e. that for a healthy economy prices have to be determined by actual costs and not by political considerations. Sasha was married. His wife obviously cared to have as nice a home as possible. They were both working and had no children, but Sasha's mother-in-law lived with them. They had a nice three-room apartment in a new high-rise building on the outskirts of Moscow. A telephone had just been installed, after two years' waiting. Now they were on a waiting list to purchase a car. Sasha had never been close to the Church and the religious reawakening taking place in Soviet Russia today had not touched him. Yet he showed the same hunger for friendship, for some kind of personal contact with a world he had known, for personal affection. Again I had gifts pressed on me and when I tried to find out what I could send them, Sasha wife expressed only one wish — a few yards of contact paper! Oh, that would be so useful in the beautification of their home.

I made an effort to find Gania's son, now married and father of two children, but he was away on some kind of summer job and his wife and children were spending their holiday in a village with the wife's mother. The neighbors were very kind and sympathetic and were enthralled at the story of a woman from America looking for the son of the nanny who brought her up. Yet I later felt it might have been a mistake on my part to speak so frankly to his neighbors, since Volodia never acknowledged the parcel I sent him from the Moscow post office. In the past, since 1958 when my daughter Olga learned in Moscow of Gania's death in 1943, Volodia and I had occasionally exchanged letters. His letters were friendly and warm, but when he acknowledged the parcels I sent him, he thanked me only for the gifts to the children, never mentioning whatever I sent for him and his wife. On the other hand, in his very first letter, he managed to make me understand that Gania did get a church funeral. The thought processes in the Soviet Union are devious, and it is difficult for outsiders to act tactfully and with understanding.

I spent a week in Moscow and then left on a plane for Leningrad, the city of my birth and childhood.

I had forgotten what a beautiful city it is. Perhaps it is more beautiful now than it used to be, for the coloring of the

palace buildings on the quays of the Neva have been restored
to their original yellow and white, pale azure and white, and
pale pink and white of the eighteenth century, instead of the
early Victorian, reddish chocolate-brown of my childhood
days. The huge empty square where military parades used to
be held ("Field of Mars") has been planted with trees and
shrubs. Curiously enough, practically all the monuments of
the imperial period are intact: Peter the Great, Catherine the
Great, Nicholas I and Suvorov continue to look at their city
in all their bronze grandeur. Wide open spaces of the big city
squares, the majestic flow of the Neva in its rigid granite
frame . . . Leningrad has maintained much of the character
of old St. Petersburg.

I was given a room in the Hotel Astoria, right in front of
the immense cathedral of St. Isaac, now used as a museum.
The porter brought my suitcase into my room just as I opened
wide the huge window looking at the cathedral. "Yes," he
said, "it is something, our old Isaac!" and he quoted the
verse of the psalm engraved around the dome. I made the
sign of the cross.

There is also a new and rather awesome aspect added to
the image of St. Petersburg: the tragic suffering of the city
during the World War II siege. People died during the
siege and their names are engraved on a huge wall that
serves as a monument to their memory.

My major contact in Leningrad was the Orthodox Theological Academy, for St. Vladimir's Seminary, where I
taught, had some contacts with their faculty. Finding the address of the Academy was quite a different matter from looking
up a name in a New York telephone book, for the simple
reason that there are no phone books in Leningrad. At the
hotel I was told that I should make my inquiry at an information booth and there was one just around the corner. The
information booth proved to be a small window opening into
the street with two or three people standing in line in front
of it. When my turn came and I asked for the address of the
Orthodox Theological Academy, the woman at the window
looked somewhat surprised and, leaning back, shouted to
someone: "Do we have an Orthodox Theological Academy

here?" The answer was positive and in a minute she gave me a slip of paper with the address. Even so, it took me quite a while, with several changes of trams and trolleys, and endless askings on the way, to find the Academy, but I must say that those travelings were one of the most enjoyable aspects of my stay. I loved listening in to conversations, looking at the books people read, trying to understand their behavior. Once I saw two boys in their late teens almost get into a fight over a book. One of them, the owner, wanted the book back; the borrower wanted to keep it over the weekend. By stretching my neck discreetly I saw the title, *Leatherstocking Tales* by James Fenimore Cooper.

The Academy was closed for the summer, but I was very kindly received by an elderly lady-typist and a young priest, who showed me all over the building. The Bishop, whose name was given me in New York, had received another appointment and was no longer there. The professor of liturgical music, whose name I was also given, had left the city for his "dacha." The priest and the typist really went to a lot of trouble; they telephoned the professor's apartment to make sure he had left, and explained in great detail how I could reach the "dacha" — in about two hours' train ride from Leningrad.

They also gave me information about churches where services were still being held. One was close by and a service would be going on right then, because it was the feast day of its patron saint. The church was referred to by a rather funny name "Kulich and Paskha" because the church building was round, like the Easter cake "kulich" and the belfry pyramid-shaped, like the Easter cheesecake "paskha." I also learned that the famous icon of the Holy Virgin "Joy of Those Who Sorrow" is now kept in this church. This name opened a flood of memories in my mind. All through our childhood, during Holy Week, we went on a pilgrimage to a church on the outskirts of Petersburg where this icon was then kept. A priest there heard our confessions. Now, by walking just a few blocks, I would see this icon again.

The church was crammed full and I had difficulty squeezing in. The crowd could only be compared to the rush-hour subway in New York. It was difficult to make the sign of the

cross and candles were passed from person to person to be lit
before the icons in the front of the church. Two young dea-
cons, slowly and with difficulty, made their way through the
crowd back and forth, carrying a copy of the famous icon so
that all the people could venerate it. Suddenly I heard a whispered cry of anguish: "Orthodox people! I've dropped my
handbag!" It was impossible to step back, to bend down to
look for the handbag, but in a minute there was another
whispered call: "Who lost a handbag? Here it is!"

Next morning I started on my trip to find the music professor. It was somewhat ambitious because by that time I knew
that tourists are not allowed to go outside the city without
being accompanied by an interpreter, but I also knew that
I was not easily recognizable as a foreigner and did not attract attention. However I almost got into a difficulty at the
station where information regarding trains is given electroni-
cally, in answer to the question asked into a receiver. It
appears there were two places of the same name, in two different regions of the Soviet Union and I used the wrong word
for "region" or "area" so that the faceless loudspeaker began
instructing me on how to get to a completely different part of
Russia. Fortunately the kindly people standing around as-
cribed my confusion to my natural stupidity and explained
everything very clearly.

I had two hours to wait for my train and settled on a bench
with a book I had bought at a booth the day before. It was interesting to note that at these book booths people always
crowded around books on art and fiction and completely
ignored the section of "ideological" literature. Two middle-
aged women were already seated on the bench, deep in conversation, and in a few minutes another woman sat down on
my other side. One of the women was complaining bitterly
about her good-for-nothing husband — never sober, always
grumbling, always angry. "Even when I went to his factory,
they told me he was a pain in the neck and they could not
see how I stood him, day-in, day-out." On and on went the
complaints, getting more and more intimate. I kept the book
open, but the conversation was much more interesting.

"Hey, you wives," suddenly said my left-hand neighbor.

"You jabber without shame, and the young woman listens to it all!" I smiled at her: "Not much of a young woman, with seven grandchildren of my own . . ." That started us off. In a few minutes I was showing her my grandchildren's snapshots. When I came to the picture of the house, I explained that it was in America, that I was a White-Russian émigré, on my first visit to my country after fifty years. The woman almost exploded with excitement: "So this is what it is! This is what it means! And I listen and listen and cannot figure out what it is that doesn't fit, that sounds somehow strange." Now she was full of questions. She wanted to know all about my house, our life, our work, our church. My train was leaving in fifteen minutes. She tried to persuade me to take another train, the one she was taking herself. It was going to some different place, but I would be able to get a bus there that would take me to where I wanted to go. I remained firm, however, and was soon comfortably installed in a clean compartment of an electrical suburban train.

My impressions in the train were no less interesting. Across the aisle was a father with two nice-looking children, a boy and a girl, some ten or twelve years old. Both youngsters were absorbed in their books; one was by Seton-Thompson, the other, also a translation, was by Jules Verne or something of the kind. I must say I had never before seen people reading as much as they do in Russia today — in trains, streetcars, and even walking in the streets.

My own compartment was full. A comfortable, cheerful, plump grandmother was taking back home with her her six-year-old granddaughter, who had just spent three weeks' vacation with her mother. Three boys, around fifteen or sixteen, were returning from examinations, given in the month of August to determine the school young people will attend. Before the train started, the grandmother opened up a paper-wrapped candy and gave it to her little girl. "The militiaman won't arrest me, will he?" she chuckled as she threw the tightly rolled-up wrapper out of the window, and she gave a questioning look to the boys. The boys grinned in a friendly way and the atmosphere remained peaceful and relaxed. I must say that throughout my stay I was impressed by the

cleanliness of the streets, the complete absence of paper or
rubbish thrown around. I saw a little boy discard a small piece
of paper as he ran along, and then suddenly stop in his tracks,
go back, pick up the paper and deposit it in a trash basket.
There was no one around.

The child was happily chatting to her grandmother and
I heard her ask whether one could still bathe in the pond.
"No, darling, too late," answered the grandmother. "God
has put an icicle in the lake and ponds and the water is cold."
I watched the teen-age boys, the quaint expression did not
attract their attention, and they did not resent it.

The train ride took some two hours, then half an hour's
walk through fields, then a village with footpaths trodden
from log cabin to log cabin. One of the houses was the professor's "dacha." First, his wife received me, to give the professor time "to make himself presentable," and then the professor, tall, portly and elderly, welcomed me and right away
I was enveloped in the typically Russian overwhelming hospitality with food and drink endlessly pressed on the guest, and
conversation that can go on hour after hour. The professor
was well informed of Orthodox church life abroad. He knew
Father Schmemann and Father Meyendorff. He was deeply
interested in the new independent American Orthodox Church.
I learned that he was not only teaching liturgical music at the
Academy, but was also a professor of ancient Russian music
at the conservatory of Leningrad. He spoke to me at length
of the young men who came today to study at the Academy.
One day, as the incoming students were going through their
physical examination, he spoke to a youngster who did not
wear his baptismal cross — "After all, you are coming to be
a student at the Academy . . ." The boy flushed as he replied:
"I was working in a factory where we worked without shirts
and it would have been noticed that I wore a cross. So I sewed
it into my belt — you see, there . . ." "And I felt so embarrassed," said the professor. "There I was picking on him when
he had to overcome so many difficulties to come here." Still
I gathered that the relations between faculty and students were
less close here than at St. Vladimir's or St. Sergius.

In the evening the professor insisted on seeing me off to

the station. His attire awakened nostalgic memories of my childhood in the country: trousers tucked into tall leather boots, a white "Russian" shirt with a buttoned-up collar and belt, over the shirt the jacket of a business suit, and a cap with a visor. His kindly courtesy, the feeling of closeness and good will warmed my heart.

There was a visitor staying at the professor's "dacha" when I came there — a middle-aged woman who was a schoolmate of the professor's wife. When I was leaving she hugged me emotionally and said my visit was like an open window into a world of light and air, a world she had known in her childhood. She begged my permission to come and see me at the Hotel Astoria. I gave it, of course, and she came to see me several times. She was very typical of a certain class of Russian women that I have often met abroad and I am sure exist as frequently in Russia. She was sorry for herself. She wanted sympathy. The professor's wife gave her two pounds of berries to make jam, and she could so easily have given her four pounds, and it would have been only right, because the professor earns five hundred rubles a month, because he gets paid both by the Academy and the Conservatory and his wife, her friend, is his second wife because he divorced his first wife and I have now come as a ray of sunlight into her life and I must come and have coffee with her and she wants me to meet her son and he is a good son, but he does not want her to live with him and her room is so dark and so damp and this is not what she was prepared for in life, and her son collects stamps and would I have some for him . . . On and on it went, with no logical sequence and no end in sight. She pressed presents on me and for almost a year she wrote me long and emotional letters. I sent her stamps and a few small gifts care of the General Post Office, for she did not want her neighbors to know that she was receiving mail from abroad. Then suddenly her letters stopped dead and I never heard from her again. This was the only happening during my stay which, with some imagination, might be interpreted as "being followed." Who knows? It might have been the Academy secretary's duty to inform someone that he had given the professor's address to a visitor from abroad, which does not at all invalidate his good will towards me. The ladyfriend might have been one of the numerous people who are told by "them" that surely, for the love of her Soviet fatherland, she would not hesitate to report anything harmful. She might have been asked to visit her friend's husband on the day I could be expected to visit him. She might have been asked to keep up a correspondence with me and see whether I was sending any messages. All this would not mean that she did not truly feel everything that she said to me, that she was not unhappy and lonely. And also it is equally possible that such conjectures are quite untrue and imaginary.

The one thing I can affirm positively is that I was never actually followed in my roamings about the city. I had occasion to leave the hotel very early, when the doors had to be opened for me by the night watchman. I crossed on foot huge empty squares to take a street car and not a soul followed me, nor was I ever asked how I had spent the day. The "Intourist" office at the hotel was always in such a state of chaotic overcrowding that I think it was actually impossible for them to supervise closely those tourists who were independent and drew no attention to themselves.

During my stay in Moscow and Leningrad I saw no hippy-looking young men with long hair and bare feet. Maybe this came later. It seemed to me that a need to make some kind of dramatic change in one's appearance did exist and I remember especially my encounter with a young man who had obviously dyed his hair. I met him in a little basement restaurant in Leningrad called "Pogrebok" which I liked. (Quite purposely I tried out all kinds of eating places, from the very cheap ones where I could get a plateful of a ravioli type of dish with butter and sour cream, coffee or tea and plenty of bread for sixty cents up to the most expensive ones I could afford.) In Pogrebok I could get an excellent and well-prepared meal for about two dollars. The restaurant was small and there were usually four or five people waiting in front of it for a place to become vacant. I took my stand there and a few minutes later another woman came up and asked how much was the steak dinner? I looked at the menu pinned to the door and answered instinctively, "A dollar and a half."

My answer came so naturally that nobody seemed to have noticed my slip of the tongue.

The only vacant place, when I entered, was at a small table which was already occupied by two very young girls and a working man, probably in his early twenties. One of the girls spoke a little Russian, the other none at all — they were both tourists from Riga. The young man had a typically Russian face — very blond eyebrows, pale blue eyes, high cheek bones, a wide nose, the kind we call in Russian "duck-billed," and his skin was pockmarked. The real flourish was the color of his hair: a boot-polish kind of dead black, obviously artificial. The young man was preening and showing off before the girls. He had brought a bottle of hard liquor hidden in his coat and now he was offering them a drink. All my grandmotherly and schoolmarmish instincts cried out for the need of a diversion. The boy was boasting of the distance he had travelled to come to Leningrad from some small town in Siberia. "Well," I commented, "this is pretty far, but I have come from still farther." "From where did you come then?" he asked doubtfully. "From America, from New York..." "You are kidding! I don't believe you, it can't be true..." His interest switched from the girls, so that my purpose was achieved. "But it is true," I insisted. "I am an old White Russian émigré, who left Russia fifty years ago and now I have come for a visit." "I still don't believe you. It just doesn't sound possible. Can you show me your passport?" "I left my passport in my hotel room, but I can probably find something." I hunted in my bag and found a dollar bill. "Will this do as proof?" The boy looked at the green bill wonderingly. "I guess it is true then," he said. And then came a regular shower of questions: is it true that life is so hard in America? Is it true that the unemployment is so bad? Is it true that poor people have such a bad time there? I answered that there was some unemployment indeed. My son, a college student, who always found jobs in construction work during the summer holidays and usually got them within a day or two, had to look for a whole week before he found one. When he did get a job he was paid three-fifty an hour (this was in 1970). This seemed fantastic, unbelievable pay to the youngster. Job offers were announced everywhere, in Leningrad and Moscow, but they were all for monthly salaries of approximately one hundred dollars. The only higher salary I saw offered was two hundred and fifty for a bus driver. The young man was also much impressed by the housing conditions. We finally separated the best of friends and he accepted with pleasure my dollar bill as a souvenir.

In Leningrad I had occasion to meet an almost forgotten member of the Shidlovsky family. In my childhood in Voltchy I used to know two distant cousins some ten to fifteen years older than myself. One of them, Sergei, was married, the other, Arseny, was fat to the point of obesity, with a good-natured smiling face, his head the size of a watermelon. In all the plays and charades we staged he always played the comic parts. I remember him especially in the part of a fat merchant's wife, sipping tea from a saucer held up with three fingers. Now, in Leningrad, I met Sergei's daughter, a middle-aged woman whose son had married the daughter of Nikita's cousin whom I visited in Moscow. The family story was typical and tragic. In 1920 Arseny made a living selling news-papers from a street booth. He had grown thin but remained outspoken and uninhibited in expressing his feelings so one day he was arrested and executed. Then Sergei and his wife Alia were also taken and shot. Their two small children were taken in by Zoya, another cousin, whose husband was also executed. The elderly woman I met was one of those two small orphaned children. She showed me snapshots of their old country home. Curiously enough it was also called Voltchy and belonged to a distantly related branch of the Shidlovsky family — we always used to say "the other Voltchy" and "the other Shidlovskys," and I suppose they spoke of us in the same way. From our visits there I remembered two attractive young women — Katia and Lilia. I learned now that both of them died from hunger, during the war-time siege of Leningrad.

Sergei's daughter Olga had an excellent apartment according to Soviet standards. Her husband was a professor of Scandinavian languages. He made trips abroad to attend inter-national conventions and was able to bring home all kinds of gadgets. Their apartment, in a solid, well-built, prerevolutionary house had three large rooms, a kitchen and a bathroom. They could boast of a washing machine and a dryer. The rooms were solidly furnished and had a kind of professorial look, carefully kept up, even though the apartment was shared by the young married son, his wife and baby and another adult daughter. I should have had a lot in common with them and yet I found the whole atmosphere and all the conversation less interesting than any I had in Soviet Russia. It was as if their well-being and comfort were a carefully built-up structure, based on avoiding any risky word, any independent thought. Participation in church life, in any form, was taboo and unmentionable. The younger couple had all the charm of their youth, and I felt that if I saw them alone we might have come closer. But the entire family showed great hospitality and again I had to accept presents.

One weekday morning I visited a church which was busy with the needs of individual believers: two or three coffins were aligned in one section waiting for the burial service; in another side section several babies were baptized. In the front of the church an elderly priest, with fluffy white hair and faded blue eyes, was serving a special short service with some thirty or forty people attending. I mingled with the group. The priest was reading the Gospel, which he obviously knew by heart, for his kindly eyes were looking at the people as he read. At the end of the service I went up to him: "Bless me, Father," I said. "I have just come from America on a visit and I bring you the good wishes of our Orthodox people there." His tired blue eyes looked at me attentively. "Pray for us in our hardships," he said, giving me his blessing.

An interesting incident took place in another church, which I also visited on a weekday. In the big basement church some two hundred faithful were having their individual needs taken care of: burials, baptisms, services of thanksgiving, etc. I asked a woman whether the main church, upstairs, was open. She told me services were celebrated there on Sundays only. "But look," she added, "they've just taken a group of tourists upstairs. You see, the door leading there is open." I hurried up the stairs and found a group of American tourists being

shown around the huge ornate 18th century church. As I
approached, one of the tourists asked in English: "Do people
still come to worship in this church?" The Intourist guide
answered without hesitation: "Well, you know, by now there
are very few people who bother to go to church." I thought
of all the crowded churches I saw, of the people downstairs
and my mouth fell open. At this moment an elderly gentleman, who might have been the church warden or the church
janitor, saw me. He obviously took me for one of the "local"
Russians. "What are you doing here?" he hissed. "Go away!
Go away!" "But she is telling such nonsense!" I protested.
The old gentleman completely lost his temper: "Go away,
go away immediately. Don't you understand? How can you
say such things? Don't you understand anything?" He practically pushed me out, repeating over and over again. "Don't
you understand? You must understand!" Yes, a Christian in
Russia has to understand a lot of things wordlessly, without
explanations. You have to bear anything, anything being said
and done, just to keep the Church existing.

Then I visited the old house that had belonged to my
parents and where I had spent all my childhood. I felt like
a ghost as I walked down the streets bearing new and unfamiliar names and suddenly recognized long forgotten landmarks. There was our street . . . the house on the corner with
the turret I had forgotten existed . . . there was our house. The
red-carpeted staircase I remembered, with palm trees in tubs
on the landing and the uniformed bewhiskered doorkeeper
who used to greet us children in such a friendly manner, were
all gone. Broken, bare, stone steps; dirty, chipped, badly-
marked walls painted bright sky-blue. I walked up the steps.
Seventeen names were listed under the two doorbells, seventeen families were living in our former apartment. I rang
the bell, my heart in my mouth.

A woman opened the door. When I told her who I was,
from where I came, she exploded in friendly excitement. She
called in as many of the "lodgers" as were around at the time.
They showed me their rooms, their poor, crowded rooms,
crammed full with cartons, bundles, little "primus" stoves.
"So this was the nursery?" "And here was our classroom!"

"You see, the bathroom is our common kitchen now!" "These were my brothers' rooms!" — the brothers who disappeared in the vortex of revolution and war ... "What was your father's name?" "Who was he?" "Sit down, sit down! I would like you to meet my children, the children who grew up in this house too ... But they are away in camp."

On the way out I suddenly stopped. My father's study ... the sanctuary of our home during my childhood. On the door there were still remnants of the padded oilcloth that insulated my father's study from our noisy games. Then I saw the door-handle ... The door handle I had forgotten — a bronze bird's claw holding a globe. I choked. "The door handle, I had forgotten the door handle ... It is the same!" Two girls were living in the room now, who had "inherited" it from their grandparents — a professor and his wife. The room still kept a faintly "academic" look. The girl who had opened the door, smiled gently at me: "No, you are wrong," she said. "The globe was a blue crystal one." (Then I suddenly saw it in my mind — yes, it was blue crystal). "When it broke we could not find another like it and we replaced it with a wooden globe." I had to make an effort to keep back tears.

* * *

My whole stay in Russia lasted only two weeks, but this short time contained experiences so meaningful that it felt like a whole lifetime. Even now I find it difficult to put into words why this encounter with Russia was so important for me. I always felt that leaving Russia, separating myself from its fate, was like an unhealed wound. I have had a full and happy life outside of Russia, but I was always conscious of this separation as a pain. Now I had again come briefly in touch with life there and suddenly I realized that there was no absolute break, no complete separation. *My life, my own* life, such as it was, came easily in touch with the flow of life that went on in Russia. I was together with Russia in the life of the Church, I was together with Russia in the search for spiritual values that is going on there. There was no dead wall between the life that went on in me and the life that went on in Russia, and we could communicate. This was a healing and releasing experience.

A taxi took me from the Hotel Astoria to the airport. The driver, a man in his thirties, drew my attention to some of the traces of war-time. He had been a small boy in 1942 and was evacuated to a village which was then occupied by the Germans. "It is strange," he said. "We speak so often of all the horrible things Germans did, and yet, as I think of that time, they were quite good chaps, these German soldiers: they played with us and gave us some of their rations. You know, I've often thought of it. There is so much evil in life, so much evil, probably more than good. But the good, little as there is of it, is stronger. Yes, good is stronger than evil."

Yes, I thought, good is stronger than evil, life is stronger than death, love is stronger than separation.